MW00829937

WILD
INTELLIGENCE

A Volume in the Series

STUDIES IN PRINT CULTURE
AND THE HISTORY OF THE BOOK

Edited by
Greg Barnhisel, Joan Shelley Rubin,
and Michael Winship

In cooperation with
Lost & Found Elsewhere / The Graduate Center, CUNY

WILD
INTELLIGENCE

**Poets' Libraries and the
Politics of Knowledge in
Postwar America**

M. C. KINNIBURGH

University of Massachusetts Press

AMHERST AND BOSTON

Copyright © 2022 by Mary Catherine Kinniburgh
All rights reserved
Printed in the United States of America

ISBN 978-1-62534-655-1 (paper); 656-8 (hardcover)

Designed by Sally Nichols
Set in Minion Pro and Bauer Bodoni
Printed and bound by Books International, Inc.

Cover design and art by adam b. bohannon

Library of Congress Cataloging-in-Publication Data

Names: Kinniburgh, Mary Catherine, author.
Title: Wild intelligence : poets' libraries and the politics of knowledge
   in postwar America / M.C. Kinniburgh.
Description: Amherst : University of Massachusetts Press, [2022] | Series:
   Studies in print culture and the history of the book | Includes
   bibliographical references and index.
Identifiers: LCCN 2021054599 (print) | LCCN 2021054600 (ebook) | ISBN
   9781625346551 (paperback) | ISBN 9781625346568 (hardcover) | ISBN
   9781613769331 (ebook) | ISBN 9781613769348 (ebook)
Subjects: LCSH: Private libraries—United States—History—20th century. |
   Poets, American—20th century—Books and reading. | Olson, Charles,
   1910–1970—Library. | Di Prima, Diane—Library. | Lansing,
   Gerrit—Library. | Lorde, Audre—Library.
Classification: LCC Z997.2.U6 K56 2022 (print) | LCC Z997.2.U6 (ebook) |
   DDC 027/.173—dc23/eng/20211203
LC record available at https://lccn.loc.gov/2021054599
LC ebook record available at https://lccn.loc.gov/2021054600

British Library Cataloguing-in-Publication Data
A catalog record for this book is available from the British Library.

An earlier version of chapter 1 appeared in a different form within
Book History 23 (2020): 206–36, by Johns Hopkins University Press.

"The Critic Reviews Loba" from *Loba* by Diane di Prima, copyright ©
1973, 1976, 1977, 1978, 1998 by Diane di Prima. Used by permission of
Penguin Books, an imprint of Penguin Publishing Group, a division
of Penguin Random House LLC. All rights reserved.

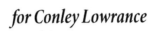

for Conley Lowrance

CONTENTS

PREFACE

WORKING WITH BOOKS and manuscripts, I often get asked about the weirdest or most wonderful thing I've ever seen. As a rare book dealer and archivist who formerly worked in special collections, I have a few ready answers: a tin of bees, Charles Dickens's cat-paw letter opener, Black Panther Christmas cards, Joanne Kyger's tarot deck, *Orifice Flux Plugs*. Though the question sometimes feels rote, I sympathize with its nature and desire. "Books" are a plural abstraction to most people, and archival papers are indiscernible in a sheaf. Hearing other people share key objects makes this vast ocean of the printed word more approachable, real.

It is good research, writing, and cataloging practice to focus on individual items. Doing so lets us describe things neatly, so that we can find them again, tell their story accurately, and revisit them accordingly. Yet in my work with books, I was always searching for the thrill of *volume*. Paradoxically, a volume is a single item—that is, a book within a larger series—and also a large quantity. I didn't just want *a* book, on my personal shelves, in my research, in my teaching at the library, or in my work as a rare book dealer. I wanted piles of them, towering stacks, endless shelves to browse. Contemplating a single superlative book lets us digest it like a piece of candy. Eat one piece, and we understand the flavor and texture. Consuming books is like eating a large handful, like I did as a kid: mawing a mass of sugar in a new sensation.

My work as an archivist and graduate student entailed visiting many poets, whose bookshelves invariably met my desire for cosmos of books. Everywhere I went, from the Maud/Olson Library, to Diane di Prima's garage, to Gerrit Lansing's Victorian house, I saw towers of books that made meaning among each other, through their placement in the house or by extension, the poet's life, and relationship to the poet's idea of what it meant to collect knowledge and information. In my search for a way of meaning-making with books through sheer quantity, I saw poets making sense of information overload by gathering books that weren't necessarily rare or expensive but were nevertheless precious. And these were *researching* poets, who honed their craft well before Internet search bars, and had experienced the censorship and surveillance of the Cold War firsthand. Their relationship to building knowledge was necessary for their survival. To that end, their shelves were lined with occult subjects like witchcraft, special handmade books by friends, historical and philosophical works, and ephemeral items like little magazines. These libraries had their own logic, beyond the individual books within them.

I was struck by the enormity of these collections, but also by their ephemerality. Institutions, for a variety of reasons, are often unable to support these types of unwieldy libraries, with their mix of rare and quotidian materials, their excessive size, and their indeterminate relationship to academic research. I understood this from my work as a librarian, but still I felt there had to be methods outside of institutional practices for documenting and preserving these collections, as well as engaging them on the poet's terms. As a rare book dealer and as a student of poetry, I tend to encounter poets toward the end of their lives when much of their work is visible and accomplished—except the work of organizing their archive and library. The question of dispersal and documentation was often imminent, and shaded my sense of urgency immeasurably.

Simply put, I wanted to help, and be of service. To create pathways for the next generation to experience what I had experienced, when there was no living room or garage to visit. This instinct formed the basis of the research for this book, and the crux of my argument: that poets' libraries are not just book collections but are rather a distinctive type of archival collation that reflects a *poetics* of information. And that in the twentieth century, this task of collecting and organizing has specific political valence for poets who worked outside of mainstream contexts: who were harassed by government organizations, denied the resources of traditional institutions, or otherwise registered on a scale of unfashionable to dangerous in an era of conformity. In this sense, poets' libraries offer us an alternative history of information management during the same century that saw this practice rise to the prominence of an accredited profession in the United States.

Of course, authors collecting copies of meaningful books is a centuries-old practice. Ben Jonson's library is one of the earlier examples of a Western

author's private collection of printed materials, and such examples only pro-
liferate as print technology evolves. Furthermore, not all twentieth-century
poets' libraries are so ephemeral; the more esteemed the author, the more
likely their library is considered to be valuable as an extension of their
archival papers. Relationships between poets and curators often ensure preservation when mainstream reputation might not suffice. Yet what interests
me—and is the subject of this book—are the libraries that are wild in their
intelligence, and have thus far evaded the legibility of being ingested into a
formal institution or offered to the literary market.

Two key poets in this book, Diane di Prima and Gerrit Lansing, passed
away as I wrote this manuscript, as did a number of their friends and colleagues, including Michael McClure and Lawrence Ferlinghetti. The archival
record of this generation is diffuse and unstable, ongoing, and in need of
custodial and critical interventions. The libraries of these poets still exist on
the peripheries, because that's where they were created.

To explore them is to forage, to hunt. And so, into the bibliographic woods.

WILD
INTELLIGENCE

INTRODUCTION

IN 1933, HARVARD student Charles Olson attempts to recover Herman Melville's library, which was sold and dispersed across the East Coast after his death. In the process of reassembly, he encounters Melville's annotations of Shakespeare. Olson begins writing a work that later becomes *Call Me Ishmael,* and argues that Melville conceptualized his seminal work, *Moby Dick,* in the margins of *King Lear.*

———

In 1942, poet Muriel Rukeyser writes to scientist Albert Einstein, inquiring whether he might compose a preface to her forthcoming book on Willard Gibbs, the late nineteenth-century scientist who discovered the rule of phase. In her letter, she writes, "I wrote this book because I needed to read it. . . . My work has been in poetry—the poetry of the years just before this war and of the war—and I know what these images mean there." Twelve days later, Einstein writes back to "Miss Rukeyser": "I cannot give my public endorsement to such an undertaking," stating "how hateful and ridiculous it is, when a serious man, absorbed in important endeavours, is ignorantly lionized" through personal biography rather than his research alone.[1]

———

In 1963, poet LeRoi Jones publishes *Blues People: Negro Music in White America.* The book traces the development of African American culture through music practices, from slavery to present-day jazz and blues. In the new introduction to the 1999 edition, titled "Blues People: Looking Both Ways," Amiri Baraka writes that when he began the book, he "was admittedly and very openly shooting from the hip," though the ideas "were forceful enough to convince me that I did know something."[2] The book was a watershed and has remained in print since its initial publication.

———

In 1961, musician and poet Ed Sanders attempts to board a nuclear submarine as an act of protest. He is apprehended by police, and incarcerated in

Montville State Jail in Uncasville, Connecticut, for most of the month of August. From his cell, he requests a copy of a book of Egyptian hieroglyphs. The request is denied over concerns of the hieroglyphs constituting Russian code, a significant threat in Cold War America. Denied also his requests for pencils and paper, Sanders proceeds to write "Poem from Jail" on hundreds of feet of toilet paper, studying the hieroglyphs he had drawn on small bits of paper and cigarette packaging.[3]

———

In 1965, poet Diane di Prima begins studying the early modern alchemist Paracelsus after receiving an offer of two hundred dollars to write the introduction to a reprint of A. E. Waite's translations. She reads both volumes of the reprint straight through. She writes in her 2001 memoir, *Recollections of My Life as a Woman*, "I didn't guess that Paracelsus would change forever my way of seeing the world."[4] She had recently established Poets Press, an imprint that went on to publish Audre Lorde, David Henderson, Timothy Leary, Michael McClure, John Ashbery, and dozens of other emerging and established poets. The printer's device is a woodcut from Horapollo's *Hieroglyphica* in 1597, an "alchemical logo" of "a dragon eating its tail, flanked by the sun and the moon."[5]

———

Audre Lorde publishes her first book, *The First Cities*, in 1968 with di Prima's Poets Press. That same year, she leaves her position as head librarian at Town School Library in New York, seven years after obtaining a master's degree in library science at Columbia University. Decades later, speaking with Adrienne Rich, Lorde says, "I became a librarian because I really believed I would gain tools for ordering and analyzing information." But she continues, "I can document the road to Abomeny for you, and true, you might not get there without that information . . . but once you get there, only you know why, what you came for, as you search for it and perhaps find it."[6]

———

Each of these vignettes recounts a poet involved in a key moment of establishing their *poetics:* a framework that the poet builds to structure the relationship between knowledge, daily life, and understanding of self. In Diane di Prima's poem "Rant," she exhorts, "There is no way you can not have a poetics / no matter what you do: plumber, baker, teacher / you do it in the consciousness of making."[7] Poet Robin Blaser remembers a formative moment in his early education, as a student of the medievalist Ernst Kantorowicz at University of California, Berkeley, along with classmates Jack Spicer and Robert Duncan: "It's from Kantorowicz that I found out poetry is noetic, that the task of poetry is knowledge . . . that it is always the re-centering of the origin of the world."[8] Don Byrd's *The Poetics of Common Knowledge* explores the idea of poetics as "not exclusively or even most significantly what appears in those peculiar and despised writings known as 'poems'" but as a type of embodied knowing shaped by material considerations.[9]

And what types of knowing were these poets seeking? Outside of the university or institutional writer's workshop—according to Amiri Baraka, the "bullshit school poetry" of "rhetoric, formalism, and dull iambics"—poets sought to recover a sense of history that could chart a way forward, through a comparative understanding of Western culture's relative amnesia toward its own origins and colonial past.[10] For instance, di Prima's *Revolutionary Letters* foregrounds the importance of learning premodern history as an antidote to the legacy of white, Christian, Western European supremacy; Lorde's *The Black Unicorn* provides a glossary of African goddesses; Olson's *Maximus Poems* explore the idea of "polis" and political community in Gloucester, Massachusetts, one of the first areas settled by colonizers in America and later populated by immigrants; and projects like Baraka's *Blues People* show how a combination of historical methodologies and intuitive practices can document aspects of Black and African American life that had never been recorded.

Or, as poet Gerrit Lansing wrote in a preface to his little magazine, *SET,*

> Disposal of you trash of memory,
> have gone / "made in Europe"
> analogies that fake the line
> like "heirlooms" / family ideas.[11]

Perhaps more succinctly, also Lansing: "European whiteness is sepulcher to us & European consciousness a museum."[12] Approximately a decade earlier, in 1951, Olson states in "The Gate and the Center": "KNOWLEDGE either goes for the *center* or it's inevitably a State Whore—which American and Western education generally is, has been, since its beginning."[13] Olson, who was educated at Harvard's PhD program, and served as a high-level official in the Office of War Information before he quit in protest of government censorship, was intimately familiar with the challenges that mainstream knowledge posed to understanding the truth of American history and the realities of its present political system.

Poets writing outside of mainstream contexts were consistently working toward the *center* that Olson references, exploring traditions and systems that had been overlooked, buried, occulted, or censored. This was not just epistemological, in terms of what could be known, but infrastructural; poets had to both collect massive amounts of difficult-to-find knowledge and also organize it. In the postwar period, the burgeoning field of information science and information management meant that *what one could know* was subjected to increasing quantification, with more research—broadly speaking, knowledge—being produced and cataloged than ever before. From the launch of the first archival processing manual in Dutch in 1898, to the establishment of the first library school in the United States one year prior, the material forms of information and their organization were subject to increasing professionalization and subsequent interrogation. In the United States, this information economy was largely shaped by the needs and effects of war. During the Cold War, information science provided infrastructure at scale to meet the rising demand for research materials at universities that had received large increases in funding for science and technology programs, and likewise cater to newly augmented enrollments as a result of the Servicemen's Readjustment Act of 1944 (or GI Bill) after World War Two.

Public and academic libraries were significant sites for this information boom. Among the information infrastructures that grew to prominence in the twentieth century, they are perhaps the most symbolically charged. With dramatic architecture and increasingly complex labor structures, libraries in the postwar era promised to provide the democratic and humanistic good of knowledge for all. Even in collections composed of materials that were considered rare or special, this symbolism was at the fore. For instance, the speeches at the dedication ceremony of a valuable private literary collection by Henry W. and Albert A. Berg to The New York Public Library in 1940 emphasized not the exclusiveness of the materials but their redemptive powers for Western culture within the context of a public space. Mayor Fiorello La Guardia intoned, "It will be perhaps a century before Europe will be able to catch up and rebuild both spiritually and materially all the destruction and the damage wrought during the past year. And therefore, extension of libraries, the increase in capacity of our institutions of higher education . . . is in keeping with this added responsibility which the mistakes of a few individuals in Europe have thrust upon us. I think we are capable of carrying on the torch of enlightenment."[14] Notwithstanding his blaming of "a few individuals in Europe" for the humanitarian crisis of World War Two, LaGuardia's comments reinforce the idea that both spiritual and material growth—in terms of "carrying the torch of enlightenment"—are obtainable through libraries and education. For this reason, twentieth-century libraries in the United States have special symbolic value in their ties to rapidly expanding wealth under industrial capitalism (as exemplified by the system of Carnegie libraries), as well as national ideas about democratic knowledge and education.

While public libraries remain a crucial resource for the distribution of knowledge, the question of *what* knowledge they house is inevitably informed by larger political forces. Thus, around the middle of the twentieth century, their collecting and policies were substantially shaped by the Cold War. For instance, president Harry Truman's requirement that state employees take a national loyalty oath effectively fired any person who was unwilling to pledge—including Jack Spicer at the University of California, Berkeley, and countless librarians at institutions that received federal funding as a result of the recent Library Services Act of 1956.[15] What libraries could acquire and make available was affected by McCarthyism and Communist panic, as well as the situation within the publishing industry, which was wracked by obscenity cases likely because this type of censorship, as opposed to blatant censorship of political ideas, was a way to target those who did not fully embody "American values." During the 1950s and 1960s, presses that were largely devoted to publishing counterculture materials, such as Grove Press or City Lights, frequently battled obscenity charges in court for books by D. H. Lawrence, Samuel Beckett, William S. Burroughs, Lenore Kandel, Allen Ginsberg, and others.

This climate played out within bookstores as well as libraries; di Prima recounts the risks of work in the Phoenix Book Shop, and the environment of paranoia: "We were in the throes of an insane, obsessive repression of the written word—you could get arrested for selling Henry Miller . . . *Howl* was on trial, and *The Love Book* by Lenore Kandel."[16] One of the primary vectors for seizing books and levying obscenity charges was the US Postal System, who was authorized to seize materials based on the Comstock Act of 1873 that made it a federal crime to transport "obscene" materials (including birth control or information about it) through the mail. Such regulations, combined with a climate of fear and enforcement, meant that di Prima and Baraka were arrested by the Federal Bureau of Investigation on obscenity charges for sending a copy of *The Floating Bear*, their mimeograph magazine, to an incarcerated friend after mail censors at the prison intercepted the issue.

Given this climate surrounding information, poets seeking to develop a poetics informed by a wide array of sources and literature soon found themselves in political crosshairs. As a result, the distribution of bibliographies like Olson's *A Bibliography on America for Ed Dorn* essentially became countercultural acts, and, as Ammiel Alcalay notes, were "part of a burgeoning revolt against the Cold War culture of containment and its particular manifestation in the academic administration of knowledge that was largely in service of state power and imperialist policies."[17] This type of activity had special stakes for topics represented in counterculture and Beat poetry, such as Eastern religion and philosophy and premodern history, as well as for those outside of the mainstream for reasons of racial difference. In the early twentieth century, a profusion of Black bibliographers, catalogers, and anthologizers helped to establish the Black experience as a legitimate subject of interest and inquiry. For example, Arturo Schomburg's *Bibliographical Checklist of American Negro Poetry* in 1916 detailed "black authorship as a specifically *literary* category," which began the bibliographic process of constructing the contours of a Black poetic tradition that had been so ignored as to be invisible.[18]

In light of the radical possibilities of bibliography outside of the mainstream, as well as the overarching political agendas that controlled public libraries and literary production in the twentieth century, we might ask, what if we looked to *poets* for our history of libraries and information management in the twentieth century? By examining the way that poets collected books and developed knowledge-building practices, this book traces a different history of information management that is structured not by the needs of government or institutional organizations but by the idea that a life of poetry is an act of political and spiritual survival.

A New Era of Book Collecting, and the Question of Archives

Olson sifting through bookshops and seller catalogs for Melville's lost volumes, di Prima xeroxing rare alchemical texts, Sanders requesting a tome of hieroglyphs, or Lorde searching libraries for a map of her mother's birthplace in the Caribbean: books shared precious information for poets completing "a saturation job"—or researching all there is to know about any given subject, as Olson describes to Dorn at Black Mountain College in what is later published as *A Bibliography on America for Ed Dorn*. The increased availability of most printed materials in the twentieth century as a result of publishing technologies for both industries and consumers (such as offset printing or mimeograph), alongside increased professional efforts in discoverability (such as cataloging), meant that collecting and finding books in the twentieth century became an accessible practice to a far greater range of people. Markets and communities emerged for the range of printing activities and archival energies at the time, too. Di Prima notes how the Phoenix Book Shop in Greenwich Village kept many poets fed, including Ted Berrigan and Gregory Corso, who would stop by, scrawl out a notebook, and sell it to the shop's purveyor, Robert (Bob) Wilson.

The significant cost of book production in earlier historical eras limited the type of individual who might consider themselves a book collector. Paul Raabe notes that early librarianship was framed as connoisseurship, and requires us to understand the history of reading before industrialization as primarily an activity related to the privileges afforded by economic status.[19] But technological developments broadly changed the nature of both book production and leisure time. By the 1880s, the publishing industry shifted from family-run businesses to larger, consolidated corporate models, with companies using mass-production techniques. After World War Two, larger cultural and technological shifts meant that more people were reading—as evidenced by book clubs, library circulation, and book sales.[20] By the 1960s, books were produced more quickly and cheaply, thanks to the ubiquity of offset printing that used phototypesetting.[21] And bookstores were key in sharing these technological innovations with wider publics; Lawrence Ferlinghetti's bookshop and publishing imprint, City Lights, championed the new popular form of paperback books when it was founded in 1953.

This profusion of innovation stands in stark contrast to the elite aspects of librarianship and book collecting during eras in which printing books was labor intensive and expensive. Using the evidence of Samuel Taylor Coleridge's working library, scholar Ralph J. Coffman argues that by reconstructing this collection, we might better understand "the tension between the democratization of the printed word and the persistence of the elitist constraints on access to information in nineteenth-century England."[22] Likewise, applying this methodology to twentieth-century American book collecting reveals specific considerations between restricted and free-flowing forms of knowledge in print, and also, significantly, changes in the type of poet who could collect a library. Poets with little income, transient housing, and no university affiliation or government resources often amassed important collections that they described conceptually, used regularly, and considered as part of their poetic practice. Some of these poets wrote extensive bibliographies as part of their poetry and pedagogy, expanding our concept of what their libraries may have actually contained. Given these qualities, postwar poets' libraries are often incomplete and permeable, yet potent portraits of their collectors.

So, where do we find such a library? Despite the rapid acceleration of the literary papers market in the twentieth century, with author archives capable of fetching upward of a million dollars, personal libraries are often not included in seller inventories or ultimately the acquisition itself. There are several exceptions to this, speaking broadly of the various strains of avant-garde writing that stemmed from New American poetry after World War Two: Kathy Acker's library, housed in its own reading room at the University of Cologne; Kenneth Rexroth's library at the Kanda University of International Studies in Japan; Robert Creeley's library at Notre Dame; Robert Duncan's library and Helen Adam's library at the Poetry Collection at the University at Buffalo, SUNY; and Hilda Morley's library at the Henry W. and Albert A. Berg Collection of English and American Literature at The New York Public Library, as well as other examples. These successes speak to the possibilities of these types of collections and reading rooms, as well as the work to be done for collections that have yet to be placed, or the collections housed at institutions but not yet cataloged. The indeterminacy of most libraries' whereabouts relates in part to their ambiguous relationship to literary papers. Instead of being treated as part of an archive and listed in the finding aid, the individual books are often ingested into a collection and cataloged by book, sometimes with no provenance note or easy way to search all the books for their single origin. This reality is noted in a recent volume of collected essays titled *Collecting, Curating, and Researching Writers' Libraries: A Handbook* (2014), edited by Richard W. Oram with Joseph Nicholson, that features an index that traces writers' libraries, as well as examples of how to engage with and preserve these collections that are often peculiarly invisible to scholars and librarians, for differing reasons.[23]

It is perhaps the technical challenges, produced by the very structures of information management that include cataloging procedures and conventions, that pose the greatest obstacle to acquiring and making visible or available poets' libraries. Literary papers tend to have a relatively established acquisitions workflow; items are stored in uniform boxes, processed according to archival series, and made available to researchers in reading rooms. However, the challenges of acquiring a poet's library as its own unit rest in large part on the fact that these collections are not quite archives, not quite collections of books. This indeterminacy also appears in archival finding aids at many institutions. Sometimes the author's books are included in the finding aid for the archive, as in the case of author Toni Cade Bambara at Spelman College, but often they are cataloged as individual items and then shelved separately according to the larger logic of the holding collection. Sometimes, the books aren't (yet) cataloged and speaking with an archivist or curator is the only way to know they are there, as is the case with Hilda Morley's books at The New York Public Library.

On the archival aspects of the poet's library: one might note that the term "archive" is somewhat diluted today, used frequently in popular culture and humanities research to describe short-term curated projects such as websites, and any number of small-scale items that do not, in fact, function as an archives or repositories in the professional and institutional sense. This appropriation of the term further dilutes the labor that goes into creating and maintaining actual archives, not to mention the frequency of "discovery" narratives of "lost" manuscripts that in fact have been carefully cataloged and managed by a repository since acquisition.[24] The poet's library—when it has been collected thoughtfully by a poet engaged in the very question of what can be known and explored—functions in the manner of a "fonds" which Terry Cook describes as "the conceptual 'whole' that reflects an organic process in which a records creator produces or accumulates series of records which themselves exhibit a natural unity based on shared function, activity, form or use."[25] The presence of *fonds,* which can be roughly translated as "depths," or the foundation of something, gives rise to the primary archival principle of *respect des fonds,* in which records should be maintained in their original order with regard to the particular dimensions of their fonds or groupings. The way that poets structured their books—particularly poets like di Prima, whose occult library was envisioned as a specific grouping or fonds, and she has stated she would like it to remain together—falls under the purview of fonds, as do their manuscripts or their correspondence. The fact that the fonds are created of books, which are governed under their own cataloging procedures, and not loose papers, which are more traditionally arranged according to archival series, accounts for many of the challenges in acquisition and preservation.

The question of visibility also informs whether poets' libraries might be viewed as archival. While not a technical manual, the influential *Archive Fever* by Jacques Derrida notes the conceptual relationship between a structure and the information housed within it: "The technical structure of the *archiving* archive also determines the structure of the *archivable* content even in its very coming into existence and its relationship to the future"—that is, the shapes of what exist determine the shapes of what can be known.[26] This is not to say that the idea of the library does not privilege the same relationship between infrastructure and discoverability, but rather, a poet's library is often more compatible with the interpretive techniques applied to primary source documents: the relationship of item to archive, and of unpublished evidence to the scholarly record, and how the materiality shows signs of creation and use.

Beyond the conceptual aspects of poets' libraries that place them at the intersection of archive, book, and library, there are very real material and financial considerations that are often barriers to the acquisition or preservation of these collections. Amy Hildreth Chen notes in *Placing Papers* (2020) that the literary archives market gravitates toward high-profile writers, and the economies of prestige that inform institutional reputations often dictate that the more well-established a writer, the more interested repositories are in acquiring their materials and the more willing they are to pay for them.[27] In addition to this, acquisition policies often foreground the importance of a collection's research value, either generally speaking or with regard to the holding institution's particular needs. Yet research and market value can easily fluctuate as a result of social or cultural capital that becomes associated with or removed from an author, and these values are not fixed entities. For instance, Herman Melville's library was dispersed after his death due to the family's poverty, since at the time, he was neither commercially nor critically successful. However, a pair of volumes from Melville's library recently cleared six figures in an auction. The worth of an author is often not defined in their lifetime (perhaps in part due to another market-based system: publishing), which makes the dispersal of archival materials particularly challenging.

Given the tendency to understand poets' libraries based on individual books, acquisition of these collections often depends on whether an institution already has copies of the titles. In instances where acquiring a poet's library would result in duplicate holdings of many volumes, it is more likely that an institution will collect only the volumes it does not have, or pass on the acquisition completely. Institutions often have limited resources for storing and cataloging author libraries as specific units, even though an author may conceive of their library as a conceptual project, or as an archive in and of itself. Without documentation of the unique materiality of these books, such as autograph annotations, they are likely to be returned to the author or estate, deaccessioned, or redistributed to general collections without readily visible attribution to their provenance.

Indeed, research on books owned by poets tends to focus on annotation, since it is a definitive textual trace that charts what Amanda Golden cites as the "material and social spaces" that inhabit the margins of books owned by writers.[28] Yet there are other ways to read across the social networks of books, as Sheila Liming notes in her work on Edith Wharton's library. For Liming, Wharton's books are "a product and agent of networked social existence" in the early twentieth century, including inheritance, association, and new structures of publishing and book distribution.[29] Indeed, Golden and Liming's work on specific instances of early twentieth-century author libraries shows the potential of contextualizing these materials wherever they are housed. Golden's work on modernist libraries focuses scholarly attention on those libraries held at special collections institutions, advocating for the importance of addressing annotated books alongside other archival materials.[30] In contrast, Liming's work traces how "implausible, and how providential, it is that Wharton's library should exist how and where it does today" at Wharton's estate, given specific difficulties with the sale but also the larger issues of selling and financing complete author libraries where they can be housed for more public-facing research or education purposes.[31]

Golden's examination of writers' libraries in *Annotating Modernism* suggests that modernism itself emerged as a discourse through its circulation within midcentury academic institutions, which can be traced through the idea of margins and annotation. It is perhaps because of modernism's entrenchment in academic discourse that early twentieth-century writers received significant critical attention as part of the literary canon, and have their libraries maintained in special collections institutions, including those that belonged to Virginia Woolf, John Berryman, Sylvia Plath, Ted Hughes, James Joyce, and others. The same cannot yet be said for poets who worked mostly outside of institutional contexts and mainstream recognition, suggesting that the already secondary consideration of writers' libraries in relation to their other archival holdings is considerably more precarious for lesser-known writers.

Beyond the institutional challenges, some libraries will never be housed at institutions for reasons related to their creators. At times, poets make no special provisions for their book collections, or request the dispersal of their libraries in their will. This dispersal, however, rarely means that the collection was insignificant to the poet in their lifetime; rather, it ensures that an already low-visibility source of evidence is all but doomed to destruction. Sometimes, this precarity is what gives a poet's library its cohesive force; Alan

Weiss suggests that "one only thinks of the totality of a library where it is depicted, catalogued, moved, sold . . . or burned."[32] In all cases, without documentation of the importance of the books as evidence of the poet's practices or as part of a conceptual project, scholars have little other option than to try and understand a library at the level of a book, using techniques such as close reading annotations, or establishing relationships between the book and the poets' work. In each instance—scholarly and institutional—the book rather than the library becomes the unit of analysis, when the very infrastructure and shape of knowledge that these libraries express is what gives them their intellectual power and historical import.

Olson, Lorde, di Prima, and Lansing

This book argues that the postwar American poet's library is a critical archival unit, or fonds, because of its deliberate arrangement and use. Through this approach, we might understand the poet's library as a radical act of knowledge production in defiance of the professional worlds and regulations of libraries, archives, and information management. To demonstrate this, I discuss four case studies: Charles Olson's Maud/Olson Library, Audre Lorde's librarianship and destroyed library, Diane di Prima's publishing and occult library, and Gerrit Lansing's house and library. For the libraries in question, I explore their material qualities, the types of history they reflect, and the ways that they connect to the poetic projects of their makers. And for Lorde, whose library, by her account, was destroyed in Saint Croix by Hurricane Hugo, I explore her thinking on librarianship and bibliography that reveals how, for her, poetry is a different epistemological structure whose capacities for information, knowledge, and understanding at times serve a comparable function to bibliography itself.

These poets are all interrelated through various degrees, though no monograph has yet placed them in close conversation. Olson and Lorde are perhaps the most studied and well-known of these writers, and whose work at times had institutional affiliations, though di Prima and Lansing are also important cohesive forces within twentieth-century American poetry and the communities that facilitated it. Lorde and di Prima went to high school together, and were part of a group of friends known as "The Branded" who read and wrote poetry and held seances for Keats, and Lorde delivered di Prima's second child in a New York City apartment. Di Prima published Lorde's first book on her poetry imprint, Poets Press, and she also published Olson, who was a close friend and, later, after his death, a spiritual companion. Lansing invited Olson to Gloucester for a reading at Hammond Castle, and the two engaged in poetic exploration of a place they both felt was *polis*—Dogtown, the Italian American fishing heritage of downtown, the rocky coasts. Lansing and di Prima were both longtime occult scholars and good friends, and their respective libraries are replete with kind inscriptions to each other on the flyleaves of books. Through the interrelatedness of these poets, we might see the connections and differences across their collections.

Each of these poets also has a semiprofessional to fully professional relationship with the organization of books. During much of her time in New York City, Di Prima worked in bookstores, where she "usually wound up doing the cataloguing . . . making sense of things, making order out of interminable piles of ancient texts," and Olson was known for conducting serious archival work even at the level of acquisitions, at one point assisting in the brokering of some D. H. Lawrence papers to the Library of Congress.[33] Likewise, Lorde's first career as a librarian spanned over a decade, which greatly influenced her approach to writing and her later professional identity as a teacher and poet. Lansing was twice a bookseller, in Annapolis, Maryland, and in Gloucester, Massachusetts—a gig that many friends note was a thin veil for his bibliophilic tendencies.

Each of the case studies in this book is somewhat ephemeral, and none of the collections mentioned have institutional affiliation at the time of this book's publication. As of 2021, Maud/Olson Library is currently planning a move and seeking additional sources of funding; di Prima's collection remains housed in her garage; Lansing's library has been largely removed from his house and its fragments are in the care of booksellers and private collectors; and Lorde's library is not a collection but rather documented in her reading lists and teaching bibliographies. Addressing these noninstitutional libraries is a political choice, motivated in part by the methods that undergird Elizabeth McHenry's call to "decenter formal education as the primary institutional force behind the reading of literature," particularly in the recuperation of those who were historically denied access to these institutions. While McHenry's work focuses on Black reading practices and bibliography in nineteenth-century America, particularly among free Black people, who established their own systems of knowledge production and literary discourse beginning in 1821, the racial dimensions of exclusion from traditional knowledge structures continued to apply well into the twentieth century; for instance, Ted Joans, in "The Book of the Best Travels To and Back from Timbuktu (1962–1978)," references researching in "the Public Library for Negroes" in 1941.[34] While Lorde's local library was the Schomburg Center of The New York Public Library, with children's librarian Augusta Baker and the extensive collections of Arturo Schomburg, as a child she still acutely felt her lack of representation and used it as grist for her librarianship, poetry, and teaching. Thus, by centering noninstitutional spaces, even as critical librarianship today has made many strides in the field toward equality and access, we might more fully consider different spaces as worthy of research, discussion, and, most importantly, preservation.

This ephemeral reality is in large part my motivation for the research that informed this book. We are in a critical moment for preserving and documenting these libraries, not only for the poets mentioned in this book but for others in their generation as well. Even if placing poets' libraries at institutions is not a reasonable goal—and in fact may run counter to the wishes of their collectors—documentation strategies that focus on the library as a whole unit of information and infrastructure can preserve our sense of these libraries for the decades to come. Furthermore, combining poets' own thoughts on their libraries and how they organize knowledge lets us understand their libraries on *their* terms—a crucial act of resistance in allowing poets to continue to write their own histories.

In this mission, I often reach for the tools of a book historian, using description, bibliography, and the historical context of the poets and their libraries. While the poetry of Olson, Lorde, di Prima, and Lansing all deserves more literary analysis and close reading than I am able to provide here—especially given that di Prima and Lansing's work has yet to receive the critical reception it warrants—my intention in these case studies is to describe their libraries and the historical context that led to their development. I want to underscore why it is important that *these* particular poets created collections, given their relationships with books, and how these affinities might lock into their poetics: that is, their worldview as contained within the structure of poetry as a life force.

With regard for the specificity of my subjects, I also do not purport to draw conclusions about *all* poets' libraries from these four case studies. Certainly at times there are shared characteristics among the personal libraries of poets working in countercultural and avant-garde communities—such as incompleteness or instability, which were often related to economic challenges, self-reflexive engagement with popular notions about libraries in twentieth-century America, tendencies toward occult materials, or narratives that decenter white European history, and so on. However, considering the poet's library as a type of archival series or fonds requires that we accept the idea of a "typical" poet's library is just as impossible as a "typical" manuscript or correspondence series in an author's archive. Rather, these collections of books or manuscripts are an intellectual grouping that makes legible a type of information that must always be explored on a specific basis. My intention in this book is to establish the importance of those poets' libraries that were made and still remain outside of institutional context, and to illuminate their work as acts of poetic knowledge. Each of these four disparate case studies refracts this argument in different ways.

My first case study addresses Charles Olson's approach to the development of his own library through his archival and book-collecting habits, especially as they relate to his research on Herman Melville's reading in *Call Me Ishmael*. I explore how his commitment to bibliography aligns with his concept of the "postmodern" (a term Olson coined in 1951, in a letter to Robert Creeley) as a profusion of information, requiring new ways to store and navigate materials. Olson's perspective on libraries and knowledge elaborates on his idea of *polis*, a key theme in his work that explores the possibilities of political community. This commitment is evident in the possibilities of the Maud/Olson Library, a collection built by Olson scholar Ralph Maud that includes a copy of every book Olson was ever thought to have read, including transcriptions of Olson's marginalia and specialized bookplates. I hone in on the William Butler Yeats section of the Maud/Olson Library—a poet who was one of Olson's first objects of study as an undergraduate—to show that while this library has been considered a "facsimile" of Olson's, it in fact has its own highly unique material qualities that can broaden our conception of how to make meaning from a poet's library as a conceptual and material unit, even in the absence of material evidence of the poet himself as the provenance. Waltzing through the stacks and specific material qualities of the Maud/Olson Library allows us to see the political and archival dimensions of poets collecting what they consider a broad scope of cross-disciplinary knowledge, and makes vivid the immensity of both Olson's and Maud's contributions to our understanding of this.

The second chapter turns to Audre Lorde, who was first published by Diane di Prima with Poets Press in 1968, the year that Olson was also published by di Prima in the anthology *War Poems*. Like Olson, Lorde exited a traditional and successful career to turn to a life of poetry and teaching, and 1968 was pivotal in this journey: that year, Lorde ended her decade-plus career as a librarian to move to Mississippi and teach as writer-in-residence at Tougaloo College, a Black liberal arts school. While much has been written about Lorde's postlibrarian life, Lorde's own writing in *Zami: A New Spelling of My Name* reveal the importance of libraries in her early life and the factors that influenced her pursuit of librarianship, which include her experiences at the Schomburg Center during a significant era of changes in collecting and cataloging practices related to the Black experience. Yet this alone was not enough for Lorde to feel that institutional libraries would allow her to find an epistemological solution for her very survival. Her essays, *Zami,* and *The Black Unicorn* reveal her own approaches to information, knowledge, and understanding that run counter to the scientific definitions of the era and are instead deeply invested in the power of poetry as a transformative force.

Lorde's reflections on her work as a librarian clearly render the mainstream structures of racism embedded in information management and institutional libraries, and thus show us more clearly what she and her contemporaries were rebelling against by developing their own knowledge-building practices. Yet, by her account, Lorde's library was destroyed by Hurricane Hugo in 1989 when it hit Saint Croix, where Lorde would live the last few years of her life with her partner, Gloria Joseph. As recourse, examining her reading as evidenced in her notebooks and teaching syllabi, particularly in light of new work on Black bibliography, proves somewhat recuperative. Yet for Lorde, poetry was the system of information management that most robustly held her webs of knowledge, in large part because of the political reality of her self-described Afro-Caribbean lesbian identity. Through this, Lorde offers us a way of understanding poets whose libraries are lost or never formed—especially poets whose identity was "forged in the crucible of difference" that was racially defined.[35]

Diane di Prima, a high school classmate, publisher, and friend to Audre Lorde, shared Lorde's investment in the importance of nonpatriarchal, non-European traditions that could be cultivated and learned as part of a poetic practice. For di Prima, possessing this type of knowledge was a primary tool for political revolution, which entailed reviving occulted knowledge in order to contact and understand "ALL LEVELS of one's own being" ("Revolutionary Letter #45"). In my discussion of di Prima's relationship with books, I situate her extensive work as a publisher of *The Floating Bear* and Poets Press to show the ways she built structures outside of traditional institutions with the intention of sharing work that was meant to be transformative: to "reclaim the planet, re-occupy / this ground," dreaming of a time when "the earth / BELONGS, at last, TO THE LIVING" ("Revolutionary Letter #35"). I trace these themes alongside her "occult library," a self-curated collection that dates from 1967 to 2020 and includes topics ranging from alchemy to soma ritual, medieval mysticism to crystal healing.

With close attention to the books, and interviews with di Prima, I explore the collection's arrangement, annotation, and evidence of use, to underscore the role of intuition in the development of her poetry and book collection. This is related to di Prima's ars poetica, enumerated in her memoir of her early years in New York City, titled *Recollections of My Life as a Woman:* "THE REQUIREMENTS OF OUR LIFE IS THE FORM OF OUR ART." She clarifies that "our" refers to women in particular, and that "requirements," a singular entity, might manifest as "the writing of modular poems, that could be dropped and picked up, the learning to sketch when you used to work in oils," no doubt influenced by di Prima's years as a mother of five young children during the height of her involvement in the Beat and counterculture poetry scenes.[36] Lorde also articulates this type of ars poetica in her call to "be aware of the effect of class and economic differences on the supplies available for producing art," discussing how the cost of materials for artworks, as well as the nature of poetry versus prose writing, determines what gets made and who is able to make it.[37] If Olson's radical contribution to postwar poetics was that poetry is created in the body of the poet, through listening and accessing "where breath has its beginnings," then poets like di Prima and Lorde make good on the fact that poetry begins in the body to explore work that resonates alongside Olson's definition of projective verse, which "involves a stance toward reality outside the poem": or perhaps, di Prima's "REQUIREMENTS OF OUR LIFE."[38] By engaging di Prima's library as a research collection that actively met her "requirements," we might more fully situate her radical poetics and knowledge-building practices.

Di Prima inscribed a number of books that I encountered on Gerrit Lansing's shelves; the two were good friends, and shared an abiding interest in the occult. Di Prima stayed with Lansing many times, including three visits to Gloucester in 1966, 1967, and 1968 to visit with their mutual friend Olson, but later Lansing would move into a large Victorian house, where he ultimately amassed tens of thousands of books. Prior to Gloucester, Lansing had numerous formative experiences: graduating from Harvard's undergraduate program with friends Frank O'Hara, Edward Gorey, and John Ashbery, and moving to New York City, where he cultivated friendships with John La Touche and Count Stefan Colonna Walewski, with whom he studied magic. Lansing brings together many streams of psychological and occult practice that had emerged in the early twentieth century. Among these, he underwent Jungian analysis, completed a master's degree on the early modern metaphysics of Henry Vaughan, and translated the early work of anthropologist Mircea Eliade, whose research on premodern alchemy was transformative for the field. As a gay man who practiced magic, Lansing's personal identity further cemented his investment in nonmainstream practices of knowing and being. These intersecting interests are revealed not only in the contents but also in the infrastructure of Lansing's library, which stretched to 1,237 linear feet, or approximately twenty thousand books at the time of his death in 2018.

This library was ordered to be dispersed in Lansing's will, and before this occurred in 2019, I documented each shelf and diagrammed each room of the library. While not a complete bibliography or catalog, this documentation suggests that Lansing's library can be understood best not by individual books but by the very structure of the house in which it was stored. Using Gaston Bachelard's *The Poetics of Space*—a text of which Lansing had two copies, in one of the most intimate rooms in the house, and was one of the final texts that Charles Olson read before his death—I suggest that even though Lansing's collection has been dispersed, the arrangement of subjects by rooms provides a way for us to work with his library even in its physical absence. With his house as a type of bibliographic cosmos, Lansing's poetic infrastructure here allows us to consider how memory itself is a generative quality of a poet's library, particularly as related to structures that are not books alone.

Cold War Containment: All Pots Are Made of Clay

In the early years of the Cold War, science and technology rose to prominence as the ultimate "rational" pursuits of truth, followed by social sciences and liberal arts such as history, with creative arts at the bottom of the hierarchy—useful by government officials for their ability to inspire patriotic loyalty through cultural production. Against the backdrop of science's supremacy, the variety of subjects and interests that poets include in their bibliographies and libraries is an eloquent rejoinder to the idea that poetry requires no research, only feeling. Their breadth also prompts us to reflect on the fragmentation of knowledge—comprehensive fields of understanding—into neatly parceled research disciplines (primarily academic) in postwar America. This phenomenon can be traced to the consciousness of a scientific era that sought to distill everything down to its minute parts: atoms, information, archives, scholarly disciplines.

Equally so, this fracturing is political, in that knowledge (or lack thereof) is embedded in governing, power, and agency. Starting in 1942 and 1943, respectively, Olson and fellow poet Muriel Rukeyser worked in the Office of War Information (OWI), where Olson eventually became the associate chief of the Foreign Language Division, and Rukeyser was a visual information specialist. In a statement regarding her work, Rukeyser writes, "By a tremendous and total effort, our civilization can grow in every part so that it can forever crush the fascist threat of brutalizing whatever good we have gained."[39] The OWI's efforts unfolded across a variety of print propaganda, including the operation of libraries in Allied nations that served as hubs of information "for the prosecution of the war" and to diffuse American values abroad.[40] And indeed, the rising tides of information management—as indicated by Rukeyser's role as a specialist in visual propaganda—meant that both Olson and Rukeyser were highly aware of the new ways in which knowledge was being created and distributed in light of information theory and cybernetics. Despite Rukeyser's optimism, the OWI was unable to provide an antidote to the rising horrors of World War Two. In 1944, Olson resigned from his post, citing the office's censorship of war news. Two years later, he composed "La Preface," one of the first poems to mention the Holocaust, for the art opening of his friend Corrado Cagli, a Roman sculptor who had been at the liberation of Buchenwald in 1945. Later, both Olson and Rukeyser were persecuted by the FBI for their time in the office—Rukeyser on suspicions of Communism, and Olson while rector at Black Mountain College.[41] As di Prima remembers, "I grew up in the world of McCarthy, of the death of the Rosenbergs and of Wilhelm Reich, of endless witch hunts"; the poet Vincent Ferrini, an anarchist resident of Gloucester and an inspiration to Olson, was targeted for his teaching and union work by the House Un-American Activities Committee hearings.

It is important to acknowledge that only certain writers were subject to this treatment; at the same time as these FBI investigations, university-based creative writing programs were booming. As Eric Bennett notes in *Workshops of Empire*, Paul Engle's fundraising for the University of Iowa's Writers' Workshop rested in large part on claims that the program fought Communism, and that these workshops functioned according to the logic of the Truman Doctrine: a cultural force that required Americans to internalize the idea of "containment" on the level of both government enforcement and individual responsibility, and fostered a cultural climate in which citizens sought "to contain themselves, restrain themselves, demanding that others live within boundaries."[42] Contrast this with the perspectives of poets working largely outside of institutional context: Diane di Prima, "Revolutionary Letter #1": "I have just realized the stakes are myself." Robert Duncan, paraphrased by Ammiel Alcalay: "I have no recourse to taste" when "the work of Olson, Levertov, and others 'belongs not to my appreciations but to my immediate concerns in living.'"[43] Adrienne Rich, in conversation with Audre Lorde about poets teaching Black studies and women's studies: "This is not just a question of being 'allowed' to have our history or literature or theory in the old power framework" but "it is every minute of our lives, from our dreams to getting up and brushing out teeth to when we go teach."[44] For poets writing outside of mainstream institutions in the United States during the Cold War, poetics was not a philosophical question but an immediate matter for survival.

Given this, it is significant that around the same time as creative writing programs were putting down roots, the Lower East Side and West Coast countercultures were in full swing with mimeographs, mail art, assemblages, poets' theaters, and experimental dance: permeable practices in which art and poetry imbued every aspect of life, spilling from classrooms and galleries into the street, bars, and cafes. Yet, too often, this history is not animated as the boundary-crossing crucible that it was; instead, it remains contained in distinct boxes—of individual memory, poets' archives that are spread across institutions and geographies, and libraries that have been dispersed. Politically speaking, this is convenient for the power structures that have made this inevitable in the United States. But ethically, for those of us who study literature, we are obligated to search across these containers for narratives that may be hidden by material circumstance.

This informational challenge was anticipated at the turn of the twentieth century by Brooks Adams, whose *The New Empire* (1902) was a formative text for both Olson and Baraka. In this work, Adams grapples with the growing influence of scientific industry on the United States' political influence, as well as with what Baraka calls the "complete domination" of the "economic sensibility" as part of a broader hostility toward artistic and creative life in American culture.[45] Adams focuses intently on books as physical and conceptual units, arguing that the overemphasis on books within libraries as a fundamental unit of knowledge limits our ability to synthesize and derive meaningful knowledge from ever-increasing bibliographies. He compares books to facts, noting that "what gives facts value is their relation to each other; for when enough have been collected to suggest a sequence of cause and effect, a generalization can be made which scientific men call a 'law.'"[46] And while the idea of knowledge organized by "scientific" reasoning is particularly charged in the early twentieth century, Adams's insistence that "no attempt has been made to digest what has been gathered," and that "libraries are no longer able to buy and catalog the volumes which appear, and he who would read intelligently must first learn to eliminate," speaks to a problem we might now characterize as postmodern.[47]

Poets' libraries embody Adams's idea in the sense that they are about not individual books but rather interrelated subjects and the meanings created between and among texts. While Adams's influence on Olson is evident, di Prima takes a similar approach but with a different teacher: Paracelsus, the early modern alchemist. In "Paracelsus: An Appreciation," di Prima writes that "the alchemists of Paracelsus's day saw unity (a single substance, or principle under many disguises) where we spend years cataloguing differences: they felt the world as organic."[48] With the informational alchemy in mind, this book also underscores Olson's, di Prima's, Lansing's, and Lorde's devotion to intuition as a method for poetic research, particularly for subjects that are fragmentary or fugitive. For di Prima and Lansing, this is an alchemical project at its core: "The *materia prima* is the single substance of which all matter is composed, as 'all pots are of clay.'"[49]

In this sense, this book attempts to build on the foundational work of Ammiel Alcalay's *a little history* by addressing certain challenges he poses, especially how we negotiate "information overload on the one hand, and containment—excluded areas—on the other," and, when it comes to our most recent generation of poetic history, "How do you categorize information, how do you deal with knowledge, how do you find it, how do you transmit it?"[50] Alcalay notes the distortion of history that literary genres such as Black Mountain, San Francisco Renaissance, Beat, and other labels introduce, where they "get us to one section of the shelf without letting us see the whole library."[51] Libraries, then, are epistemological and political recourse—for poets assembling knowledge, and for those of us who seek to understand history not as sections on a shelf but as a vast and rhizomatic extension of multiple voices across material forms. In particular, libraries that belong to poets are some of the most potent and unmediated artifacts available for us to achieve this type of understanding. With little surprise, they are also some of the most precarious and low-visibility collections that stand in the balance today. To rectify this, in what follows, I seek to sketch the contours of a few key poets' libraries as imaginative, intuitive, and liberatory acts of knowledge building. By characterizing them thus, we might better understand the poetics—or, in di Prima's alchemical metaphor, the clay—that gives these objects their unity, meaning, and distinctive material force.

FIGURE 1. Books in the Maud/Olson Library, Gloucester, 2019.
—Photograph by M. C. Kinniburgh.

CHAPTER 1
"BIBLIO. & LIBRARY"
Charles Olson and the Maud/Olson Library

BOOK HISTORY FOLLOWS the principle of an entropic universe: cohesion succumbs to eventual diffusion. As Ammiel Alcalay notes, the flow of historical materials between people, institutions, and spaces renders our records "atomized, pulled apart, stored in separate containers, making it much harder for us to inhabit coherent stories, to make sense of ourselves, our history, and the times we live in."[1] In the mid-twentieth century, the poet Charles Olson came to a similar conclusion during his scholarship on Herman Melville, and in particular Melville's reading practices. Because of financial troubles, after Melville's death in 1891 his family sold his richly annotated library to dealers all over the East Coast. Beginning in 1933, Olson began to identify and gather these books from booksellers. In reconstituting this collection, he was one of the first scholars to encounter Melville's reading notes—sometimes mere "x" marks in the margin, but, as in the case of his copies of Shakespeare, sometimes revealingly annotated.[2] During his graduate work in Harvard's History of American Civilization doctoral program from 1936 until 1939, Olson analyzed these annotations alongside Melville's research on the New England whaling industry, and argued for their fundamental connection to *Moby Dick* (1851).[3] Harvard scholar F. O. Matthiessen (who brought Olson to Harvard) praised Olson's 1937 essay "Lear and Moby Dick" in his classic *American Renaissance*.[4]

Olson completed a book-length draft of his scholarship on Melville's reading practices and library in 1940, placing this material aside as he joined the Office of War Information in 1942 as the assistant chief of the Foreign Language Division, a post he resigned in 1944 in protest of government censorship policies. Olson's manuscript was later published as *Call Me Ishmael* in

1947, and he turned his comprehensive list of Melville's books over to Merton Sealts, who completed *Melville's Reading* (1948) by building on Olson's inventories.[5] During the height of anti-Communist panic in the 1950s, C. L. R. James composed *Mariners, Renegades, and Castaways: The Story of Herman Melville and the World We Live In* (1953) while detained for months on Ellis Island under political suspicions of subversion.[6] In *Mariners, Renegades, and Castaways*, James explored the political dimensions of *Moby Dick* and Melville, particularly on the shifting edges of totalitarianism and democracy that became so immediately relevant while he was detained. While Olson's and James's fates were radically different, their shared interest marks the political and historical relevance of Melville at the time—at once neglected by mainstream scholarship and politically salient, if not downright subversive.

In light of this, Olson's attempts to physically regather the books of this little-understood author likely raised eyebrows at the time—though at a 2019 auction, a lot containing two of Melville's annotated books cleared one hundred thousand dollars. Yet Olson's collecting proved essential to scholars who recognized Melville's literary merits—such as Raymond Weaver, whose work helped launch the "Melville revival"—and Olson was an active participant in this community of scholars. David Herd, in the introduction to *Contemporary Olson*, describes Olson's fundamental contribution as no less than "alter[ing] the field of Melville studies, both as archivist (re-assembling Melville's library) and through his radical re-contextualization of *Moby-Dick*."[7] This "re-contextualization" of Melville's work takes place both materially and conceptually, setting the stage for a methodological lineage; Olson's approach to Melville would become a template for scholars to one day address *The Maximus Poems* through Olson's own sprawling piles of books. As Ann Charters notes in her *Olson/Melville: A Study in Affinity* (1968), which traces Olson's approach to Melville, Olson's work amounts to more than that of a "scholar or academic critic," but, more dramatically, a "basic restructuring of the entire human universe."[8] As Charters and others have argued, Olson's utilization of Melville, books, and bibliography as part of a larger cosmological and poetic project is one of the hallmarks of his influence. Projects such as Richard Grossinger's *Olson-Melville Sourcebooks* (1976); Albert Glover and Jack Clarke's decades-long chapbook or fascicle series, *A Curriculum of the Soul*; Charters's aforementioned work; and, perhaps most monumentally, Ralph Maud's *Charles Olson's Reading: A Biography* (1996) all follow the impulse to map Olson's reading practice as a way to understand his work, just as Olson did with Melville.[9]

Ralph Maud, however, set out on a quest to match Olson's extreme biblio-philic impulse. Over the course of his own lifetime, Maud collected copies of books that he deduced Olson had read, drawing on evidence in his poetry, correspondence, teaching materials, and even his apartment at 28 Fort Square in Gloucester, Massachusetts. Maud's letters to and from friends and book dealers testify to the obsessive and painstaking nature of this project, with printouts of catalog entries from the online rare book website AbeBooks, receipts from local bookstores totaling hundreds of dollars, and back-and-forth banter about specific copies and volumes. After Maud's passing in 2014, this collection of books, comprising over three thousand volumes, was trans-ported to Gloucester and named the Maud/Olson Library. The collection now lives with Ralph Maud's personal papers, anchored by Charles Olson's own massive, cigarette-burned, paint-streaked writing desk.

The Maud/Olson Library (MOL) is an idiosyncratic resource to say the least. As a physical library of the book-based knowledge of a man, it is not just a facsimile of a legacy library belonging to Olson (the books possessed by Olson are mostly at the University of Connecticut–Storrs with the rest of his literary papers) but a conceptual project in its own right. The conceptual aspect derives from the library's close relationship to enumerative bibliography, which for Olson—who first coined the term "postmodern" and its concomitant connota-tions of fragmented, expanded, unknowable narratives—was a crucial practice. In particular, bibliography relates to the idea of thoroughness in ways that Olson addresses in his advice in *A Bibliography on America for Ed Dorn* (1964). By telling Dorn to "saturate" and "beat" a single subject until it is fully known, Olson argues that "the point is *to get all* that has been said on given subject" and not just through "*books: they stop*" but also through archival documents, primary sources, and other premises that expand the small world of published material.[10] Completeness of Olson's own material traces is elusive, as it is for many other authors; his materials are housed in multiple special collections across North America, including the MOL. Yet if, after Benjamin Friedlander, we consider Olson's work as a "borderless archive" that rejects the idea of "the book as ultimate horizon," we might more fully explore the iterative, possibly dialectic relationship between knowledge and its material form when the ques-tion of completeness or saturation consistently eludes us.[11]

Charles Olsen lived, worked, and wrote during an era dominated by a physics-heavy consciousness of the atomic bomb that sought to distill every-thing down to its minute parts: atoms, information, archives, scholarly disci-plines.[12] The question of the atomic bomb was that of "scale," according to Leo

Szilard (the Hungarian American physicist whose inventions led to the initiation of the Manhattan Project), in the knowledge that led to its production and in the destructive effects it produced.[13] This micro- and macro-consciousness had particular stakes for conceptualizing knowledge not unlike a mushroom cloud: how do we contain a rapidly proliferating body of knowledge in stable material form, and how are our practices influenced by the ramifications of information overload? While recent scholarship increasingly addresses Olson's approach to knowledge building in the era of information overload, we have yet to fully address the archival implications of these forms of understanding.[14] The MOL affords an opportunity to examine not just Olson's knowledge-building practices and how they might reflect a postwar American sense of information management but also the archival elements that render this process visible and will preserve it for future generations of poets and scholars.

This focus on archives and materiality is tied directly to Olson's poetics and epistemology; for him, knowledge was always embodied, buried in the soil, material and real. The MOL's material qualities are experimental grounds to consider Olson's priorities as a "historian of ideas" and also, in the words of his mentor, Edward Dahlberg, a "historian of realities."[15] Olson's work relied on a symbiotic approach to the material considerations of his world—Gloucester, Mayan potsherds, research in England on the colonial period—combined with the question of how we can touch what can be known. Even for Olson's cosmological approach, "space, like myth, had to be as actual, solid, and factual as everything else," and characterized by "insistence upon the concrete and literal condition of all cosmic forms."[16] We might then take Olson's work in book history and the resulting archival traces as the bedrock of his very poetics and relationship to knowing, and part of a larger response to the dematerialization of knowledge in postwar America, after N. Katherine Hayles's call to see information as material and embodied (which I will discuss more extensively in relationship to Audre Lorde's work).

Thus, while the premise of the MOL speaks specifically to scholars of Olson and New American poetry, as a special collection it is part of a larger conversation that concerns the visibility and interpretation of postwar American poets' libraries, particularly as subjects that warrant the scholarly toolkit of a book historian. While the MOL's idiosyncratic structure does not necessarily make it a typical example of poet-generated libraries from this era (since it is not in fact generated by the poet itself), the very uniqueness of this resource allows us to think broadly of the institutional and material qualities of what we might conceptualize as a poet's library. In particular, this collection's dual representation of Olson and of Maud makes vivid the possibilities of what happens when the material paradox of the bibliography as a conceptual act—summoning books that are materially absent but intellectually present—is challenged by being made physically present. With regard to Olson's own interest in enumerative bibliography, a practice of inventory in which books shape (or limit) the field of what is possible to be known, the MOL provides insights into how Olson's conceptual project of shaping the "human universe" or postmodern knowledge itself relates to and operates on specific material conditions. By negotiating the conceptual and the material in the MOL, I will contextualize the possibilities of the collection as a model for the very real physical considerations of noninstitutionalized archival spaces and holdings, in an era marked by the proliferation of knowledge with increasingly destabilized structures in which to house it.

Material: Making the Maud/Olson Library

In his 2016 essay "Driving Charles Olson's Brain," Gregor Gibson, an author, antiquarian book dealer (who in fact sold certain volumes to Maud for his collection), and founding member of the Maud/Olson steering committee, recounts the odyssey he took in 2015 after Maud's death in 2014 to pack up and relocate the library from Vancouver to Gloucester, where Maud's bequest had donated it to the Gloucester Writers Center.[17] Joined by Henry Ferrini, the director of the Gloucester Writers Center, documentary filmmaker, and nephew of Vincent Ferrini (addressee of the first *Maximus* letters), Gibson describes the transcontinental drive and its deep reveal of America's "sprawling, gorgeous, deep, murderous, inscrutable" self. Gibson then applies this same litany of adjectives, in the very same order, to "Olson's Brain," his term of affection for the Maud/Olson Library. This repetition weaves together the vastness of the American landscape and of Olson's knowledge, invoking the sublime ("gorgeous," "murderous") and conceptualizing the immensity of Maud's project and its possibilities.

The books, as Maud envisioned them, forge direct lines back to Olson. Maud spent decades hunting down copies of books Olson had read and accessioning them into his collection via annotation and bookplates. When possible, Maud transcribed Olson's own marginalia into the books he had collected. Maud also created a bookplate for each item, containing a summary of the book's relationship to Olson, and sometimes page numbers where annotations had been carefully inscribed. The bookplates offer a preliminary template for understanding the collection itself; each plate is titled "Charles Olson Collection," with a picture of Olson's book-strewn table and office, and captioned: "The main working area in Olson's apartment. He usually slept here. From his chair at the desk he could look out and see Ten Pound Island, the outer harbor of Gloucester, and out to sea." Below that were four dotted lines for Maud's contextualizing annotations, and centered at the bottom of the plate, "Ex libris ~ Ralph Maud." The bookplates document the intimacy of Maud's connection with Olson's work through his books. Thus, the MOL not only represents "Olson's Brain," using books as metonymy for the knowledge they provided Olson, but also "Maud's Brain": the obsessive scholarly and personal project of assembling such a vast corpus of materials.

The MOL inventory was comprehensively published as issue numbers sixty-four, sixty-five, and sixty-six of *The Minutes of the Charles Olson Society*, in conjunction with the Charles Olson Centenary Conference at Simon Fraser University on June 4–6 in 2010. This publication crystallized, to some extent, a complex acquisitional and bibliographic history that is now materially solid-ified and accessible on the shelves of the MOL, which was originally housed in an upstairs commercial space on 108 East Main Street, down the road from the Gloucester Writers Center (housed in Vincent Ferrini's old framing shop and home). Launched in spring 2016 with support from André Spears, the MOL holds the Ralph Maud papers as well as Olson's writing desk. Ann Charters donated paintings by Theresa Bernstein, and Thorpe Feidt paintings line the hallway. The poet Gerrit Lansing, a close friend of Olson's, also donated mate-rials and even annotated Maud's bookplates with his own personal knowledge of Olson's reading. The collection is community-oriented, with the scholars, writers, and artists who know the most about Ralph Maud and Charles Olson serving on the steering committee or advising in various formal or informal capacities. Thus, the MOL is not just a museum of Maud's collection but con-tinues to be curated collectively by those who understand its context best.

Maud donated the collection to the Gloucester Writers Center before he passed away, with the understanding that it would be housed and displayed in a dedicated space in Gloucester for at least five years.[18] The books might well have remained in Vancouver, but in October 2015 an agreement was reached and Miriam Nichols, Alan Franey, Peter Grant, Henry Ferrini, and Gregor Gibson brought the MOL to Gloucester in a U-Haul.[19] The shape of the Maud/Olson Library remains to be determined; neither its location nor its funding is permanent. Efforts to contextualize the MOL and seek scholars to animate it continue; the Gloucester Writers Center provides key contextualization and an audience for the Maud/Olson Library, in the former's mission to offer extensive curricula and community that supports local writers across education levels and genres. And in 2019, the MOL brought sixty volumes to the Graduate Center, CUNY, for a pop-up exhibition and conversation about independent special collections, with the sponsorship of the Community Grants Program from the Bibliographical Society of America. As of 2021, the books are slated to move into a newly renovated Gloucester Writers Center, where they will serve as the working library of this organization—a move that requires significant fundraising but would increase the financial stability of this project immensely.

To fully understand the capacities of the Maud/Olson Library, we must understand the collection as a vector into understanding each word in its title: Maud, the scholar; Olson, the poet who approaches knowledge as fundamentally material; and the library as an institutional unit that can be reframed in light of the conceptual qualities of the men whose brains it purports to represent. Assessing the interplay across these categories gives us greater insight into the possibilities and limitations of "Olson's Brain," as well as lessons on formulating special collections spaces and experiences that reflect their creators and contents.

Conceptual: Making the Maud/Olson Library

While two short years passed between Maud's death and the establishment of the Maud/Olson Library, the scholarship represented on the shelves of the MOL has been culminating for decades, fed by Maud's own talents and the synergistic fact that scholars who study Olson tend toward Olson's own principle of a saturation job in their staggering thoroughness. George Butterick, a student of Olson's and the curator of Literary Archives at the University of Connecticut during the acquisition of Olson's materials, had produced a "Preliminary List" before the full bibliography appeared.[20] Butterick, too, had extensive interest in Olson's books, and augmented the collection at Storrs that was based on Olson's volumes from Black Mountain with additional volumes of books Olson was thought to have read. Maud's project, though, is a unique combination of Olsonia and collecting chops. No stranger to building large-scale book collections, he is largely responsible for the Contemporary Literature Collection at Simon Fraser, where he acquired pamphlets, chapbooks, little magazines, and other ephemeral items representing the years from 1945 to 1965. Thus, while the MOL currently does not have an institutional affiliation, its generator was highly skilled in navigating traditional environments for acquiring and maintaining special collection resources.

In particular, Ralph Maud's papers within the Maud/Olson Library offer a close-at-hand means of contextualizing the efforts that went into the development of his collection. The papers, currently being cataloged by Gregor Gibson, consist largely of correspondence that reveals the deeply networked nature of the project of collecting Olson's books. A crucial player in this story is Jack Clarke, and his visit to 28 Fort Square in 1965 after Betty Olson's death in a car accident. To lure Olson home again (he had not been back in the apartment since her death), Jack and Sue Clarke went in to help with the basics—cleaning floors, placing books back on shelves. In this process, Jack Clarke began to create an inventory of Olson's books in a series of small notebooks. He recounted the process to Maud in a 1989 letter, housed in the Ralph Maud papers located at the MOL:

> When we arrived the back door was open, the padlock broken, so it had been entered by unknown persons already. Jean and I secured the place. As far as she could tell, nothing was missing. I assume the library was fairly intact at the date of the inventory. Later, when George [Butterick] actually took possession of the books, things had by then come up missing (why he made use of my list in the archive magazine), some before his death, especially from the other side where he had boxes (Linda Parker might know about this period), some after, to family, etc. Kate and Connie were there directly—unfortunately things got disposed of—not books, but things—which I know George wanted for the archive. Not big things . . . but simply, say, a shirt to show size etc., or a table used to write on, an old wobbly throw-away anything. The big things got sold anyway, so neither archive nor family has them, though George was always looking out for stuff that might come up for sale in N.Y. this way to buy back for the archive (though resources always slim post-Olson #10.). Jean has some books of Charles that never entered the archive. Of course this works both ways, e.g., Charles had many of Harvey's books on loan which George would never let him have back, like 2 sets of the Historica Highways. So, along with Linda, Harvey, & Kate, Boer was also in and out of the Fort in this time frame (though his memory leaves a lot to be desired, to put it mildly), but I'm afraid you'll only get 'stories' if anything as to discrepancies between my list of 1965 and the actual situation, 1970. So I guess it's quite fortunate that more were not lost in this period (mainly because of annotation, obviously), because the place was never secure except when he was occupying it.[21]

This passage highlights the basic question of household security in gauging the accuracy of Olson's library, since his home had been broken into by "unknown persons" by the time Clarke began his inventory. This instability is accompanied by tension between how archivists and families approach objects; Butterick had wanted a shirt to show Olson's size, for instance, while Connie and Kate (Olson's former wife and their daughter) had disposed of many personal belongings in cleaning out the apartment. The passage contains a variety of names, highlighting the dense social structures that govern the distribution of Olson's books or evidence of them having been there, including Jean's books that "never entered the archive," and Olson's borrowed copies that Butterick claimed for Storrs. Finally, Clarke characterizes the list as highly permeable, since Olson's place was "secure" only when Olson himself was in it, and otherwise the flow of books between people in Olson's milieu can be characterized only by disparate "stories." For Clarke, while the list technically solidifies Olson's collection at a certain time, its entire premise is marked by instability and permeability.

This impossibility of completeness is matched only by the intensity of our desire for it. Reflecting on a moment when he arrived at Olson's apartment, only to interrupt him in the act of writing in a poem, Maud asserts that observing Olson's desk and room scattered with books gave way to the "conviction that to follow the evidences of Olson's reading—the books he kept, the books he stored or gave away, the books that the poems, essays, and letters reveal he used, the significant articles in magazines he was sent or read at the drugstore counter or whatever (there is so much evidence, and the abundance is to the point)—to follow Olson's movement within these source works is the best way to get into the poems, which, as I witnessed, are often a direct extension of his reading. The life of the poet was a life within books."[22] Parentheticals often paradoxically set aside a key point—here, the question of "abundance" of evidence in the sheer variety of scope of Olson's reading. Of primary importance is the manifold nature of the material, much of it ephemeral or possibly inconclusive. Items that we might traditionally conceive of as "ephemera," including the descriptions of "drugstore counter" or "whatever" magazine article, are calcified in Olson's letters, lectures, and poems, meticulously reconstructed and traced by Maud. The very materiality of some of these items resists completeness, and it is a testament to Maud's skills as a collector that so much of it remains preserved.

Thus, the MOL's current incarnation in Gloucester is only a moment of temporary stasis in a long history of such moments. This can make its interpretation challenging at times, especially to broader audiences. While the MOL has welcomed dozens of visitors and researchers, from local high schoolers to

Olson translators, André Spears also acknowledges that there exists a "possible alternate view of the Maud/Olson Library as a waste of time and money, a collection of replicas that are basically fakes, from which are missing the bibliophilic items of true value."[23] The skeptical alternative, however, does not stand up to close examination of the history and structure of the MOL. The books are not replicas of Olson so much as they are originals from Maud: a material testament to his conceptual project while they gesture also toward Olson's own knowledge and reading practices. The lack—rather, impossibility—of completeness in a bibliographic project such as this is fundamental to the conceptual work of the MOL in its representation of Olson's knowledge practices. It underscores, in material form, that knowledge building is *always* in process, despite the appearance of fixity in material instantiations such as libraries or archives. This indeterminacy, this in-processness, reminds us of Olson's own always-unfinished epistemological work: scoping fields of knowledge, negotiating the postmodern problem of information overload. Fortunately, the MOL offers us a few sense-making techniques.

"Biblio. & Library"

On the one hand, the question of completeness thus far refers to the collection of the books in the context of a full library. On the other, completeness

FIGURE 2. Ralph Maud among the Maud/Olson Library, sitting at Charles Olson's desk, 2012. —Photograph courtesy of John Faulise.

and its impossibility in the context of the MOL also refers to Olson's reading practices: that is, what was actually *read* and why it matters. Of Olson's master's thesis, Maud cautions that we need not be "gulled into assuming that everything mentioned has been read," noting that Olson's passing allusions to major literary works do not appear in his later library or even necessarily in his poetry.[24] Likewise, Gerrit Lansing annotates the Maud bookplate of *Phenomenology of Perception* by M. Merleau-Ponty (translated by Colin Smith) with the simple "Did O see the book?"

The difficulty of comprehensiveness over the course of a lifetime means that there is no stable, material concept of a library that was expanding ever-outward; the only evidence we truly have of Olson's reading practice must be obtained through multimodal sources, given its existence in his actual books, Maud's Olson library, and Olson's letters, lectures, poetry, interviews, and other material traces. Olson's ever unstable financial circumstances as well as his intellectual interests shaped his library as a living thing. And, of course, very few individuals have a stable library over the course of decades. How, then, do we negotiate the conceptual project of the MOL alongside an understanding of Olson's own library? In his letter to Maud, Clarke described the difference between his and Butterick's lists of Olson's reading:

> Butterick's list in Olson doesn't include all the books here because:
>
> A) As you ask, some of the books are not his.
>
> B) Many of these titles, especially specialized, expensive ones, were borrowed from the SUNY library by Charles, so though 'his' he didn't own them—the dif. between biblio. & library.
>
> C) Furthermore, many books recommended along the way were from memory, once he had seen or used previously, but not possessed at any time.

Here, Clarke identifies a key premise, expanded over points A, B, and C: the difference between "biblio. & library" as a result of many of Olson's books not being his own property. Clarke notes, "Though 'his' he didn't own them," characterizing the "his" as Olson having intellectual command although not material ownership over the items. "Library," for Clarke, implies some sense of material ownership.[25] However, one can "own" a book without possessing it materially, given the symbolic value of the book as metonym for Olson's knowledge and his distillation of the contents within it. Within this paradigm, the word "library" in the context of the Maud/Olson collection is indeed fitting—Maud established actual ownership over all of the books he assembled for the project—but Clarke's distinction highlights the conceptual paradox of the

MOL. The MOL is a synthetic fabrication, a conceptual unit materialized by Maud that would not otherwise have ever become incarnate. To that end, in terms of technique, the only way to stabilize the concept of "Olson's Library" or, as Gibson calls it, "Olson's Brain," is enumerative bibliography—a practice closely tied to book collecting as well as Olson's own critical work.

Enumerative bibliography entails the listing of publication and bibliographic (that is, book as physical object) information on items that relate to a specific subject, with the goal of author- or subject-specific comprehensiveness. It is perhaps one of Olson's earliest and most persistent literary forms. In the beginning of his master's thesis, Olson provides "the first complete bibliography of Herman Melville ever attempted," bringing together unpublished letters, doctoral theses, and published works from across US libraries.[26] Later, in 1955, at Black Mountain, at Edward Dorn's request he writes *A Bibliography on America for Ed Dorn*, which circulates privately for years until its printing in 1964 by Donald Allen as a pamphlet by the Four Seasons Foundation in San Francisco.[27] While for the MOL, bibliographic knowledge of Olson underlies the conceptual and material unit of the "library" itself, for Olson, bibliography functions not as evidence of reading that has been accomplished but rather as mapping the contours of what can be known based on textual evidence at a certain point in time. This practice of bibliography as testing the limits of what can be *known* in the future, as opposed to evidence of what has been read or digested in the *past*, is essential to understanding Olson's relationship to materiality—and thus, the way this understanding crystallizes on the MOL's shelves.

In *A Bibliography on America for Ed Dorn*, Olson advocates for a "saturation job" of a subject—"to dig one thing or place or man," either archaeologically or enthusiastically (dig it?), until one's knowledge is exhaustive. Olson advocates for this process occurring within "primary documents," as Maud reprints:

> Repository #1: THE NATIONAL ARCHIVES, Wash., D.C.
>   " #2: Senate Documents (published)
>   " #3: Bureau of Am. Ethnology Reports & Bulletins
> (pub. by the Smithsonian Inst.)[28]

Not only does Olson use the institutional language of the "repository," the overarching term for an organization that holds archives, collections, libraries, and other cultural heritage collections, but he advocates first and foremost for an archival approach.[29] Books, he argues just prior to this list, contain finite information that requires supplementation, interrogation, and further digging. Olson practiced what he preached; he recounts to Ann Charters in *Olson/Melville* how he chased a lead in a book to the Shaw Papers at the Massachusetts Historical Society by sitting in their donor's kitchen, realizing the connection, and then making a beeline for the archive.[30] Not only proficient in the interpersonal dealings of archival research, Olson was involved in archival creation. In a 1950 letter, he recounts going into a bookshop to find a copy of D. H. Lawrence's *Fantasia* and instead finding the bookseller in possession of a collection whose sale he then facilitated to the Library of Congress.[31] While the worlds of archivist and academic can be disparate today, as a result of efforts for professionalization in both fields over the course of the century, Olson offers a fluid model—more common in the first half of the twentieth century, during an era of interest in establishing special collections and also public libraries—that generatively blends researcher and collector roles in the service of the subject at hand.

While characterized by an archival impulse, Olson's thinking was often shaped by information science, especially by Norbert Wiener's *Cybernetics* (1948), which shows up almost wholesale in "The Kingfishers" (1949).[32] In an echo of atomic theory, a popularly known development of modern physics, Wiener framed humans as machines, in which all elements of information and communication could be reduced to their parts. Olson's work with primary sources shows a strong interest in taxonomies of information and materials; Maud recounts Olson's 1953 handout to freshmen that states *"fiction is only one form of storytelling"* and lists other forms: "the dictionary," "the encyclopedia," "the library card catalogue," and *"Reader's Guide to Periodical Literature,"* then "Herodotus's *History*" and the daily newspaper.[33] The variety of reference genres here as generative, *narrative* forms is striking for its dissonance with contemporaneous literary studies. I. A. Richards in *Principles of Literary Criticism* (1924) cites *Britannica*-style resources as "negligible," while Olson wields them to great effect in "The Kingfishers," where he includes language from the *Encyclopaedia Britannica* to describe the bird's life cycle.[34] For Olson, returning to primary sources, to dictionaries, to library catalogs, to the fundamental *units* of information offers an opportunity to seek information at its *source*, recombine it on the atomic level, and develop new fields of understanding based therein.

For Olson, source information was an intellectual priority, and its presence in his work is reflected with varied degrees of "processed" and "unprocessed" information. After the traditional archival definition, "processed" collections have been fully accessioned by their repository, include a finding aid or other catalog record, and are served in a dedicated space in a particular manner based on the policies of the institution. Olson, sitting at the kitchen table of a literary executor and then pawing through boxes at the Massachusetts Historical Society, or wandering a bookstore only to broker a significant collection, engages with primary sources at a highly unmediated and unprocessed level—he often intervened actively in the sources themselves. Thus, a possible parallel emerges between Olson's archival approach and his approach to reference. His approach to knowledge development is to build information up close to its source, before interpretation, in the act of collating its fundamental material or definitional existence.

This re-*source*-fulness as a strategy for assembling knowledge is fundamental to Olson's approach to bibliography as well, especially in his *Bibliography on America for Ed Dorn*. Dorn reflected on the *Bibliography* in his Olson Memorial Lectures at Buffalo in 1981, noting its meaningfulness to him, and specifically that

> the value for a student in a well-conceived bibliography is not in the bibliography's comprehension, or completeness, if such a completion were possible, but in the engagement of certain of its—I don't want to say "genes." But in the engagement of certain of its—I'd like to say here that the lighthearted depreciation of some of Olson's sources on the basis that some of them are dated—for instance, I've heard this charged against the Pleistocene work—or not up to date, leave me cold, and unimpressed. The value of a working instructional bibliography lies in its net of connections. It isn't concerned with the latest so-called "corrections" and insights of the latest worker, or the latest hot number. The value for a student in a well-conceived bibliography is not in the bibliography's comprehension, but in the engagement of certain of its genes.[35]

Dorn speaks iteratively here, looping back on his definition multiple times to refine the difference between the content and the connections within a bibliography. Fundamentally, the bibliography offers an opportunity to explore a "net of connections" that is not necessarily comprehensive but demonstrates a path to certain foundational ideas, traditions, circumstances, or individuals—what Dorn deems "genes." This biological approach envisions bibliography as a living organism, in possession of genetic matter that can be queried and explored, as well as a vector to return to a source, to the cellular level of knowledge in this metaphor, by way of examining the interconnectedness of textuality.

Dorn goes on to suggest that the source-based quality of bibliography means it functions like a "map" that can be read in manifold ways, since maps are used to "go different places" and "do different things" depending on their users.[36] Indeed, this is a useful template for the Maud/Olson Library on the whole, whose contents can be animated in a variety of ways depending on its audience. In the MOL, multiple prisms of intellectual depth filter the experience itself. These prisms—Olson's approach to reading, the actual subjects of his library, Maud's approach to Olson's reading, the depth of his research on this topic—exist in a vast array of archival materials, from Olson's reading lists and correspondence and even his poetry, to Maud's letters, conversations, research, and more. Olson and Maud's bibliographic obsession adds still more layers of meaning to the MOL. Like Dorn's "net of connections," each book is a vector to another, by means of its own bibliography, its presence in another's bibliography, or its relationship to a primary source. From this and from Clarke's definition, we might define "bibliography" as a fundamentally conceptual practice that negotiates the presence and absence of materials simultaneously. Thus, it stands that when this conceptual form is made incarnate—into a library, like the Maud/Olson—the materiality itself becomes a site for rapidly expanding meaning.

This Is Yeats Speaking (through the MOL)

The reading environment of contemporary special collections in general is characterized by a sense of isolation from the visual and material scope of the collection. While open stacks became a symbol of access in university libraries after World War Two, and while all library access policies are individually set according to the regulations and resources of their institution, special collections often operate on a reading room model in which materials are not available for the researcher to self-select but must instead be paged from a (presumably) more secure location.[37] This process often exists in complex interplay with open stack models, often within the same institution; Terry Belanger, summarizing student reports on special collections between 1976 and 1985, notes an "ancient New England library" in which many rare American first editions were discovered and subsequently "locked up," but not so a collection of incunabula that remained on the open stacks until 1967, with "scandalous" circulation cards affixed within—"scandalous" because the very cards themselves, glued to centuries-old open-shelved books, undermine the collection's mission of secure preservation and limited access.[38]

In this access model, a researcher first scrutinizes catalog records, inventories, or finding aids to identify materials of interest. Of course, this step requires that materials are cataloged in the first place, or, depending on the researcher's location, that digital records are available for remote access. Then, once relevant materials have been identified, they are paged by a specialist, and delivered in a limited amount for the researcher to examine methodically. Since all special collections may operate according to their own guidelines, often set by a curator, the amount of material that may be accessed at any given time varies. Certain collections offer an archival folder at a time, an archival box at a time, or only a few books, and it is almost impossible for the average researcher to see the scope of the collection in its physical, material form, since browsing archival boxes or rare-book stacks often constitutes a security violation. The only way that an average researcher can ever gain a sense of scope in terms of the collection is through its metadata, whether that be a catalog record or a more extensive finding aid. Once again, this also covers only materials that have been cataloged, meaning that there is always a backlog information or acquisitions that a researcher can never account for at all (unless they are telepathic, or, perhaps more likely, have an inside connection to the repository).[39]

In contrast to this, while it remains a special collection because of its mix of rare book and archival materials, the rooms of the MOL simply *are:* drawers of archives to be opened and stacks of alphabetized open shelves, all ready to be browsed at the researcher's leisure. Maud's meticulous bookplates are tucked in each book's pastedown, and while they each lead to worlds of correspondence, research, and Maud's life work, a visitor to the Maud/Olson Library is initially confronted only with spines, an assortment of titles and subject areas, browsable but almost impenetrable. Metaphorically speaking, most archival collections present a building brick-by-brick, making available to users only a partial view to assemble a perception of the whole building. The MOL offers the whole building first, and we look up at its immensity, experiencing the awe of that confrontation.

The gesture of open stacks in a special collection, while it may be born of the community basis of the MOL and indeed, its smaller budget, is significant rhetorically. The experience of awe and immensity at sight of the scope of the books, while still being unable to perceive the density of their connections to each other, raises the question of affective response in special collections, and even in terms of scoping knowledge as part of Olson's project. While not yet a predominant theoretical lens in the archival and special collections community, "the affective turn" is gaining traction as an interpretive tool for our experiences within archives, and indeed, the critical value of identifying emotional encounters with documents.[40] In these conversations, the question of affect, or emotional experiences in archival spaces, touches on the intersection of the political and personal, on erasure and precarity, and is especially relevant to engaging endangered archives in war-afflicted communities, or interrogating LGBTQ+ archives for silenced histories. In this instance, we might interpret the affective experience of the MOL as part of the energies of Olson's own interest in the body as a site of experience. In Miriam Nichols's indispensable *Radical Affections,* she cites Martha Nussbaum and Charles Altieri to explore the ways "that poetry may catch and hold our experience of the world as larger than ourselves" to reanimate the terms "love, cosmicity, the practice of the outside" in the works of Charles Olson, Robert Creeley, Robert Duncan, Jack Spicer, and Robin Blaser.[41] Of Olson in particular, she states, "Document plus affect: these are the coordinates of Olson's map."[42] And indeed, within the MOL's open stacks, "document plus affect" is a potent formulation not just for Olson's work but for a visitor seeking to make sense of the space as well.

This affective quality necessarily plays out across and within bodies. In the 1953 work "The Resistance (for Jean Riboud)" Olson argues that man has to fundamentally contend with "his own physiology . . . it is his body that is his answer, his body intact and fought for, the absolute of his organism in its simplest terms."[43] This process was not just theoretical for Olson: he even performed ballet at one point, taken by the critical and expressive possibilities of the body.[44] This bodily appreciation of experience itself as a site of knowledge is key in affect theory on the whole, and discussed to great effect by Teresa Brennan's *The Transmission of Affect.* Articulating that the "transmission of affect" is "social in origin but biological and physical in effect," Brennan describes how energies are transmitted across bodies and spaces from either individuals or the environment.[45] She further argues that because of the permeability of affects within spaces, that this possibility "undermines the dichotomy between the individual and the environment and the related opposition between the biological and the social."[46] While still accounting for the particulars of individual experience, Brennan's work ultimately destabilizes the idea of the "self-contained Western identity" that separates the self from the "Other"—often with political consequences. This, too, constitutes an important aspect of Olson's own knowledge-building project, which he enumerates in "Human Universe" by condemning mere acts of "demonstration, a separating out, an act of classification" to constitute "a stopping," arguing that instead, "any of us, at any instant, are juxtaposed to any experience, even an overwhelming single one, on several more planes than the arbitrary and discursive which we inherit can declare."[47] This concept—that experience need not be contained arbitrarily, since it can simultaneously stretch in manifold directions—is in part a guiding principle of the material conditions of the MOL itself, and part of its force as an act of knowledge production.

Considering this focus on experience, alongside Clarke's idea of "library" and "biblio," we might think of the MOL as part conceptual art, part performance art that is cocreated by its users as they engage in a conceptual piece that demonstrates the contours, limits, and possibilities of bibliographic knowledge. André Spears highlights this quality in "Maud/Olson and Me," noting that Maud's work does not simply function as an "Olson source library" but also as a "conceptual art installation . . . designed to highlight Olson's library as a space through which and around which a community or 'polis' might come to life," or "an open invitation to enter a growing and evolving network of texts that would cohere as social body."[48] It is this invitation, and the mechanisms of it, that feels most immediate to the reader on entering the collection.

Given the overlap and creative friction between galleries, museums, libraries, and other spaces of performance, the idea of performing a library is especially charged. Writing in the edited collection *Fantasies of the Library*, Anna-Sophie Springer notes that the concept of the library is particularly well-suited to acts of performance, given the private connotations of reading an individual book, juxtaposed against the idea of a library as a "public place of reading" and thus "a hybrid site for *performing the book*."[49] In fact, there are many instances of artists using the idea of the library to create site-specific installations and performances. For instance, Scottish artist Katie Paterson's project *Future Library* (2014–2114), based in Norway, consists of a library of one hundred pieces that will not be printed until 2114, at which point one thousand trees that were planted for the occasion will be processed successively to create the one hundred pieces that have been commissioned by an author.[50] The artist Buzz Spector has done many art installations that play with the idea of the library, notably including *Unpacking My Library* in San Diego and Tijuana in 1994. The exhibition consisted of a 155-foot shelf that extended along four gallery walls, with all of Spector's books (3,951 volumes at the time) taken directly from his house.[51] Additionally, Micha Ullman's memorial installation *The Empty Library*, created in 1995 beneath the Bebelplatz, with enough empty shelves to hold the volumes destroyed in one of the most devastating book burnings during the Nazi regime in Germany in May 1933, shows another example of the library as an installation, a performance completed by the viewer of the empty shelves.[52] These examples, among many others, show the active possibilities of considering a library not just as a research site but also an embodied space to play with the question of what type of knowledge is contained, memorialized, or made possible by the infrastructure of the library.

The conceit of the MOL, with its open shelves full of rare books and periodicals that hide their bookplates (and thus conceptual worlds) within their covers, generates a provocation to the researchers that casts them as performers: find your starting point. Which book do you pull, in this body, space, and time? Contemplating his library, as well as his intolerance for organizing and categorizing systems, printer and poet Alan Loney asks a question that interrogates the possible performances of his library: "What is the dance to be done with the library in order to make both of us work. Yet I still do not have an answer to the question: what does it mean, to take a book from the shelf."[53] Choosing a book off a shelf is not necessarily a revolutionary act. Yet, that first choice is significant from the perspective of a reader "performing" the collection: the only way *in*, to begin to create an understanding of the totality, is to start somewhere.

And once you've pulled that first book, the network of meaning in the collection starts to reveal itself through the materiality of the book, the Maud bookplate, the secondary sources and experiences that surround the collection. But to return to the revolutionary: choosing to build structures of knowledge in a particular way is always a political act, especially within Olson's criteria. In his opening sentence of "The Gate and the Center," as I cite earlier, Olson writes, "KNOWLEDGE either goes for the CENTER or it's inevitably a State Whore—which American and Western education generally is, has been, since its beginning."[54] The conceptual structure of the MOL—as "Olson's Brain," in material form, yet a conceptual piece in and of itself— means that addressing any arc enables the reader access to a central core. This core is as unstable as the material paradox of libraries and bibliography, in which the knowledge they metonymize is located in bodies, not in the books. In this capacity, each and every item may be utilized as a vector into a core of meaning—Olson's universe—and outward, into possibilities suggested by the books' very materiality.

As a study in examples, we might start with William Butler Yeats, an author that Ralph Maud pinpoints as inspiring Olson's critical approaches to literature and whom Olson later activates in his essay "This Is Yeats Speaking." Yeats, for whom Ezra Pound served as secretary, is part of the hermetic lineage of modernist poetry (along with others, like H. D.), that poets like Olson, di Prima, Duncan, and Spicer often engaged in their work. Olson's study of Yeats occurred early on in college; Maud notes that Olson wrote an essay on Yeats for Wilbert Snow's "modern poetry course" in 1930, and observes that the books he was likely to have purchased included *Early Poems and Stories* (1925), *Later Poems* (1928), *The Tower* (1928), and a poem of Yeats's that Olson had spied in *The New Republic.*[55] This discussion takes only a page of Maud's *Charles Olson's Reading: A Biography,* but the material works of Yeats occupy far more conceptual and physical space in the MOL itself, particularly given the question of influence and poetic lineage. In some ways, the Yeats section of the MOL illustrates Olson's own point: that books have artificial stopping points or arbitrarily contained subjects. Maud's inventory is only a paragraph, compared to the ample shelf space Yeats occupies; however, the very materiality of the Yeats books themselves offers extensive vectors outward.

W. B. Yeats's *A Packet for Ezra Pound* (1929) is one of the first books in sequence on the shelf that contains Yeats, and Maud's bookplate indicates that the book was "used in [a] college paper." The MOL volume is stunning, with lettered signatures and a red ink colophon that notes that "four hundred and twenty-five copies of this book have been printed and published by Elizabeth Corbet Yeats on paper made in Ireland at the Cuala Press, 133 Lower Baggot Street, Dublin, Ireland. Finished in the first week of June 1929." On its flyleaf, a small penciled dollar amount remains: "250." The book is a very fine copy of a first edition of Yeats: a lovely acquisition by the MOL, far exceeding student-grade material. While it is ambiguous whether Olson actually read certain books in the MOL, this particular book cannot ever have been read by *anyone:* its pages remain uncut. While the book represents what Olson learned from it, its actual materiality—its uncut pages—shows that would have been impossible.

The question of uncut pages appears frequently as a paradox in writers' libraries, and is a phenomenon cited in the library of James Joyce, whose justification for preservation and cataloging may well have influenced Maud's methodologies. Bibliographer Thomas Connolly, along with other scholars, was convinced of the significance of Joyce's reading practices to the author's densely allusive work, and in 1955 Connolly conducted a complete descriptive bibliography—with annotations and all, as did Maud—of the so-called Paris Library, with 468 items that are now part of the Poetry Collection at the University at Buffalo, SUNY. Connolly undertakes this in an effort to determine what has been read, and cites uncut pages as evidence of Joyce not having engaged with the text, though he conversely notes the limitation of cut pages in revealing this information.[56] Likewise, di Prima's occult library contains books that she definitely read (based on evidence in letters and teaching materials) but that show no signs of reading through trace and otherwise. While the MOL's books were not the copies that Olson read, and we cannot examine their materiality as evidence to this effect, the question of what it means to have "read" a book always operates at the level of bibliographical paradox, toggled between the physical book and the "work" within it. A poet may have read the *work*, just not *that* book.

In this same vein, Yeats's *Last Poems and Plays* (1939) is inscribed "To mother with love from Lois / May 1940," while Maud's bookplate states "Olson took the BMC copy. Storrs," indicating that Olson "borrowed" the Black Mountain College library version, which is now housed at University of Connecticut. Maud's bookplate highlights the disparateness of Olson's pilfered copy with the material life of the book Maud obtained for his version of Olson's library, preserving a certain Lois's dedication to her mother. Like *A Packet for Ezra Pound*, as well as many others in the collection, this book is marked as a first American edition, printed by Macmillan in 1940. Its sale price is noted as eighty-five dollars, likely far too extravagant for Olson. This price, once again, highlights the disjunction between Maud's first edition *library* and Olson's at times *bibliographic* possession of the material, after Clarke's distinction.

Indeed, the Yeats section of the MOL contains numerous fine copy editions, many of them very lovely finds indeed. Yeats's *Ideas of Good and Evil* (1903), published by A. H. Bullen, also contains unopened signatures and unique typographic details, including page headers in the margins as opposed to the top. *The Tower* (1928), by Macmillan in London, has gold stamping on the cover, unopened introductory pages, deckled edges, and a penciled-in dealer price of $105. The bookplates notes "Clarke's list," a reference to Clarke's inventories of Olson's work in 1965 at 28 Fort Square, reframing this fine copy as a reference to one of the many books scattered across Olson's apartment.

Not all of Maud's acquisitions are of rare stock; while Yeats's *Autobiographies: Reveries over Childhood and Youth and The Trembling of the Veil* was published in New York by Macmillan in 1927, the flyleaf reveals that the book is a library discard, last checked out on October 26, 1999, from the duPont-Ball Library of Stetson University in DeLand, Florida. And indeed, not all books in the MOL are early imprints. Catherine E. Paul and Margaret Mills Harper's edited volume of *The Collected Works of W. B. Yeats*, specifically the thirteenth volume that features the original 1925 version of *A Vision*, was published by Scribner in 2008. The bookplate notes that "Olson consulted the 1925 edition for his college paper." Two very different print materials, then, are substituted for each other in a symbolic manner, as evidence of Olson's reading. The 2008 date of the edition also illustrates the lifelong nature of Maud's collecting, as it signals his fifth decade of acquisitions for the project.

The presence of Maud's penciled-in annotations only augments the unique material considerations of the MOL, speaking to Olson's knowledge on the one hand, and to radically different vectors of materiality on the other (Lois's inscription, the unopened pages). In the Maud/Olson copy of A Vision, one of Yeats's most esoteric works, Maud's bookplate states that the pen notes in Maud's hand were "taken from the Storrs copy," and in parentheses, he notes that half-erased pencil markings in the book belong to another owner. Published by Macmillan in 1961, this text is heavily annotated throughout as Maud reproduces Olson's own annotations from the 1938 Macmillan edition copy held at Storrs. On the back flyleaf of the MOL copy, Maud copies out a passage from "The nail of the cross" poem, citing "see 'Crown of Nails' A Nation of Nothing But Poetry p. 20 poem based on p. 278 and 294 . . ." The notes go on to engage with this notoriously complex text, asking on page 278 "where a nail of the cross became the bit of Constantine's horse" and citing "neoplatonism," then underlining Yeats's description of the world becoming Christian as a "fabulous formless darkness" with the question "as fascism?" Through Maud's annotations, we might also see how Olson engages with the premise of the work, annotated as "the confusion of spirits over material location" in which Yeats describes his method of receiving dictation.[57] The front flyleaf further highlights Olson's depth of engagement with this text, as Maud reproduces annotations that demonstrate the interconnectedness of Olson's reading practice, including "soft immortal bounces stream Euryodocles (?)," "Dying each other's life, living each / other's death—Heraclitus," "Leda 267," "gyres," "How great the gulp between / simplicity + insipidity Blake 72," and "discarnate (follows incarnation) 79." Maud's transcription, however, differs in key ways from Olson's annotations. While Olson's annotations are concentrated in the upper corner of the back flyleaf, Maud's are arranged in a more projective way on the front flyleaf, almost as poetry. Maud's confusion over "Euryodocles" may be referring to "Empedocles," which is mentioned within Yeats's text, "bounces" is "boundless" in the original annotation, and "gulp" is "gulph" in the original Olson annotation.[58] While these differences show slight errors in fidelity on Maud's part—with Olson's admittedly challenging hand—this does not seem to alter their purpose as part of a facsimile library.

After all, Maud's annotations are not meant to substitute for those within the original books but rather to gesture to their importance within Olson's life of reading. As a result of annotation's paratextual qualities, marginal notes almost always point outside of the text to other referents; likewise, Maud jots down Olson's observations about the text in a way that encourages an observer to return to Olson's books that are held in a repository, or to seek further information about their possible meanings.

Olson draws out resonances and key themes in his annotations, not just for *A Vision* but with regard to his larger cosmological interests in the discarnate and immaterial versus incarnated, gyres as a Yeatsian cosmological schema, and leaps across large swathes of text and time—Blake, Heraclitus, Empedocles. While the semantic content of the Maud/Olson annotations invites further exploration at greater length, their material presence, like the unopened pages of the Yeats or a stamped library insert, embodies the generative paradox of the collection.[59] At once pointing to an original annotation in Olson's hand, in another book in another library, the annotations now point to Maud's hand and must be reconciled alongside other (half-erased) markings, imprint details, and considerations of materiality in the books themselves. Yet, as per Clarke's formulation, they are no less a part of Olson's *bibliography*, or scope of his knowledge, because of their differing materiality. Rather, they represent almost infinite possibilities outward based on their unique material conditions—toward Olson, and also toward other vectors.

Postmodern Paper

Thus far, I have described the present and the history of the MOL, including how it began as a conceptual project whose material form exponentially expanded and challenged its scope, and how it relates to Olson's own ideas on embodiment and knowledge. This, however, leaves open the question of the future, or, in the parlance of special collections, preservation. The question of archival proliferation goes hand in hand with preservation, since the presence of the former limits the institutional opportunities of the latter. Since the twentieth century, during which archives first became professionalized in the United States, archivists working in government, private industry, and cultural heritage institutions have faced exponential increases in deposits of materials. This is evidenced by the turn to "More Product, Less Process" (MPLP) processing practices described by Mark A. Greene and Dennis

Meissner as necessary for institutions in the face of extreme backlogs of material that pile higher with each new acquisition.[60] We might consider this proliferation as twofold. Firstly, mass-market reprographic technologies, from the Xerox to the printer, create a proliferation of paper for an archivist to negotiate, and even the relative inexpensiveness of books during the twentieth century often means that an author's library contains thousands of volumes. The decreasing cost of paper goods—the stuff of books, drafts, and writing between the decline of parchment manuscripts and the rise of the personal computer—dramatically increases the possible volume of an author's collection of materials, challenging the archivist to determine what materials may be significant (and therefore worth preserving), or not.

Secondly, for many authors writing in the twentieth century, the growing consciousness of archival practice in its first century of archival professionalization and the rise of (a few) special collections acquisition budgets means that most authors born in this century are aware of their own archive, preserve it and structure it to some degree, and often participate in the terms of its sale over the course of their lifetime. This twofold aspect of archival proliferation—in terms of the paper itself, whether in manuscripts or published books, and also in terms of authors conceiving of their own archives along with possible institutional futures—dovetails with the postmodern question of knowledge proliferation in general, especially after World War Two. As a result of the increase in availability of mass-market and personal print technologies, print knowledge was produced and disseminated at a faster rate than any historical era prior. Now, in the digital age of keyword searches, Wikipedia, and the sprawling knowledge of the Internet, we can conceive of this information overload only as big data that can be visualized, mapped, or otherwise rendered legible through a format other than its raw, sheer scope. Information overload as a postmodern condition is at the heart of contemporary archival practice, especially with regard to preservation and custodianship.

Literature in the archival sciences field suggests a few avenues of redress. One is more stringent collecting and deaccessioning policies, in which materials deemed to have little scholarly value are "weeded" from collections or not accessioned in the first place. In the case of author libraries—a challenging format with a mix of mass-market paperbacks, first editions, autographed editions, and a variety of other print forms, such as journals or magazines— these collections are generally on the chopping block when institutions weigh the "research value" of unannotated pulp fiction alongside Yeats first editions. Likewise, certain types of ephemera or multiple copies of items are often weeded as per best practices in most archival manuals, although items such as brochures and flyers may one day prove to be valuable—as in Charles Dickens's broadsides, advertising his reading tours—should they become rare enough. In a similar vein, Andrew Stauffer's ongoing project since 2014, *Book Traces*, addresses the precarity of nineteenth- and twentieth-century books in general stacks that are deemed not rare enough for special preservation, and are at times possible candidates for digitization and deaccessioning.[61] While these conversations are often fraught, they expose an incredible reality: that somehow, academic scholarship and institutional repositories (whether archives, libraries, or museums) are the dominant infrastructures of cultural preservation and interpretation, with limited resources that often dictate their practices. And that participating in these infrastructures necessarily requires professionalization (another infrastructure) and is subject to boards of trustees, government funding, and institutional accreditation, rather than our shared communal and cultural responsibility.

In the MOL, fine copies of Yeats share the same shelves as *The Price of Salt*, Patricia Highsmith's lesbian romance from 1953 (under pen name Claire Morgan) that Audre Lorde taught in one of her classes at City University of New York, according to bibliographies in her notebooks. Mimeograph magazines, archival documents, Gloucester maps, and Greek philosophy primers intermingle. Because of the autonomy of the MOL, outside an institutional repository, its conceptual project and material form are safe from what would be a damaging and obfuscating process of weeding. While I have demonstrated that especially for the MOL, completeness is a paradox, this ensures the MOL's ability to preserve not just what *seems* significant now but also what might become significant in the future, for a variety of reasons. Given the restrictions of institutional repositories, based on budgets, backlogs, staffing, and other limitations, maintaining a community-based archive may offer the greatest flexibility for housing unique collections.

However, community archives also pose specific challenges in their precariousness. Despite the prevalence of recommendations for developing community-based repositories as opposed to considering institutions as the be-all and end-all, the practice of creating a community collection is arduous. Cataloging systems must be built from scratch, modified from open-source software, or purchased for steep fees; staff must be trained to catalog, serve rare materials, and otherwise manage a reading room; and marketing, curriculum development, and outreach all make the work of a community archive visible and possibly sustainable. While institutional repositories are required to have long-term stewardship plans, few community archives can hope to do so unless they are acquired by a larger institution with the capacity to support them.

For community-based repositories, traditional modes of preservation do not always apply. For instance, the literature of collections management cautions us against sunlight, pests, food and drink, and even the handling of materials themselves. At the MOL, you can read on the patio while drinking a beer on a sunny day. Sunlight and alcohol are not the primary threats to global archival holdings today. However, the widespread destruction and pillaging of Iraqi archives during the US invasion, and the impact of war on institutional repositories more generally speaking, represents a totalizing and enormous degree of cultural destruction. In such events, the only thing that often survives is the secondary scholarship on items and/or their catalog records. The MOL's thorough catalog—digitized by Judith Nast, and available as a dataset for exploration—is available in numerous material forms and could theoretically be used to reconstruct another MOL at a future point. However, given the unique materiality of the current collection, a future iteration would not be the same. Like a conceptual art project, this instantiation of the library—with Maud's own notes, the bibliographic particularities of the books themselves, and even its location in Gloucester—is irreplaceable.

Rebecca Knuth, in *Libricide*, states that all libraries, of any kind, symbolize human culture.[62] The particulars of the MOL demonstrate that all books are materially unique vectors that point toward their relationship to the library and further afield. The poet's library as an archival genre is just as significant a historical tool as literary papers. For Olson, his library was a material collation of the type of knowledge building that could generate a *polis,* an ideal society. Maud's scholarship collected these tools of *polis* and arranged for them to exist in a format that could truly make good on their promises, in open stacks, currently overlooking Gloucester Harbor. This type of collection and curation is a model for how we might think through the archival precarities of author libraries by embracing a mode of cataloging and access that does not seek to shoehorn them into current systems of classification—as unique rare book items or as part of archival papers that must be served in a reading room—but rather considers them as their own archival type, and makes them visible and available with respect to this. On the scholarly side, the best way to encourage this type of preservation and access is to develop critical methods that are well suited to contextualize and theorize the importance of a poet's library as a cohesive project, ensuring that narratives exist about the importance of an author's books and their interconnectedness to their life and works.

With this, the material itself is only half of the story. Ammiel Alcalay notes that "having the courage to take up the historical burden also means knowing how precarious and open to manipulation cultural materials are, how necessary it is not just to preserve them but to reanimate the contexts in which they were created."[63] Thus, an even more important part of collections management, beyond the handling and preservation of special collections materials, is generating comprehensive records and creating narratives in which primary sources will live on in secondary scholarship. This chapter is an attempt to "reanimate the contexts" of the MOL from a variety of angles—Maud, Olson, and even my own perspective as an embodied user of the collection. In doing so, I hope to solidify a historical and critical milieu in which this collection can be legible to those who stand to benefit by seeing it—whether scholars of Olson, the subjects in his library, Maud, bibliography, special collections management, or ideas not yet articulated.

In 1931, around the same time that Olson began his own book collecting in earnest, Walter Benjamin wrote "Unpacking My Library: A Talk on Book Collecting" to explore some of the processes that create what he calls the "magic circle" created by books as they enter a collection. Benjamin notes that for a collector, "an acquisition of an old book is its rebirth," and that for private collections, the absence of the collector himself begins our understanding of what he has accomplished.[64] Through this possibility of rebirth, collections can become transformed in their uses and meanings, even as we learn from their assemblers. Thus, while Maud's efforts were part of his admiration of and fidelity to Olson's work, thanks to the comprehensiveness of Maud's project our explorations need not be limited to the MOL's original collecting mandate. Rather, we might view this collection as part of a wider array of resources related to poets writing after World War Two that we might examine, engage, and indeed advocate for. This work is necessary as we attempt to understand the book history of our most recent era of poetry, whose material traces require our active care to settle into patterns of visibility and meaning. As Olson states in his *Bibliography on America for Ed Dorn*, "It is not how much one knows but in what field of context it is retained, and used."[65] Through Maud's scholarship, and the stewardship of those involved in the Gloucester Writers Center, we have the opportunity to dance—literally, if we wish—in some of Olson's own retained fields so that we might reanimate them, in a new millennium, for our own edification.

FIGURE 3. "Audre Lorde in her study." Taken in her home in Staten Island, ca. early 1980s. —Photograph courtesy of the Lesbian Herstory Archives.

CHAPTER 2

"DON'T FORGET I'M A LIBRARIAN"

Information, Knowledge, and Understanding
with Audre Lorde

A PHOTOGRAPH OF AUDRE Lorde, browsing her bookshelves in her home in Staten Island in the 1980s, reveals a study room full of books, with piles on the shelves and on any open surface. The networks that would have brought books to Lorde, and Lorde to books, were numerous. She was a poet, activist, and teacher, whose work and identity as an Afro-Caribbean lesbian made her a pioneer within political movements of the 1970s and 1980s, during which she spoke alongside Coretta Scott King, James Baldwin, Adrienne Rich, and other figures of international stature. Lorde's political and poetic contributions were informed by her research practices, experiences traveling to Africa and the Caribbean, and relationships with activist communities. Seeing Audre Lorde with her books, one perceives the enormity of her relationship with them as sources and resources. The photograph brings to mind Ralph Maud's choice of bookplate for the Maud/Olson Library, the intrigue of a poet at home with their resources. With Lorde, a similar provocation arises: somewhere, among those stacks, are the clues to a life of poetry.

In the poem "Future Promise," Lorde explores the Staten Island house in which this photograph was taken, purchased in 1971 with partner Frances Clayton and the place where she raised her children. Lorde notes that "the roof leaks," and that the staircase sometimes gives her children splinters. Despite this, the function of the house is bound by her need for it. She imagines the silent stairway, "with no more need for changelessness," and concludes:

freed from constancy
this house
will not stand
forever.[1]

The prophecy proves correct. That house, which held Audre Lorde's books, papers, and children, no longer exists as Lorde knew it. In 1988, Lorde sold the house and moved to Saint Croix with Gloria Joseph, where she lived until her death from cancer in 1992. In 1989, Lorde and Joseph encountered disaster when Hurricane Hugo devastated Saint Croix—an event whose consequences she enumerates in her introduction to *Undersong*, written from 1990 to 1991. She notes that Hurricane Hugo destroyed their "house, library, and whole way of life" in one night, and that few of the books were salvageable.[2] In the midst of this destruction—which left her and other residents with no food, water, power, or phone lines—she found a soaked copy of *Chosen Poems*, a prior anthology of her poetry. Lorde began workshopping the poems therein over the next three months, committing "each day to a brief discipline of refeeling, reliving, and revising these poems."[3] One might imagine that these poems served the same function as the library itself—an opportunity to revisit texts, to pull them off the shelf (or page), to engage. And this anecdote also provides an *ars archiva* as we lament the loss of Lorde's library for her, and for ourselves and future scholars.

The introduction to *Undersong* provides evidence that yes, there was an "Audre Lorde library" developed over the years as Lorde bounced around apartments in the 1950s, found stability in her Staten Island family home, and subsequently distilled, packed up, and moved to Saint Croix. However, any cohesive physical unit known as "Audre Lorde's library" is no longer extant, and her relationship with books is documented only in her archives at Spelman College, the Lesbian Herstory Archive, the Schomburg Center, and other repositories with her primary sources.[4] Her archives are not insignificant; Spelman College has over forty linear feet of material, donated to the college through Lorde's will and received in 1995.[5] Indeed, Christina Olivares notes that "the sheer volume of material available is extraordinary, even overwhelming," as she explores its holdings of ephemera, including an old wallet with Hunter College stickers, scuba gear, hats, and even a box that contains Lorde's locs.[6] Despite this richness, and while there are a few boxes of ephemera and inscribed publications by Lorde herself, there is no "library"—a large collection of books she would have read, that she considered a working resource for herself. And while sometimes institutions decline to collect personal libraries, this is likely not related to Spelman College's collecting practices; Lorde's archival neighbor, Toni Cade Bambara, has a finding aid that enumerates titles for nine boxes of assorted books, and additional boxes of magazines and smaller publications.

With over sixty unpublished journals in her archives, containing reading notes, bibliographies, and reflections, and much mention of reading and libraries in her published work, Lorde's relationship with books is deeply articulated.[7] At the same time, the contours of her library are no longer physically collated. Beyond those books that were physically destroyed in Saint Croix, Lorde's library is an evocative presence that exists in the memories of people who knew her: her friends, her children, and those who saw her house in Staten Island.[8] While we cannot explore Audre Lorde's relationship to knowledge-building practices and information infrastructure through her personal library, in cases like this it is important to note that significant evidence still remains. Namely, Lorde was a librarian.

Lorde's choice to step fully into the life of poetry in 1968 coincided with the final year of her decade-plus career in this profession. She left Town School, a private elementary school on the Upper East Side where she was head librarian, and embarked to Mississippi to teach as writer-in-residence at Tougaloo College, a Black liberal arts school. There, she found herself immersed in the challenges of teaching a cadre of radical students, and in doing so, accounting for the central role of poetry in her life. This experience was a crucial link in the chain of events that marked Lorde's full-time switch to teaching and writing as her primary activities. In an interview with Adrienne Rich, Lorde remembers, "From the time I went to Tougaloo and did that workshop, I knew: not only, yes, I am a poet, but also, this is the kind of work I'm going to do."[9] Lorde had worked on and off in libraries since 1955—starting as a clerk, returning after the birth of her children to work night shifts, but after her experience in 1968, she would not return.

The absence of Lorde's library as an archival resource, and the relatively understudied prehistory of Lorde as a librarian, suggests an intersection and perhaps even tension between institutional forms of librarianship and poetic adaption of these principles for personal book-collecting. What is clear is that librarianship on the whole deserves greater critical attention for the ways in which ideas about and within the profession have shaped literary studies, especially for figures like Lorde who are both librarians and writers. Despite Lorde's extensive work in libraries, Shawn(ta) Smith-Cruz cites the lack of comprehensive publication on Lorde's time as a librarian, noting that "brief autobiographical sketches from interviews or secondary-sourced chronologies" are at present the available resources. While Ethelene Whitmire's "The Audre Lorde Librarian Project" has begun undertaking a deep dive into Lorde's relationship with librarianship, work on Lorde's librarianship remains ongoing, and for good reason; as Smith-Cruz argues, Lorde's years as a librarian left indelible marks on her teaching and writing—particularly in relationship to the principles of reference assistance.[10] Still, the fact that Lorde was a librarian is mostly an anecdote that precedes the post-1968 work for which she is more widely known.

The cultural and professional climate that cultivated Lorde's desire to become a librarian, and the context of professional information management in the 1960s, provide fundamental contexts for us to understand Lorde's librarianship. In particular, her accounts of learning to read and working in libraries show that her desire to become a librarian was shaped by certain expectations about libraries as sites of comprehensive information and infrastructure in the twentieth century more broadly, buoyed by promises of facilitating democracy and public education. As a result of the increase in research on the history of libraries and bibliography, and especially through the auspices of groups like the Black Bibliography Project, we can more clearly see the efforts of Lorde's librarian contemporaries in attempting to create more comprehensive information that reflected Black experience and history, which Lorde found so lacking in her early years and which motivated her own career path.[11] Lorde's participation in this era of librarianship, as well as her discovery of its failures and shortcomings, situates her relationship to the information infrastructure of libraries, and, in particular, reveals how she turned to poetry to augment the aspects of professional library infrastructure that she found inadequate for her work.

In this chapter, I also explore how Lorde's writing and interviews articulate clear and practical differences between information, knowledge, and understanding. I argue that we must read these ideas according to their context, in a scientific era shaped by information theory and information science, which were a growing part of librarianship during Lorde's time in library school. As I will discuss, information theory generally refers to the early roots of cybernetics and communication theory, which described information as disembodied data, particularly for use by computers; in contrast, Lorde's own definitions of information and knowledge are decidedly embodied, and often developed through her poetry in her postlibrarian life. This is, in part, because of the failures of research that she encountered as a librarian and in libraries, and her desire to discover new forms of knowledge, especially those related to recovering the Black experience through history and mythology. While some evidence of her reading practice is preserved in her notebooks as bibliographies and syllabi, the textual infrastructures of her poetry—such as the presence of a glossary and bibliography in her poetry book, *The Black Unicorn* (1978)—suggest in the absence of her library, we might read Lorde's poetry as its own information architecture that preserves her relationship with books and structures of knowledge, and that this might be a template for other poets whose libraries have been lost or destroyed.

While libraries symbolized a certain democratic freedom of knowledge in the twentieth century, Simon Gikandi reminds us that libraries can be interpreted as an "essential mark of bourgeois identity and privilege" that creates meaning differently "for those not born in the house of culture."[12] While this statement flags the elitist constraints of certain institutions, the statement can also be read in reverse: a library can be a profound tool of intellectual and social mobility when its resources are extended to those outside "the house of culture." Audre Lorde learned to read at her local library, like many poets and people of her generation; Vincent Ferrini, whose father told him he was from the wrong social class to become a poet, sought his education from the Lynn Public Library and later built his own meticulous collection on his miniscule budget.[13] Despite Charles Olson's high-ranking positions in the US government and his education at Wesleyan and Harvard, his admittance to these libraries and institutions were hard-won; his father was a Swedish immigrant who worked at the post office, and his mother was the daughter of Irish Catholic immigrants. Poets seeking knowledge at institutional libraries relished the possibility of learning and knowing, even as they noticed the absences and omissions in collections—and indeed, how the structures of libraries permitted and augmented these gaps. Along these lines, Lorde's observations about the inadequacies of librarianship are closely related to her experience of being an Afro-Caribbean American and the daughter of immigrants, a position that she considers fundamental to her identity as a poet.[14] Her embrace of the possibilities of the library, centering these key aspects of her identity, ultimately led to her understanding of its shortcomings for the work that she needed to undertake. Yet through the library, Lorde found poetry: a full-fledged system of knowledge that she could cultivate, articulate, and inhabit.

Lorde as Librarian, Histories of Black Librarianship

Lorde was the daughter of two immigrants from Grenada, and she was born and raised in New York City. She was a promising student, and later a successful librarian; yet turning her attention to teaching and poetry allowed her to develop the body of poetry, speeches, essays, and prose that makes her a celebrated writer today. As Lorde herself has noted, the road to "becoming" herself was fraught with racial and economic challenges—factory work, living alone downtown in the 1950s, and navigating being gay and Black in a political climate that long predated intersectionality. In this growth, 1968 was a pivotal year. While battling severe illness and navigating some of the most explosive years of the civil rights movement, Lorde received a phone call from Diane di Prima, her friend since high school. Di Prima insisted it was time for Lorde to have a book, and offered to publish it. Titled *The First Cities*, and published by di Prima's Poets Press, Lorde's first book crystallized her identity as a poet, which had been building over the years—beginning with a high school publication in *Seventeen* magazine, and continuing with inclusions in anthologies edited by poets such as Langston Hughes.[15] That same year was the last that Lorde would ever work as a librarian.

Lorde's road to librarianship was complex, and unfolded over many years of her early life. Having originally wanted to be a nurse, Lorde found that Black women were not eligible for fellowships, and her eyesight posed an additional challenge. Instead, librarianship was a more accessible path to stable living, and Lorde pursued a graduate degree and professional training in the field.[16] While the terms "library" and "librarian" do not even make it into the index of her biography, libraries and information feature prominently in Lorde's writing, especially *Zami: A New Spelling of My Name*, which underscores that librarianship was neither a brief career for her nor trivial to her growth as a person. Lorde received her master of library Science degree from Columbia University in 1961, the birthplace of library school in the United States. Prior to this and beginning in 1955, Lorde had been working in some capacity (at least intermittently) in public libraries, particularly with children's collections—as a clerk for The New York Public Library's Children's Services (1955), and as young adult librarian at NYPL's Mount Vernon location (1960). After her degree, she would work night shifts at the St. Clair School of Nursing (c. 1965, while she raised her children), and was later head librarian at the Town School in New York City, a private school for children located on the Upper East Side.

Lorde came of age in an era that was shaped by the recent professionalization of library sciences and information management, ushered in by Melvil Dewey's creation of the first graduate degree program in library sciences in 1887 at the School of Library Economy at Columbia University, where Lorde received her degree decades later. Dewey's conception of library school, developed with the American Library Association, considered librarianship as a profession (rather than vocation) that should require an academic education within an institution.[17] In earlier years, collections were governed by untrained "genteel" individuals whose main desire was protecting books from use, but the rise of library school signaled a certain democratizing effect on who could staff a library—including an Afro-Caribbean American like Lorde—based on the qualifications of the degree rather than on pedigree alone.[18] Given Dewey's influence, by the 1910s, numerous other programs were established internationally to train individuals in the administration of knowledge infrastructures.

The early years of library education were marked by certain assumptions about librarianship, its demographics, and its intellectual potential. The fact that librarianship as a profession attracted primarily women was key in the first program's establishment at Columbia; the then-president saw a library school as "a most useful device for achieving one of his own goals—women students at Columbia."[19] After significant stalling and debate, the program was allowed to commence with the understanding that it would cost the institution nothing, and Columbia would gain an inexpensive labor force to staff the college's libraries in the form of professional training for paying students. In addition to this, the choice to set up a school within an academic institution was a rhetorical move on Dewey's part not only to establish the professional nature of librarianship but also to imbue within it the sheen of academic respectability.[20] However, the close ties between the American Library Association and the founding of the school, per Dewey's own devising, meant that the technical nature of librarianship persisted instead of shifting to more philosophical or critical perspectives on the field—though this would happen later, and continues today.

In the decades before Lorde attended library school, many significant Black women librarians were active across the country in the twentieth century, in subfields ranging from children's librarianship (Lorde and Augusta Baker at The New York Public Library) to curatorship (Bella da Costa Green, at the Morgan) and cataloging (Dorothy Porter at Howard University). Increased scholarly attention to Black women librarians has recovered crucial information that reveals how many of these women, like Dorothy Porter, had significant influence on the development of classification systems or collection materials.[21] Lorde's choice to pursue librarianship was part of this important legacy of Black women librarians; Baker taught her how to read. Her time as a librarian also echoes the well-established connection between poets and the "day job" of librarian; Robin Blaser, Jack Spicer, and Amiri Baraka (a night librarian, as was Lorde for a time) also found themselves among the stacks, and Frank O'Hara was an art curator, among other examples. Dudley Randall, an early champion of Lorde's work and publisher for the Broadside Press, one of the most influential Black presses of the postwar period, had also been a librarian in the 1950s.[22] Randall in particular demonstrates the close connections between librarians and literary production in the 1950s and 1960s; he used his proximity to libraries to market his books, writing to Robert Hayden regarding the publication of *Poem Counterpoem*, "I think we could sell an edition of 500 or 1,000 hard-bound copies. I could push it with all my energy into the library and college field and locally," and noting that he had shown the "order librarian" at his work a copy of a publication, to find out that it had been ordered shortly thereafter.[23] As Erin Dorney chronicles in "Librarian as Poet / Poet as Librarian" on the *In the Library with the Lead Pipe* blog, the poet/librarian combination is often a generative intersection of interests; poets are surrounded by examples of unique publishing on their shelves, and opportunities to relate creatively to language in their daily work.

Yet racial difference in librarianship, and particular the presence of racism in a field that was largely female and white, stymied some of the utopian possibilities of being a poet in the library for Lorde. At the Mount Vernon library, Lorde encouraged young Black teenagers to check out books, and provided them "with stories about black adventurers she hid in her desk," despite suspicions by the head librarian that these were not serious students.[24] At the same time as Lorde witnessed racism toward library patrons, she also experienced it as a result of her differences within the Black community. These included being a lesbian who did not strongly identify as butch or femme, as well as her decision to wear natural hair. She remembers a group of Black colleagues who collected money to purchase her a hot comb and straightening iron that they obtained on lunch hour and then placed in Lorde's locker, only to be discovered by Lorde on a coffee break as it fell out of the locker, and "all ninety-five percent of [her] library coworkers who are very very white want to know what it's all about."[25] Remembering other Black gay women in her social scene at the time, Lorde recalls, "Self-preservation warned some of us that we could not afford to settle for one easy definition, one narrow individuation of self," and that "at the Bag [local gay bar], at Hunter College, uptown in Harlem, at the library, there was a piece of the real me bound in each place, and growing."[26]

Amid the racist interpersonal interactions occurring within them, libraries as institutions are often built on racist infrastructures that undergird their systems of acquisition and also classification. Many institutional acquisitions focused on white, Western-centric topics, a reality that Lorde quickly discovered in her first futile attempts to locate her mother's town of origin in Grenada on a map in a library. And while the infrastructure of the Dewey Decimal System was praised for allowing collections to expand in size through organization, when materials that represented the African American or Black experience were acquired, the technical vocabularies used to describe these materials framed them immediately within an outsider context.[27] In particular, the Dewey Decimal System offered scant opportunity to richly classify information related to Black or African American experience beyond its relationship to slavery, or without classifying Black people as foreign-born.[28] Laura Helton explores how Dorothy Porter, the inaugural curator of the Howard University Negro Collection, created her own supplementary classification scheme to describe the materials in her care, and how her effort to mimeograph this in collaboration with the Dewey Decimal System was flatly refused, because Porter's work "would quickly result in destroying all standardization."[29] Likewise, the American Library Association, still the predominant professional organization in the field, was known for hotly debating the use of double hyphens even as it could not agree on a path forward for a professional school.[30] Together, these details suggest that the technical aspects of library classification were not in place to categorize diverse forms of knowledge but, perhaps more accurately, were meant to center whiteness and white people as authorities in the stacks.

Porter's work at once represents the possibilities of librarianship, and also its limitations based on professional organizations. These limitations were further defined by the political climate of the Cold War in the United States, since many libraries received federal funding and were designated as public institutions. In the era of loyalty oaths, such as the one required in California that caused Jack Spicer to lose his job for noncompliance, Lorde's participation in libraries was a crucial part of her political development. At Mount Vernon, where Lorde worked from 1960 to 1962, the mayor required all public institutions to participate in a civil defense drill. Lorde refused to participate, citing her beliefs as a chapter member of the National Committee for a Sane Nuclear Policy from her time in library school at Columbia. Even though her supervisor led her to believe this could cost her her job, she was only verbally reprimanded as a result. Lorde's biographer, Alexis De Veaux, who recounts this incident, cites this act of political protest as a first for Lorde in bringing her a feeling of self-confidence and self-determination.[31]

The very symbolism of libraries, on an international scale, had particular stakes for marginalized and Black voices. Gikandi remembers the "young revolutionaries" he met at the University of Nairobi, who "reminded me that the goal of literature was to change the world and that most of the books in the library were custodians of the old order," prompting him to ask: "Could one be a revolutionary and still love the library?"[32] Lorde was likely asking herself these same questions during her tenure in libraries—her famous essay "The Master's Tools Will Never Dismantle the Master's House" by title alone might suggest the futility of resistance within an institution like a library, or a cataloging system like the Dewey Decimal System. Returning to Lorde's refusal to participate in the air raid drill: this act shows that she felt her participation in libraries to be a political act, and a site for experimentation with gestures of political resistance that would later define her identity.

This step may have been defining for Lorde on a path away from the library, as well; as Smith-Cruz notes, it was likely her political awareness of the close relationships between the library and the state, after Louis Althusser, that precipitated a professional break with librarianship.[33] Nevertheless, Lorde remembers her early years of librarianship as joyful, pleasurable work that allowed her to connect more deeply with her relationship to language, in direct contrast to the stifling dread of working at the Keystone Electronics factory in Stamford, Connecticut. Yet her career eventually became unsustainable as Lorde discovered the inadequacy of librarianship for the political and poetic work she felt she needed to do. Lorde left her career in librarianship for a variety of reasons, but they were informed in part by "the horror, the enormity of what was happening" in 1968, which Lorde characterizes as an experience of "living on the edge of chaos." She continues, "Whatever we were doing that was creative and right, functioned to hold us from going over that edge"; these activities were "the most we could do, while we constructed some saner future." But in this acknowledgment, Lorde states, "I knew then that I had to leave the library."[34]

Before this realization, though, Lorde's autobiographical writing suggests that in her early years, the library was a space where she had been able to believe in "some saner future" from early childhood onward. As she recounts in *Zami*, Lorde learned to read from the children's librarian Augusta Baker. Baker has her own legendary status in the history of Black readership, and is acknowledged today for assembling important bibliographies of children's books whose key criteria were that they portrayed Black youth in a positive light during an era in which minstrel aesthetics dominated illustrations and Black characters were disproportionately assigned negative roles in children's books.[35] Lorde vividly remembers the emotional effects of encountering racist books during story hour at the public library, when she was a child: "The Story Hour librarian reading *Little Black Sambo*. Her white fingers hold up the little book about a shoebutton-faced little boy with big red lips and many pigtails and a hatful of butter. I remember the pictures hurting me and my thinking again there must be something wrong with me because everyone else is laughing and besides the library downtown has given this little book a special prize, the library lady tells us."[36] Lorde's recollections prove the necessity of bibliographic work like Baker's, and the importance of having a positive influence on Lorde's understanding of her own Blackness as a child. Lorde mentions Baker by name, as well as "the old 135th Street branch library, which has just recently been torn down to make way for a new library building to house the Schomburg Collection on African American History and Culture." Lorde claims that Baker's gift of reading "saved my life, if not sooner, then later, when sometimes the only thing I had to hold on to was knowing I could read, and that that could get me through."[37]

In fact, Lorde's first words by her account are "I want to read," after Augusta Baker shows her kindness after a tantrum (brought on by her mother's anxious pinching and Lorde's screaming in response) and reads her *Madeline*, *Horton Hatches the Egg*, and "another storybook about a bear named Herbert who ate up an entire family, one by one, starting with the parents," which clearly pleased young Lorde. Lorde continues, "By the time she had finished that one, I was sold on reading for the rest of my life . . . I said, quite loudly, for whoever was listening to hear, 'I want to read.'" Lorde's mother responds with delight, kissing Lorde in "an unprecedented and unusual display of affection in public . . . for once, obviously, I had done something right."[38] This outpouring of affection, which Lorde notes was unusual, combined with the respectability of reading, meant that Lorde would keep this library-oriented validation close at hand. In a 1982 interview, Lorde remembers her parents "respected her book learning" and "were influential in the fact that I learned to read and write," noting that "when you're born Black and almost blind, in Harlem during the depression, that's not easy" (though Lorde's parents didn't "respect the books that I wanted to read," she acknowledges, "there has to be a parting of the ways someplace").[39]

From her location in Harlem, Lorde was a benefactor of an unprecedented effort on the part of Black librarians and bibliographers working within a radical tradition to increase the amount of information on Black experience available at institutions. Yet for Lorde, whose Caribbean identity and relationship to Blackness in segregated America was a lifelong source of interrogation and struggle, the *idea* of the institutional library and the realities of its deficiencies are at the heart of her turn toward poetry—a way to structure books, reading, and information that Lorde found sustaining. Her departure from librarianship is not unlike Charles Olson's departure from the Office of War Information and the Democratic Party, or even the artist Jess's apocalyptic vision that caused him to leave his career as a scientist working on the Manhattan Project.[40] These moments symbolize an emerging poet's or artist's rejection of upper-middle-class values and a forfeiture of a traditional career for the pursuit of knowledge through poetry. In the case of Olson, Jess, and Lorde, this was not done to be romantic but rather as an act of political urgency in the face of the collapse of the planet as it was known. As Smith-Cruz notes, Lorde's "identity as a librarian who chose to depart from the library as a means of survival" is critical for us to understand.[41] In this act of survival, Lorde's accounts of her professional participation in libraries in the 1950s and 1960s informs our understanding of what noninstitutional book collecting and knowledge infrastructures were rebelling against.

Failures of Information

In *Zami*, Lorde recounts the difficulties of her entrance into school: her need for glasses, her mother's strictness, and the racism of the predominantly white Catholic schools Lorde attends in order to receive the best possible education. Despite these challenges, she remembers wanting to do well, please teachers, and, essentially, learn the right answer. While this was possible in subjects like math and Latin, as Lorde found herself asking more complicated questions—How can I locate my mother's birthplace on a map? How does pregnancy work?—she quickly encountered the limits of finding any answer at all. The racism present in her early education produced even more questions that books couldn't answer. In the poem "Brother Alvin," Lorde mourns an elementary school classmate's death and the confusion of his disappearance, seeking the index of "each new book / on magic / hoping to find some new spelling / of your name."[42] Spelling, also invoked in the full title of *Zami: A New Spelling of My Name,* is critical in information infrastructure—it is essential for locating entries in indices or resources. In "Brother Alvin," even when Lorde uses books for reference as she has been taught, to navigate the traditional structures of information infrastructure, she cannot find the answer. Importantly, though, the structure of the poem provides redress—a knowledge structure that can contain the emotion that goes along with information's failure.

This clarity and concreteness contrasts with the importance of *knowing* as a type of knowledge without a clear book antecedent for Lorde. Knowing as a type of intuitive or mythical practice is often directly related to Lorde's Black identity, particularly in the way she describes the perspective and knowledge of her mother, Linda. This knowledge is intricately tied to her mother's status as an immigrant, and as a light-skinned Black woman in New York during an era of racial segregation and discrimination. Lorde notes that Linda knew to take them to the Museum of Natural History, because it was a good place to cultivate curiosity and knowledge for young minds, despite her fear of the "pale blue eyes" of the museum guard, "staring at her and her children as if we were a bad smell." In the next paragraph, "What else did Linda know?," Lorde shares two evocative pieces of folk knowledge: how to choose a good grapefruit and what to do with the bad ones, and how to use black elm leaf to heal wounds, knowledge that had been passed down to Linda from her own mother.[43] Yet each time Lorde mentions this inherited information, she notes how its transposition from Grenada to New York City rendered it unusable—no pigs to throw grapefruit to, and no black elm to use in Harlem.[44] Lorde's early relationship with her mother's knowledge is specific to Grenada and folk knowledge, showing the vastness of these traditions even as they falter in America's lack of similar contexts and resources. Lorde's biographer notes that these pieces of information appeared in Lorde's journals while she visited Grenada for the first time; that even for this knowledge to surface, it had to be reanimated on the soil that fostered it.[45]

Lorde's mother's home is a critical nexus for Lorde's relationship to information. As Lorde grows up, she searches for the specific place of her mother's former home—Carriacou—and notes it "was not listed in the index of the *Goode's School Atlas* nor in the *Junior Americana World Gazette* nor appeared on any map I could find, and so when I hunted for the magic place during geography lessons or in free library time, I never found it, and came to believe my mother's geography was a fantasy or crazy or at least too old-fashioned, and in reality maybe she was talking about the place other people called Curacao, a Dutch possession on the other side of the Antilles." This inability to find formal documentation—that is, validation—of knowledge that she possessed through her family lineage was formative in Lorde's studies at library school. She continues, and notes in an asterisk that "years later, as partial requirement for a degree in library science, I did a detailed comparison of atlases, their merits and particular strengths. I used, as one of the foci of my project, the isle of Carriacou. It appeared only once, in the *Atlas of the Encyclopedia Britannica*, which has always prided itself upon the accurate cartology of its colonies. I was twenty-six years old before I found Carriacou upon a map."[46] This search for validation of self and history through information—maps, genealogical information, historical dates—is at the core of most libraries' functionalities, but the Western-centric and colonial approach to the West Indies meant that information on these places was quite literally not on the map. The lack of validation and history made Lorde wonder if her mother's memory was "a fantasy or crazy or at least too old-fashioned"; it is only because Lorde investigated further that her family's history was confirmed and endured.

While deeply personal to Lorde, this combination of imagined exoticism and lack of Western resources on non-Western topics was a broader theme in American culture at the time, particularly within the Beat and counterculture poetry scenes. Growing interest in traditional spirituality in countries like India, as well as increasing awareness of Indigenous groups and their traditions, were associated with the hippie movement. While the mainstream appropriations of these traditions often constituted white erasure, at times, this search for knowledge that was not encompassed by the Western canon was practiced quite earnestly and with influential cross-cultural exchange—resulting in the foundation of the first Buddhist college in the United States at Naropa University in Boulder, Colorado, or Olson's fieldwork in the Yucatán and study of Mayan glyphs. In an undated letter from Allen Ginsberg to Ted Joans, Ginsberg begs Joans to write a book about his pilgrimages to Africa, writing,

You're the only one I know's been pilgrimaging all over Africa, will you ever write a book of geographic/ tribal/ ritual/ travel/ fact/ politics/ local religion/ gossip/ guide/ reflections/ roads? The religious and rituals are just as old or older than any, anywhere, and so's important for you to record living traces of them now for possible hip adaptation in West, as I've adapted some Indian ritual/tricks to U.S. use, like mantra & meditation & grass customs—i.e. as West mind returns to Nature as it must to survive, all the old tribal knowledge will be more & more helpful to the lost tribes of U.S.[47]

While the question of "hip adaptation" is now usually interrogated as appropriation, Ginsberg's connection between preserving local knowledge and the survival of culture is apt. Knowing one's history, especially when Black in America, was a matter of survival. For instance, Lorde acutely remembers finding out about Crispus Attucks during her blossoming relationship with Ginger at the Stamford factory. Lorde wonders how it was possible that she did not know this, having completed "supposedly the best high school in New York City, with the most academically advanced and intellectually accurate education available," where she had been taught by prominent historians yet "never once heard the name mentioned of the first man to fall in the american revolution, nor ever been told that he was a Negro."[48] Of this revelation, Lorde asks, "What did that mean about the history I had learned?"[49]

Lorde's experience of this failure of information—of the failure of traditional libraries to provide adequate information due to racist structures—was common, and not limited to her circumstances or generation. In response, around the turn of the twentieth century, Black historians were beginning to assemble collections and libraries that specifically spoke to the African-Diasporic experience and history. Most notable was Arturo Schomburg, who was told in elementary school in Puerto Rico that Black people had no history, and cites this insidious statement as the impetus for his assembling of research collections that documented Afro-Latin and African American histories and experiences.[50] Importantly, the activism and skill of private collectors like Schomburg laid the groundwork for public collections; his collection was and remains one of the foremost in the world, and was sold to The New York Public Library's 135th Street branch in 1926.[51] This was the same library where Audre Lorde learned to read, though she notes generally, "the library in Harlem used to get the oldest books, in the worst condition."[52]

Assembling libraries, particularly in regarding to the African American experience, has historically been an act of recovery and challenge. Laura E.

Helton, in her studies of Dorothy Porter's cataloging practices, describes her attempts to pull together the Howard University's Negro Collection (Porter was inaugural curator) as "tracking down a neglected, partially lost library" that had been in the stacks since 1867 but never assembled as such.[53] Collecting and cataloging efforts were closely related to this expansion of "curiosity about Negro life," that "turned urgently to profounder interest in Negro cultural background and history," which Helton finds identified in the Moorland Foundation Annual Report of 1939–40.[54] As Helton interprets, according to the efforts of Schomburg, Porter, and their colleagues, "the contours of what could and could not be known underwent revision," preparing a body of knowledge that would one day transform into Black or African American studies.[55]

While Lorde's librarianship, from what we can construct, seems more invested in reference assistance—connecting people with the right books—than with the technical details of cataloging, her coming-of-age at the Schomburg Center, her relationship with Augusta Baker, her attendance of library school, and her teaching at institutions starting in the late 1960s all mean that she was part of a complex ecosystem of information theory, collecting practices, recuperative cataloging, and librarianship that sought to consider information not as a disembodied feedback loop but rather as insights that could affect lived experience and Black peoples' conceptions of themselves. In the midst of an unprecedented boon of Black bibliography, and efforts to place Black experience within the infrastructures of information at institutions, Lorde learned to read and seek information. Librarians like Porter "exhibited full faith in classification" and its possibilities, and as such, from within institutions they became revolutionaries.[56] Celebrating women like Porter is just as crucial to our understanding of this history as is identifying reasons why women like Lorde sought to establish the contours of knowledge outside of institutional walls, or in new ways using the techniques of poetry.

Information, Knowledge, and Understanding: The Road to Abomeny

Indeed, much of Lorde's work is shaped by the failures of information, knowledge, and understanding at various points within the intellectual architecture of libraries or systems of knowledge production, such as the university. In the 1960s, when Lorde attended library school, "information science" was beginning to appear in degree program names, aligning libraries with the more technical aspects of communication theory.[57] Intimately related to information theory, which explored the statistical and information-based possibilities of communication from electronic perspectives, this field coalesced around the idea that there could be a "science" to the structuring of data for various research and administrative uses. Indeed, Lorde's own degree was in "library science," and dealt with concepts for structuring, storing, and accessing information.

In 1948, Claude Shannon developed what would become the dominant theory of information, which was defined as a mathematical quantity legible through its patterning.[58] As a result of the wide acceptance of Shannon's theory as well as ongoing cybernetic discourse, N. Katherine Hayles notes that at critical moments in the post–World War Two development of this field, information was interpreted to be immaterial and disembodied, merely a feedback loop that was channeled through carbon or silicon components—a sign of the rising "posthuman" condition and deeply entwined with its militaristic uses.[59] Much of Hayles's work argues for the impossibility of a dematerialized theory of information, as do projects such as Nicole Starosielski's *The Undersea Network*, which traces the physical cables that undergird the World Wide Web by exploring the communities who make and maintain them, or Mara Mill's exploration of the "hearing glove" and how disability can challenge the disembodied paradigm of information.

Lisa Nakamura, in "Indigenous Circuits: Navajo Women and the Racialization of Early Electronic Manufacture," delineates the establishment of the Fairchild Semiconductor and its specific recruitment of Indigenous women as part of the circuit of technoscience, which requires the labor of women, especially of color, to function.[60] Audre Lorde was intimately familiar with this reality; she worked at Keystone Electronics in the early 1950s, where she processed quartz crystals for use in radios and radar machinery. The work conditions at the factory were terrible, and endured by poor women of color with few other job prospects; Lorde was exposed to such significant amounts of carbon tetrachloride and X-rays that it may have influenced her later development of cancer.[61] Thus, when we consider Lorde as librarian, or even her approach to information, we might consider her as part of the embodied circuit of information on multiple levels: from factory floor to reference desk. And at every turn, particularly when we listen to her *own* formulations of what constitutes information and where to find it, we must remember: she removed her body from the labor of the technoscientific circuit of production, in both factory work and librarianship, for her very survival.

Lorde's interviews and writings are frequently punctuated by the words "information" and "knowledge," and she uses these words technically. For Lorde, "information" is a basic unit of observation or sensation that can be acknowledged and filed for future use, and is deeply tied to both verbal and nonverbal forms of communication that occurred early in her life. Far from the mathematical quantity that defined information for Shannon—primarily so it could be transferred easily among machines—Lorde's definition of "information" is acquired through distinctly intuitive means. In an interview with Adrienne Rich, Lorde remembers how she "learned how to acquire vital and protective information without words" as a way of staying safe and tuned in to her mother's changing moods. She carried this habit throughout high school, where she "found out that people really thought in different ways, perceived, puzzled out, acquired information, verbally," noting that she never studied, never read assignments, but "intuited" her teachers to "get all of this stuff, what they felt, what they knew."[62] In response to Lorde being asked a direct question, she remembers, "I would recite a poem, and somewhere in that poem would be the feeling, somewhere in it would be the piece of information" in the form of a poetic device, such as a line or an image.[63]

As a secondary resort to the information of experience, books were an avenue for Lorde to gain information that was otherwise not meted out to her or revealed in the body language of others, particularly in regard to her growing body and menarche—a pivotal moment for Lorde. Concerned by her mother's fears about Lorde's delayed period, at the age of fourteen, Lorde remembers obtaining a "hard-to-get-book on the 'closed shelf' behind the librarian's desk at the public library" to read about menstruation, after bringing a forged note that allowed her to read the book at a special desk under supervision. She remembers, relatably so for anyone who has read these type of books during puberty, "Although not terrible informative, they were fascinating books, and used words like menses and ovulation and vagina."[64] She returned to the 135th Street library with further forged notes to read about sex and childbirth—"when [she] wasn't getting whippings"—confused about the relationship between menstruation and childbirth but clear about the role of penises, wondering if this disconnect was because she "had always been a very fast but not a very careful reader."[65]

In contrast to this illicit compiling of information, Lorde describes the relief of finally getting her period with an extended scene *Zami* of her pounding *souse,* a spice mixture from her mother's lineage. Observing the phallic process of pounding herbs and spices with a mortar and pestle, Lorde describes the erotics of her awakening to the status of womanhood within her body, writing of a "thread" that runs along her body that empties into "a basin that was poised between my hips, now pressed against the low kitchen counter before which I stood, pounding spice. And within that basin was a tiding ocean of blood beginning to be made real and available to me for strength and information."[66] In particular, this use of the word "information" contrasts its more formal definitions, defining information not as something obtained from the secret shelves of the library but something experienced in the body that becomes a tool for further inquiry.

Often, research took turns into imagination and experience, hallmarks of Lorde's relationship to knowledge that would privilege intuition beyond just "the facts." This approach is likely the result of repeated efforts at research that resulted in Lorde leaving empty-handed. For instance, despite extensive research in a local repository, Lorde was never able to find an official record of her father's birth in Barbados. Instead, she sought out experiences on the island to connect her to him, such as the shared sight of the ocean, local animals, and plants.[67] These imaginative modes of redress are a critical part of Lorde's relationship to knowledge and her former life as a librarian, whose limitations she confronts in an interview with Adrienne Rich: "I became a librarian because I really believed I would gain tools for ordering and analyzing information. I couldn't know everything in the world, but I thought I would gain tools for learning it. But that was of limited value. I can document the road to Abomeny for you, and true, you might not get there without that information. I respect what you're saying. But once you get there, only you know why, what you came for, as you search for it and perhaps find it."[68] In this paradigm, information without understanding of *why it is sought* is inherently incomplete, and unsatisfying for Lorde. In her early years at library school, the validation of finding Carriacou on the map may well have been enough—locating the information that was so hard to come by. However, as her relationship with poetry as a way of knowing deepens, she draws a distinction between obtaining the facts from books and understanding that the real information comes from experience and interior observation.

The choice of Abomeny as an example here is significant; the "road to Abomeny" references a trade route in the former kingdom of Dahomey, from the port to the royal capital, that was known even to European travelers as a marvel. Lorde traveled to Africa to connect with her ancestral heritage, and received a vision of her "maternal, spiritual bloodline" to the goddess Seboulisa there, a motif that would become part of her poetry and an important part of her spirituality.[69] Thus, this road was something that Lorde had traveled—a destination that could be located on a map, perhaps in a library—but Lorde would not know that "she felt Dahomey was home" until she arrived.[70] For Lorde, this place was characterized by a symbolic and spiritual experience—a firm example that what you could learn in a library was wholly insufficient without experience and intuition.

As poet-librarian Sam Lohmann points out, the influence of Russell Ackoff's well-known "DIKW pyramid," which provides a basic hierarchical schema that places data, information, knowledge, and wisdom in succession, is prevalent in contemporary understandings of different forms of sense making. Lohmann sees poetics as a possible site of resistance to the prescriptive aspects of this schema—a perspective with which Lorde would agree.[71] Lorde's writing and interviews show her own development of a sense-making schema, in which information is a unit that creates the possibility of *knowledge,* which can then facilitate *understanding.* Or as Lorde states, "Understanding begins . . . to make knowledge available for use," which entails making language—poetry or prose—that articulates a reality that has no extant textual record, for herself and for others.[72] Information is not an inferior object in this workflow, particularly in the ways that information appears in Lorde's poetry. In her essay "Poetry Is Not a Luxury," Lorde argues that poetry is far more than just a literary activity, but is rather an engagement with "deep sources of information and power"— speaking specifically to the editorial controversy at *Chrysalis* magazine, which had stopped featuring poetry in its feminist magazine due to budgetary concerns.[73] In her essays, Lorde often uses the words "information" and "power" close together—or "strength" and "information," as with the souse-pounding scene in *Zami*; likewise, "The Uses of the Erotic" explores a "consideration of the erotic as a source of power and information."[74] This poetics of the power of information, developed by a poet in her postlibrarian years, becomes a signature technique in Lorde's own writing—perhaps in direct response to the way that the popular and scientific connotations of "information" became so dematerialized and disembodied in the postwar era.

Lorde's informatics are poetic at their core. Information appears in Lorde's poems, such as the "Conaiagui Women" in *The Black Unicorn,* who "wear their flesh like war / bear children who have eight days / to choose their mothers."[75] The presence of this information, much like the distinctive glossary and bibliography that accompanies *The Black Unicorn*, is designed to chronicle forgotten histories within the architecture of poetry, embedding this information to be adapted into knowledge by the poet and the reader. Importantly, this occurs within the purview of poetry, not historical writing. Lorde notes that she received a critique of *The Black Unicorn* that stated she didn't fully document the goddess figure in Africa. Lorde recalls responding, "I'm a poet, not a historian. I've shared my knowledge, I hope. Now you go document it, if you wish."[76]

Information, documentation, and knowledge exist in complex interplay, particularly in relation to Lorde's ideas about race and feminism. When Rich and Lorde discuss this in their interview; Rich notes, "If I ask for documentation, it's because I take seriously the spaces between us that difference has created, that racism has created," and Lorde responds, "I'm used to associating a *request* for documentation as a questioning of my perceptions, an attempt to devalue what I'm in the process of discovering."[77] Lorde goes on to note that "documentation does not help one perceive, at best it only analyzes the perception," or "at worst, it provides a screen by which to avoid concentrating on the core revelation, following it down to how it feels." Lorde notes that knowledge and understanding "function in concert, but they don't replace each other," and at that point, reminds Rich, "Don't forget I'm a librarian."[78]

For Lorde, who managed information as a librarian, and participated in the technoscientific infrastructure of electronics development as a factory worker, "information" or "knowledge" can be considered reclaimed terms related to feeling and lived experience. When she describes the "core revelation" as "how it feels," she does not juxtapose her response against rationality or objectivity. Lorde notes in conversation with Rich that "rationality . . . serves the chaos of knowledge [and] feeling," and that Lorde doesn't "see feel/think as a dichotomy" but rather "a choice of ways and combinations."[79] What is truly transformative, and brings revelatory meaning to information and knowledge, is their center in the affective experience of the body. Or, as Lorde states, "If we are to create a new order, we must go back, back, to what is primary, and those are our feelings."[80] While di Prima's "Revolutionary Letter #33" asks "how far back are we willing to go after all" in the search for premodern knowledge, this search for Lorde happens at an emotional level of experience, feeling, and sensation.

Black Bibliography and Teaching

Lorde's approach to information and knowledge deeply influenced her teaching, which was an essential activity in her life as a poet and activist. As she reflects on her development as a teacher in the City University of New York (CUNY) system, Lorde notes that her style was not to give "chunks of information" but rather to treat the learning process as "something you can incite, literally incite, like a riot."[81] In fact, her librarianship was her only somewhat-formal preparation for teaching. Lorde recounts being "terrified" at Tougaloo of her first time teaching, with no prior classroom experience and her self-professed lack of formal knowledge of poetic theory.[82] In an interview with Adrienne Rich, when discussing this part of her life, Lorde exclaims, "Adrienne, I had never read a book *about* poetry! Never read a book about poetry. I picked up one day a book by Karl Shapiro—a little thin white book. I opened it and something he said made sense. It was, 'Poetry doesn't make Cadillacs.'"[83] At Tougaloo, Lorde began by asking her students about their own desires for writing, and feeling "they needed access to literary models beyond those offered in their English courses," which Lorde provided by "mimeographing and distributing to them poems by other black poets."[84] Her participation in creating and building alternate structures related to literary models for these students drew on her librarian talents—assembling and structuring information, although this time, the recipients were Black radical students who were inspiring and generative for Lorde, instead of the "lily-white atmosphere" of Town School where she still held her librarian position back in New York City.[85]

Lorde's teaching, as documented through her journals, contains significant evidence of her reading practice and use of books not as units of information but as gestures toward broader themes and topics. A key resource for our exploration of Lorde's reading practices is available through *Lost & Found: The CUNY Poetics Document Initiative,* who recently published excerpts from Lorde's journals and archives related to her teaching at CUNY in the Search for Education, Elevation and Knowledge (SEEK) program. Created in 1966 to accept low-income students and increase the ability of minority students to pursue a college education, SEEK was initially populated at the instructor level by talented poets, many of whom were involved in some type of countercultural poetics in New York City, including Adrienne Rich, David Henderson, June Jordan, Toni Cade Bambara, Aijaz Ahmad, and others. A friend of Lorde's showed Mina Shaughnessy, director of the SEEK program at City College, Lorde's *The First Cities,* and thus secured her place in the program.[86]

After participating in SEEK, Lorde began teaching at Herbert H. Lehman College in the Bronx in 1969, and in 1970 became the first Black faculty member of the English Department of John Jay College of Criminal Justice within CUNY. Due to open admissions, a greater percentage of Black and Puerto Rican students enrolled, sitting alongside police officers in training (the school's specialization) who visibly carried guns in Lorde's class.[87] There, she taught a course specifically on race, including stereotyping, middle-class values, and structural oppression. Later, Lorde would teach at Hunter College, where she had received her undergraduate degree, and to which she was happy to return. Her journals document this rich history of teaching, including bibliographies, syllabi, and other notes, which form the basis of *"I Teach Myself in Outline": Notes, Journals, Syllabi, and an Excerpt from Deotha,* which was edited by current CUNY doctoral students.

In assembling the chapbooks, the editors frame Lorde's "reading lists, lesson plans and hastily penned notes on her students in class" as evidence that primarily points to her teaching practice, though it also relates to her reading practice.[88] While enumerative bibliography is a relatively straightforward practice in a librarian's toolkit, it has particular stakes for Black and African American communities in tracing the history of American reading. As Helton notes, the development of African American bibliographies, catalogs, and indexes occurred at the same time that the United States was formalizing many of its archives, libraries, and cataloging standards—the information science and management systems that undergird the distinctive relationship poets have to knowledge. Laura Helton's research explores published documents—namely, the acknowledgments of African American literary anthologies—as crucial sites of information that identify collectors, bibliographers, and library workers. She argues that these people within the field of information management, broadly speaking, were involved in "the making of infrastructures for inquiry" that are embodied in "lists: bibliographies, catalogs, and indexes," citing the bibliographic work of W. E. B. Du Bois, Paul Laurence Dunbar, Nella Larsen, Langston Hughes, and Audre Lorde as participating in these systems, from bibliography production to cataloging.[89] These entwined worlds of the Black anthology and Black bibliography worked together to establish the literary category of Black authorship, according to Helton—a category that Lorde worked within and beyond during her lifetime. By way of example, in the 1960s, Langston Hughes deliberately sought out Lorde to contribute to a Black poetry anthology that he was editing—an act related to his broader practice of seeking out Black authors to anthologize them and thus establish what Helton terms "the shape of a Black poetic tradition."[90]

For those developing bibliographies within professional institutions in the early twentieth century, the profession had particular and politicized limitations in regard to vocabulary for nonwhite subjects, especially in cataloging or describing what were termed "Negro collections." This necessitated improvisation to better describe the materials at hand, without perpetuating the racism embedded in standardized vocabulary and taxonomies.[91] Helton credits these "catalogers and list makers," both inside and outside of institutions, with building their own systems and architectures of Black thought.[92] This capacity of enumerative bibliography, and the talents of Black knowledge builders in using it, did nothing short of establish and trace arcs of reading and poetic traditions as a political act to establish a Black American literary history.

Lorde's bibliographies, as they appear, are roadmaps to their subjects. In the *Lost & Found* chapbook, her bibliographies on "Race and the Urban Situation" at John Jay College and "The Other Woman: Lesbian Voices in 20th Century Amer. Literature" at Hunter College are divided into conceptual units, with both required and suggested texts. For the John Jay course, in addition to Barry Schwartz and Robert Disch's *White Racism: Its History, Pathology, and Practice*, and Lerone Bennett's *Before the Mayflower: A History of the Negro in America 1619–1966*, Lorde also suggests texts by James Baldwin, Toni Cade Bambara, Eldridge Cleaver, Malcolm X, LeRoi Jones, and others. The readings have an immediacy to them; far from discussing long-published canonical texts, Lorde explores race from an ongoing perspective, collating poetry, history, and social sciences in her resources for students and taking advantage of recently published material. By observing these bibliographies, one cannot help but want to attend the class. Lorde's syllabi read, to a large extent, like the academic documents they are: designed to provoke conversation in the classroom and receive illumination from their instructor. Just like Lorde's road to Abomeny, one can point out the right text, but only the true experience of it in context will get the reader where they need to be.

Lorde notably describes poetry as "the skeleton architecture of our lives," citing its ability to "form the dreams for a future that has not yet been and towards which we must work when we speak of change."[93] In line with this infrastructural characterization, Lorde's definitions of poetry mirror many definitions of bibliography—namely, Ed Dorn's idea of a bibliography as a road map, as in Olson's *Bibliography on America for Ed Dorn*. In an interview, Lorde states, "Poetry is a roadmap, a way of putting together, in a new way, the pieces that we carry around within us . . . what I call that knowledge."[94] Poetry's ability to map the terrain, to serve as information, power, and a resource, is why it serves as Lorde's primary knowledge-building and organizing structure throughout her life. Despite her long affiliations with universities and public institutions through her teaching and librarianship, she acknowledged the "narrow and restricted interpretations of learning and the exchange of knowledge that we suffered in the universities or that we suffered in the narrow academic structures," particularly in relationship to the dearth of Black knowledge and the constructs of institutional racism. In the face of this, Lorde knew that "different tools in the exchange of information" were necessary to redefine the possibilities of the future.[95] She found these tools through fostering discussion and dialogue, in her classes and conferences, but also through her poetry.

One such technique is her inclusion of a glossary and bibliography in her poetry collection *The Black Unicorn*. At the end of the book, "A Glossary of African Names Used in the Poems" includes definitions—some a paragraph or two—of eighteen ancient capitals of African Kingdoms, as well as goddesses and cultures. Beginning in the first edition published in 1978, and included in all subsequent editions, the glossary is accompanied by a bibliography of four sources on the Yoruba, Dahomey, and African gods. This inclusion of reference material in a book of poetry invites the reader into the process of researching the possibly unfamiliar names within, and also shows that these two forms of knowledge (poetry and reference) are intermingled textually.

The choice of names in the glossary also dates the present moment of the book—contemporaneous political events or people, such as Assata Olugbala Shakur, are not glossed, and contemporary readers must step outside the text for greater context on its many references to civil rights movement struggles and events. Yet the glossary is a powerful tool for Lorde, one that reframes the relationships between named entities in the text. Poems such as "125th Street and Abomey," by virtue of their title, juxtapose Lorde's present and her geographically distant history. The poem "For Assata" reimagines a mythic blend of historical worlds in its address of Assata Olugbala Shakur, who was convicted as an accomplice to the murder of a police officer during a shootout. As Lorde addresses "Assata my sister warrior," she imagines that "Joan of Arc and Yaa Asantewa / embrace / at the back of your cell," blending the Ashanti queen of Ejisu who waged war against British colonialism in the early twentieth century with the medieval French saint who led the French revival against England in the Hundred Years' War.[96] The kindred nature of these two figures, which Lorde imagines as guardian spirits to Assata Shakur, is striking in part because of the fame of the canonized Joan of Arc in Western European culture and the obscurity of Asantewa by comparison, despite their shared fight against imperial and colonialist rule. Asantewa is in the glossary, for the unfamiliar reader; Joan of Arc is not. Glossaries can provide information that is generally assumed readers might not know, but at the same time, they also establish what information is important in a text. By reestablishing the marginalized historical figure at the center of the glossary, Lorde's poetry draws correspondences and also revises the historical context of a warrior woman.

This process is part of Lorde's deeper mission to step outside of white patriarchal European consciousness, a project also undertaken by her friend Diane di Prima at length. Lorde felt that "living in the European mode" was not just a problem to be solved, because to do so would be to focus on the Western-centric connection between ideas, innovation, and freedom. Rather, Lorde notes that as "we come more into touch with our own ancient, non-european consciousness of living as a situation to be experienced and interacted with, we learn more and more to cherish our feelings, and to respect those hidden sources of our power from where true knowledge and, therefore, lasting action comes."[97] While this process can be plagued with lack of sources and resources—as Lorde's own research efforts show—there is no substitute for its pursuit.

In "An Open Letter to Mary Daly," Lorde articulates her frustration that Daly's book, *Gyn/Ecology,* focused only on Western examples of the goddess figure. She writes, "Simply because so little material on non-white female power and symbol exists in white women's words from a radical feminist perspective, to exclude this aspect of connection from even comment in your work is to deny the fountain of non-european female strength and power that nurtures each of our visions."[98] In works such as *The Black Unicorn,* Lorde uses the historical record to correct an absence of information and role models in her own life, showing historical realities of collaboration and bonding among African women, women-centered communities, and women warriors. In this capacity, Lorde's poetry is a system of information management that facilitates knowledge, understanding, and deeper connections to lived experience. In particular, Lorde's work on her identity, as seen within her poetry, shows how her "lesbian consciousness operates on both the historical and the mythical levels," and her understanding of the political reality of her current moment through historical corrective lenses makes her work doubly significant.[99]

Lorde's quest was shared by her contemporaries, who often visualized this practice of incorporating new realms of knowledge, or working across disciplines and traditions, through the metaphor of doors. In *Polis Is This*, Henry Ferrini's film on Olson and Gloucester, Amiri Baraka flags "the whole question of putting the hinge back on the door," or "trying to find out what had been hidden from us by the emergency of this new one-sided society" in twentieth-century America.[100] Baraka is referring to Charles Olson's statement in *Proprioception*, which lays out a series of seven historical "hinges of civilization to be put back on the door" that consist of "leaping *outside* as well as connecting *backward*" through language and history, engaging both Indigenous and Western practices to illuminate a present understanding of North America.[101] The metaphor of hinges and doors shows the importance of poetry and thus becomes a way of thinking, a method of inquiry into larger systems that shape the historical record and our reception of it.

Libraries Destroyed

Audre Lorde's unpublished novel *Deotha*, excerpted in the *Lost & Found* chapbooks, begins with a scene of self-care—a term that Lorde coined, which argues that taking care of oneself within a heteropatriarchal capitalist system is an act of political revolt. The protagonist, Dee, takes a hot bath with sandalwood essence and a stick of incense that is held "between two books in the tiny bookcase beside the toilet" so that the ash can fall neatly in the toilet bowl.[102] In the poem "Touring," Lorde writes, "I leave poems behind / dropping them like dark seeds," noting that she won't "harvest" them or grieve their destruction, since "they pay for a gift / I have not accepted."[103] If we substitute "poems" for "books," these two vignettes show how we must read for Lorde's books now—as evidence in her writing, rather than items on a shelf.

Returning to the circumstances that surround Lorde's own library and its destruction, the failure of libraries as adequate infrastructures feels all the more acute. Any library, by virtue of its existence on a planet in ecological decline, is vulnerable. Lorde's move from Staten Island to Saint Croix, an island that has been subject to the global forces of colonialism and imperialism, whose infrastructures and geographic position created an added layer of ecological danger, relates deeply to her identity as an Afro-Caribbean woman, and the destruction of her library—while not a personal affront from Mother Nature—can be read only along these lines. In an interview with Karla Hammond, Lorde notes the ecological challenges that face her generation: "It's important to keep the whole place floating long enough so that we have somewhere to evolve upon," and "we live with the knowledge that we're an endangered species because we're killing the earth, the water, the air." She continues, "Unless we're very careful, we're not going to have any place to evolve on. And building space stations is not the solution."[104] Lorde knew that women of color in developing and/or colonized countries are particularly underrepresented and vulnerable to the systems of patriarchy and imperialism that built the world as she experienced it, and her lifelong work was to seek out other women and represent their differences as a site of mutual power. In doing so, she and her library moved to the ecological crosshairs.

The destruction of Lorde's library is also an opportunity to comment on the vulnerability of Black poets that Lorde felt during her lifetime, which is echoed by colleagues such as June Jordan. When Lorde writes, "We were never meant to survive" in *A Litany for Survival,* she speaks to this political reality and moral failure of racism in America. Racism created significant barriers to achieving economic stability and general well-being, particularly during the civil rights movement, with its ongoing violence. For those bearing its full brunt—such as Bob Kaufman, whose constant run-ins with police led to involuntary electroshock therapy, head trauma, and more—collecting a library might have seemed a luxury.

Yet, Lorde herself is an apt poet to remind us of what gets counted as a luxury and why this matters. In "Poetry Is Not a Luxury," Lorde tells us that poetry "forms the quality of the light within which we predicate our hopes and dreams toward survival and change, first made into language, then into idea, then into more tangible action."[105] These continual steps toward embodiment of self are critical in Lorde's formulation, and can be read alongside the idea of assembling a library, a bibliography, or any sort of collection of book-related knowledge. The power of these reactions is related to the individual infrastructure that undergirds them. Considering Walter Benjamin's library as he unpacks his own, Homi Bhabha notices the surprising juxtapositions of books against each other, and the "subtle ways that disorder challenges the shelved order of the study, and displaces the Dewey decimal system," allowing Bhabha to contemplate the "dis-ordered historical 'dwelling' bestowed upon us" by the book collections we create and use.[106] Indeed, the purpose of the Dewey Decimal System was to eliminate the need for individual librarians to develop classification schemes in the rapidly expanding field of public libraries; the personal library brings this crucial element back to the fore.[107]

The importance of eclectic organizing, and the possible freedoms therein, reminds us of the intricacies of Lorde's lived experience that defied any sort of categorization throughout her life. She was a Black lesbian who had children with a white man; she was not at home in the "gay girl" scene in New York City bars that was predominantly white, nor was she at home in the Black Arts Movement that she saw as heteronormatively driven; she was a poet who was best known for her essays and prose works; she was a warrior Caribbean descendent of the goddess Seboulisa who had been a children's librarian on the Upper East Side. Walt Whitman's joyful cry of "I contain multitudes" can be a celebration, but only if one has a home in which to celebrate it.

Beginning in the 1950s, finding an epistemological schema that could accommodate her felt sense of self became a lifelong project for Lorde, and one that caused her to embrace the quality of difference as a political act. Citing the range of scholarship on this topic, Linda Garber notes that Lorde's approach to identity is often described as postmodern, given its appreciation and acknowledgment of multiple selves through her identity as Black, feminist, and lesbian.[108] Yet the theoretical lens of postmodernism is not wide enough to orient us toward the complexity of Lorde's achievements. When Lorde states, "I am a black feminist lesbian poet, and I identify myself as such because if there is one other black feminist lesbian poet in isolation somewhere within the reach of my voice, I want her to know she is not alone," she reveals to us her audience and the political, lived stakes of representation.[109] At the same time, Lorde notes that being a poet is the one aspect of her identity that cannot be separated from any other facets of it, in which poetry is "the strongest expression I have of certain ways of making, identifying, and using my own power."[110] Her greatest contribution to the idea of information management in the twentieth century relates to di Prima's idea in the opening of *Revolutionary Letters:* "I have just realized the stakes are myself," which casts the body as a site for compiling meaning and difference. As an embodied system of information architecture, in which Lorde negotiated her own visibility and clout in a world that was hostile to this, her achievement remains outstanding.

FIGURE 4. Bookcase within Diane di Prima's occult library, housed in her garage, San Francisco, 2018.

—Photograph by M. C. Kinniburgh. Permission of Sheppard Powell.

CHAPTER 3

"THE REQUIREMENTS OF OUR LIFE IS THE FORM OF OUR ART"

Diane di Prima's Publishing, Cosmology, and Occult Library

IN AUDRE LORDE's archive, on a piece of brown cardstock—
"Strathmore artland tan," to be exact—Diane di Prima has
typed publishing notes for Lorde for *The First Cities.* The sheet contains possibilities for hand-tooling, including calligraphy, tipped-in autograph sheets,
or other special limited-edition features, as well as suggestions about different
ways to approach the cover. Di Prima seeks Lorde's input at each turn, while
also demonstrating her technical knowledge of book production: the colophon to the half title, the structure of proofs, and the timeline to send to the
printer. She ends the note with words anyone who has published a book will
know well: "Sooner we get it together, the sooner it goes to press."[1] Lorde and
di Prima had been friends since high school as members of "The Branded,"
a group of girls who held séances to summon Keats. Over their lives, they
often visited each other, hosted each others' children at their houses (Lorde
in fact delivered di Prima's second child in New York City), and wrote back
and forth. Here, that friendship takes the form of careful attention to aspects
of publishing Lorde's first book.

By the time that Diane di Prima sent this undated card, likely circa 1968
around the publication date of *The First Cities,* di Prima had been a publisher
in some form since 1961, when she began mimeographing *The Floating
Bear,* and 1963, when she bought a press and began Poets Press. Yet di Prima
remembers understanding the connections between printing and politics

from an early age, raised in a self-described middle-class Italian American household in Brooklyn, with an anarchist grandfather, Domenico Mallozzi, who was a strong influence on her upbringing. She recalls that "the anarchist dream of being a printer had long been in me," and dedicated her work *Revolutionary Letters* to Mallozzi.[2] This anarchist impulse led di Prima directly to poetry, after dropping out of Swarthmore College at eighteen and moving to downtown New York City, where she lived alone and participated in what would become the Beat poetry scene. In *Recollections of My Life as a Woman*, di Prima writes, "Choosing to be an artist . . . in the world I grew up in, the world of the 40s and early 50s, was choosing as completely as possible for those times the life of the renunciant."[3] In di Prima's hands, this role was ultimately liberatory in her search for knowledge and experience outside of mainstream culture, and printing and publishing were crucial activities in her self-directed education.

While di Prima's activities as a poet on the whole are understudied—including her founding of Poets Theatre, a performance space in New York City; her decades-long practice of Buddhism; her teaching of occult and esoteric wisdom for healing; and, of course, her poetry—her underacknowledged role as a publisher is essential context for her relationship with books. One of the most influential projects she undertook as publisher—for both herself and the postwar American poetry community—was begun in her twenties, when she began editing and printing *The Floating Bear* with LeRoi Jones in 1961. With a total of thirty-eight issues by 1971, the *Bear* was unprecedented in its velocity for a poet-made little magazine. Sixteen issues were published and distributed in the first year alone, and with di Prima and Jones's mailing list, which grew from approximately two hundred poets to a print run of roughly two thousand copies per issue, the *Bear* served as a proving ground for emerging poetry, away from the conformity and oversight of traditional publishers and journals.

As typesetter and printer of the *Bear*, di Prima typed up all the stencils for mimeographing, at which point friends and apartment visitors would pitch in with collating, stapling, addressing, and stamping. Speaking with David Hadbawnik about how her own poetry was influenced by the community that coalesced around *The Floating Bear* and other projects in the 1960s, di Prima notes that other than Ezra Pound's *ABC of Reading*, typing poems for the *Bear* was one of the most influential learning experiences for her as a writer: "The place where I learned the most about poetics . . . was actually typing those poems for the *Floating Bear*, onto those green stencils. . . . By the time you start, since the *Bear* was the same size as a typewriter page, once you copy exactly the line breaks and the spacing that Olson had done, it gave you plenty of time to absorb it and to ponder why did he do it that way."[4] Di Prima's careful copying of Olson's work, among works by many other poets, for *The Floating Bear* suggests that attentiveness functions as a type of conversation between poets, ephemerally occurring in the space between the page and the typist. During the Beloit lectures, Olson explores the word "typos" from a printer's perspective, describing moveable type and notes: "Really, to imagine a printer doing it . . . he's under your words in order to make the letters of them. Which always delights me, literally, as a problem of creation. In fact, literally, I would go so far—if you will excuse my Americanism—to think that you write that way. That you write as though you were *underneath* the letters . . ."[5] For Olson's work, di Prima is "under [the] words," reading carefully, learning. In Olson's own formulation, he's writing in that manner too—up underneath his own letters, composing. One imagines Olson's pieces in *The Floating Bear,* with di Prima and Olson both beneath the print, holding up the piece as we read, as if on the other side of a space-time dimension.

Sometimes, di Prima would retype materials not for publication but instead for her own use. She recalls a "priceless collection" of poetry books that Fielding Dawson left at her house, containing material from "Black Mountain College: early Creeley and Olson texts which I perused, and in some cases copied poem by poem, entirely on my electric typewriter. . . . So when I gave them back I would still have a copy for myself."[6] The preciousness of those words, to warrant the painstaking act of typing them out, attests to the importance of possessing a material copy to revisit, explore, and learn further from. Di Prima maintained this instinct well through the era of xerography; for Robert Duncan's once-elusive and important *The H. D. Book,* not edited for publication until 2011, Diane di Prima was instrumental in its clandestine circulation; she collated the pieces and distributed them as a single volume for others to read and share.[7] While this speaks to di Prima's long-term centrality in her poetry communities, it also speaks to a consciousness of reprography—of the uses of technology to distribute and document—that was part of a contemporaneous bookmaking revolution in which di Prima played a key role.

The Floating Bear was one project among many emerging publications that formed the "mimeograph revolution," resulting in a flourishing of poet-run small presses and magazines. Like the earlier so-called print revolution, its innovation was its rate of production, which in turn created the possibility for increased readership and distribution. In the preface to *A Secret Location on the Lower East Side: Adventures in Writing, 1960–1980,* a compendium of the small press and mimeograph revolution, poet Jerome Rothenberg links the importance of self-publication to the very identity of poetry, from Walt Whitman's self-published *Leaves of Grass* in 1855 through the "writers who sought new ways & languages" and "took charge of their own publication," such as Gertrude Stein, alongside poet-run and noncommercial presses from Black Sun to early New Directions.[8] After this heyday, Rothenberg revisits how the Cold War era marked a newly fragmented world of poetry that was homogenized and sterilized by McCarthyism, New Criticism, and commercial publishing practices that elevated only a few approved voices. Against this backdrop, he demonstrates how "the actual topography of the new poetry (circa 1960) was at a necessary distance from the commercial hub of American publishing," and newly possible thanks to cheap rents and newly affordable printing technologies, including mimeographs, ditto, Xerox, photocopy, and offset presses. Rothenberg's preface underscores that "the lesson of the works presented here [in *A Secret Location*] is the reminder of what is possible where the makers of the works seek out the means to maintain & fortify their independence."[9] And indeed, Steve Clay and Rodney Phillips enumerate over one hundred such examples of this type of publication, including di Prima's *The Floating Bear* and Poets Press, as well as Totem Press (who published her first work), alongside other highlights—Oyez Press, *Yugen, Semina, Fuck You: A Magazine of the Arts, Umbra, The Poetry Project Newsletter, The Black Mountain Review, Evergreen Review,* Grove Press, and New Directions.

Thus, after Rothenberg's characterization, self-publication and independent modes of publishing in Cold War America were political gestures: refusals to edit poetic language to fit the mold of commercial or university life. This political gesture is sometimes misinterpreted in a "chicken or egg" manner, which suggests that counterculture poets could not attract commercial attention, when it was often the case that they resisted it outright. For instance, Brenda Knight, in *Women of the Beat Generation,* underscores di Prima's role as a publisher, noting "Diane di Prima, considered by many to be the archetypal Beat woman, started her own press rather than wait for a publisher to come knocking."[10] While di Prima reflects on the difficulties of creating and sharing art in the 1950s, asking "how to carve a niche for it, if one doesn't have access to galleries, to publishing houses? How make a place if one doesn't speak the language of the critic?," she has nevertheless captured significant interest in her lifetime from trade publishers such as Penguin, who printed *Loba* and *Recollection of My Life as a Woman.*[11] Knight's statement oversimplifies, if not mischaracterizes, *why* di Prima developed a deep relationship to printing and printing technologies, since she was not holding out by any means for traditional representation of her or her colleagues' work. It is not, as Knight might indicate, solely because there is an absence of major publisher interest but rather because the primary value of the work is not in its legibility as a "famous" publication by a larger publisher. Rather, as Rothenberg states, what matters is the poet's ability to write and print for herself, in her time, in her community.

Di Prima's work in publishing was indeed part of her larger rejection of institutional structures of knowledge distribution, including academic institutions, and it was also a deep part of her poetics. She describes using a multilith press at Columbia University, working in its Electronic Research Lab, as a mystical experience, comparing herself to a "bee tasting a hundred kinds of flowers."[12] Later, while learning the entire workflow of publishing from Aardvark Press (who agreed to publish her debut book, *This Kind of Bird Flies Backward*, if she did the typesetting and printing), she describes being "caught up in the wonder of offset printing" and "hooked, though [she] didn't realize it" on the process.[13] In her lecture as poet laureate of San Francisco, she reflects how "poetry led me to . . . learn offset printing and raise the money to buy my Fairchild-Davidson press," and how she "was very proud of it. It came secondhand with a week of printing classes."[14] She began her imprint, Poets Press, with a "Davidson 241 and put it in a storefront. . . . I went to 'printing school' for a week and learned how to run the machine (I was the only woman in the class), and I got on with it."[15] Through Poets Press, she published John Ashbery, Jean Genet, Audre Lorde, Gregory Corso, David Henderson, Kirby Doyle, and her own work, as well as an anthology of poems protesting Vietnam, titled *War Poems*, featuring Charles Olson among many others.

In a funding letter for the press, the National Foundation of Arts and Humanities acknowledges di Prima's work in foregrounding "authors of significant works who have difficulty in being published through the usual commercial channels," and how Poets Press contributed directly to efforts "in advancing the cause of the unknown, obscure or difficult writer, and in the publication of books visually and typographically distinctive, thereby helping to advance the cause of the best in American art."[16] (Di Prima remembers that the last book she printed with funding of this sort was in Kathmandu, Nepal, on very nice lokta paper, which her funders saw as a waste of money on non-American materials and thus ensured the end of her grants from such organizations.) Adding to the reach of the press, some titles remain in print today through other publishers, such as Timothy Leary's *Psychedelic Prayers*. Curator Jolie Braun notes that Poets Press books were often mentioned in underground magazines and newspapers of the day, including *LA Free Press, Olé, Margins, Quixote, The Berkeley Barb,* and *The Paper,* as well as the National Foundation. As a women working in the editorial and printing community of New York City in the 1960s, and later on the West Coast, di Prima's voice as an editor, publisher, and poet is unique and also essential to our understanding of the radical possibilities of this era.

As I explore in the previous chapter, Audre Lorde's reflections on her time as a librarian allow us to recover, in the absence of her library, her conceptualization and organization of information against mainstream forms of information architecture. Likewise, di Prima's background in printing is an important backdrop to our understanding of her book collecting as an extension of a certain type of work: gathering the necessary knowledge for poetry and survival. Shaped by her early years in Manhattan running Poets Theatre, and participating in a dynamic scene of dance, performance, painting, and poetry, di Prima's work as poet and publisher was embedded in the praxis of everyday; the art she and her contemporaries created "existed beyond the studio, the typewriter, the apartment . . . that it—even briefly—changed the world."[17] The multifaceted intentions of di Prima's works such as *Revolutionary Letters*—meant to be sung on the steps of City Hall, or shared via mimeograph as fuel for anger or consolation—rejects the idea of poetry as a solely hermeneutic practice, or the idea of a book as an encounter just between the reader and the object. Rather, di Prima's relationship with books and what is within them calls for radical transformation of life itself. This effect relates to Ammiel Alcalay's observation that di Prima has refused to give over the "paradoxical complexities of plain language"—a significant act in a critical milieu that uses "specialized terminologies that attempt to control things that might defy control."[18]

Di Prima's refusal to work within mainstream institutions for the duration of her life—with the exceptions of accepting funding for her publishing projects—is a key part of understanding the importance and independence of her contributions to twentieth-century poetry. Jed Rasula, in *The American Poetry Wax Museum: Reality Effects, 1940–1990,* argues that poetry's "dominant condition . . . in the second half of the twentieth century is its subsistence in administrative environments," from New Criticism to Associated Writing Programs.[19] By contrast, di Prima's institutional affiliations are with her ideas and her community; she has described New York City as her "school" or "university" during her first decades as poet.[20] In *Recollections of My Life as a Woman,* she makes clear the importance of her own abdication of formal academic education at the age of nineteen, giving up "the notion of college degrees" to pursue poetry. This was a firm choice, despite her extensive coursework as a student in New York City, and also due to the economic realities of her father refusing to fund a formal degree after she left Swarthmore.[21] With this, we have much to learn by noting how thoroughly di Prima's work has always existed outside of formal academic structures, informed by a wide range of knowledge traditions.

"What Is Saved . . . Is Saved by a Few"

Di Prima's reflections on her work as a printer are also tied to her views on the preservation of history. Her instincts to copy, collate, and otherwise preserve sources of information—not just by buying books or typing mimeograph stencils, but also by xeroxing, typing, writing, or other otherwise copying for her personal use—is archival in nature, and its motivations might be traced to a 1956 conversation she had with Ezra Pound. In *Recollections,* she recounts a lesson on cultural preservation that she learned early in her life as a poet while visiting him at St. Elizabeth's Hospital:

> Ezra told us of copying Vivaldi scores in the library of the Dresden Museum, copying them for Olga Rudge, his love. When the Museum was destroyed in the bombing of Dresden, they were the only copies of those scores that remained. They were being transcribed even as we spoke about them.
>   Stories like this made a deep impression on me. They made me realize that what is saved, the shards we call civilization, is saved by a few. By people photographing, or copying by hand. Today as I sit here writing at my computer, I think of the library I've put together since then, the alchemy books old and new I've xeroxed for students. Stuff I've copied by hand. How much of that came out of the Vivaldi story.[22]

This type of message, from Ezra Pound, is particularly unique given his role in poetry around the war. As the only American tried for treason in World War Two, Pound was held as a political prisoner by his own government for thirteen years, on account of demonstrations of fascist ideology on radio broadcasts in Rome and later from charges of insanity. While Pound was held in St. Elizabeth's, the US government was hiring ex-Nazi scientists and organizers at a rapid pace after the war concluded. Alcalay notes, "Never a real trial, the Pound case played an important cultural, historical, and political role" that "established the shadowy image of the poet through whom art's relationship to politics can be administered and cordoned off, and used as a surrogate form of debate."[23]

Within this larger context, Pound's presence in poetry, and indeed in di Prima's and Olson's life during the 1940s and 1950s, reveals critical moments in their poetic development. Both di Prima and Olson visited Ezra Pound in St. Elizabeth's Hospital early on in each of their respective lives as poets— Olson after resigning from the Office of War Information, and di Prima in 1956 after having corresponded with him for a few years. Di Prima remembers her visit to Ezra Pound fondly in *Recollections*, noting his generosity and courtesy to her and her poet friends while also observing the intense racism of Washington DC, at the time; Olson's memory, consolidated in the volume *Charles Olson and Ezra Pound: An Encounter at St. Elizabeth's* and edited by Catherine Seelye, is more vexed, although Olson dedicates his first major work, *Call Me Ishmael*, to the poet. For Olson and di Prima, what Olson calls Pound's "collapse of judgment brought about by hate" does not cause them to jettison his prior work, including his *ABC of Reading* that proved so influential to the next generation of poets. Their relationships with him, primarily of poetic lineage, remained critical sites of inquiry for both Olson and di Prima in their own poetics. Within the University of North Carolina at Chapel Hill archives, one of the largest repositories of di Prima's archives other than her own home, a single postcard from Pound to di Prima notes, "All I can do is wish you luck, can't guarantee it, E.P."[24]

Thus, it may be not so much Pound's exact notion of what deserved to be saved but the weight of his poetic vision that necessitated poets intervening in the very cultural record during war that seemed to last a lifetime. In Ed Sanders's *Investigative Poetry,* the work begins with a clarion call "that poetry / should again assume responsibility / for the description of history."[25] Through a modernist poetic lineage, and alongside poets like Sanders, Olson, and many others, di Prima learned quickly: in order to describe that history, you might need to save it yourself. Doing so is a matter of political urgency, so that knowledge itself does not get destroyed as collateral for global warfare.

The Requirements of Our Life Is the Form of Our *Library*

Diane di Prima's house that she shared with her partner, Sheppard Powell, was structured by books. In a flashback dated May 15, 1995, in *Recollections*, di Prima writes,

> As I write about leaving Topanga Canyon in 1963, my own household in San Francisco is under siege: a new owner is trying to evict us and move into my pad. I mentally see my four thousand books in labeled boxes, me trying to manage that, to find what I need when I need it in a great catacombs of "storage." ... Now there is a storm about me, storm of regret, storm of definition and redefinition of lifestyles for myself, for my partner, Sheppard. We stare at each other down long corridors of Art. Or stand silent in rooms whose walls are awash in books.... Which life to salvage out of the many that surround us.[26]

While di Prima was thankfully able to stay in her home in this instance, this quote indicates the scope of her book-collecting project: "four thousand books," which she dreads the thought of "trying to manage," as a "great catacombs." Indeed, di Prima's house was "awash in books," and her personification of their energies as "life" that requires salvaging speaks to the intimacy of her relationship with books that has spanned her lifetime.

Among her whole collection of books, there was a particular subset of books that di Prima conceived of as her "occult library." This library remained in use until di Prima's death in October 2020, with volumes residing throughout the house, but was stowed almost exclusively on custom-built shelves in di Prima's garage, carefully arranged by topic over hundreds of volumes. Di Prima and Powell invited me to their home in California while I was a graduate student working with *Lost & Found: The CUNY Poetics Document Initiative* and while working as a librarian at The New York Public Library, with the idea that I could use these intersecting proficiencies to begin cataloging this collection. This library had not been documented at the time of my arrival, and as of 2021 was little-known beyond di Prima's circle of friends and students.[27]

Within this collection are the photocopied and bound alchemical texts that di Prima references in her Vivaldi story, as well as the canonical texts one might associate with mysticism and occult practices in the twentieth century—Aleister Crowley, Rudolf Steiner, Frances Yates, and George Gurdjieff. And on the first few shelves alone, materials address how to read the tarot, gemstones and crystals, medieval hermeticism, Atlantis, Egyptology, the Dogon, medieval female mystics, Meister Eckhart, Gnosticism, and biblical apocrypha. While cataloging, I found myself getting lost in a handbook on practical magic, or while peering at di Prima's extensive handwritten annotations. The material is unique in the first place, but as with the Maud/Olson Library, browsing it in person creates a web of unprecedented connections.

Beyond this physical distinctness of shelving (excepting books migrated upstairs or elsewhere, for the poet's use), di Prima marked this facet of her library as conceptually distinct. Written in di Prima's hand, on the back of a cardboard shipping box packed with newspaper clippings and chapbooks from Timothy Leary in prison, is the label "Pamphlets + Book by Timothy Leary," and the instruction "add to occult lib @ house." She envisioned her collection as a "reference library" with its own mode of cohesion, meant to be used at her home but eventually to be placed elsewhere and hopefully kept together.[28] Like any poet's library, we might infer that it contains materials di Prima has used for teaching, writing poetry, researching for lectures—the work that allowed poetry to flow freely through her.

The occult themes of the library are particularly purposeful in light of di Prima's larger poetic project, and indeed, the work of her contemporaries. In "Some Notes on Maximus," Creeley contextualizes Olson's use of sources, arguing that "the use of historical materials in *Maximus* will not be realized until one understands that they are being brought into a context of the *present*—no one is 'going back' to them, nor is there any question of the 'good old days.'"[29] Likewise, in his essay "Gnostic O," Kenneth Warren notes that "Olson's efforts to reach back to Sumer, to Pleistocene, and to races of men who existed before the dawn of history is not really an attempt to escape from the West but rather a variation of Western occult tradition."[30] Di Prima, like her friend and mentor Charles Olson, is a voracious reader and 'istorian with decades of experience. For instance, projects such as *Seven Love Poems from the Middle Latin*, published by Poets Press in 1965, are not titled evocatively. Di Prima translated Middle Latin works into a facing-page book of poetry, publishing the volume herself after its first publisher, Simon & Schuster, failed to deliver. She remembers working "hours every day" among "Latin texts and dictionaries and a reference grammar," "often uncovering the hidden sexual meaning of a metaphor, or a place where a stanza or two had likely been cut in copying by a prudish monk," and drawing from her four years of Latin as a student at Hunter College High School.[31] This type of intellectual and poetic work does not come without research, familiarity, and effort. Likewise, di Prima's teaching schedules from New College in California, the San Francisco Institute of Magical and Healing Arts, and other workshops show that beyond her devotion to poetry as a craft, she had assembled a formidable body of knowledge in her lifetime.

The questions of sources and research are essential to contextualizing di Prima's intellectual genealogy and the importance of her library, particularly in relation to her reworking of "the progression of European thought" as a means of answering the question of how historical knowledge can be activated in the present moment.[32] In "The Birth of Loba," she lists: "Paganism, Gnosticism, alchemy and then what—where do we go. Way-seeking Mind, 'that which is creative must create itself.' I want to say that the old religion and the old forms that we're all studying with such total devoutness—Eastern and Western—they have a lot of information and they have a lot of the means, but where we're all going they haven't mapped yet. We're mapping it now—or it's mapping us. If Buddha really had done it, we wouldn't be here."[33] Here, di Prima draws on her decades-long training as a Buddhist—in both the Zen and Tibetan traditions—to engage the idea of "way-seeking mind," or the principle of the self that is motivated to look for something larger, greater, or "more than." She contrasts devoutness toward the past with the ongoing indeterminacy of the past, noting importantly that the question of the future is being mapped by us, or mapping us, since no single knowledge system (such as Buddhism) has satisfactorily projected a way forward. In this dimension, di Prima does not reify mythological, spiritual, or historical knowledge—in what Alicia Ostriker might call the nostalgia-based "Modernist mythmaking of Yeats, Pound, Eliot, and Auden," who place faith in the past as a "repository of truth, goodness, or desirable social organization."[34] Ostriker, in her work on Alta, Margaret Atwood, Sylvia Plath, Anne Sexton, and H. D., articulates that women writers in the twentieth century who heavily address mythology in their work do so by "treat[ing] existing texts as fence posts surrounding the terrain of mythic truth but by no means identical to it," as "enactments of feminist antiauthoritarianism opposed to the patriarchal praxis of reifying texts."[35] Within her own paradigm, di Prima focuses on the generative possibilities of what these knowledge systems have yet to delineate that we—by mapping or being mapped—must actively cocreate.

In "Light / and Keats," di Prima answers an audience question about the importance of poets knowing the work of others. She responds,

> Look, the more you read and fill up your head with cadences, with rhythms and vowel patterns of other poets, the more of a repertory you have to draw on, conscious and unconscious, when you're writing. A lot of what you do is variations on riffs you've already heard. In this sense, poetry, like jazz, is a kind of dialogue that extends through time. . . . The more you've refined the instrument, the more gradations of tonality you program into it, the more information—history, myth, biology—you program into it, and the more you increase your capacity for carrying energy—literally carrying current—then the more you'll have available when the poem seeks to move through you.[36]

A voracious reader and architect of her own intellectual curricula, di Prima's advice to stoke the furnace of the mind with as much information as possible is why the presence of her books is so important. Materially, they attest to this lifelong practice of reading as an act of preparation for poetry, a jazz-like dialogue between di Prima and the information she has ingested through books and other writers. Importantly, di Prima does not posit a direct mode of influence between her sources and her poetry—rather, she is the alchemical crucible through which sources are heated, cooked, and transmuted in poetry. This is particularly important in the context of di Prima's studies on the history of religion, science, and, broadly speaking, the occult.

While Diane di Prima's life is characterized by in-depth research in a variety of fields, she credits Robert Duncan with the impetus to dive deeper than before on the topic of "hidden religions," or occulted practices. In particular, New College was a site to teach not just poetry as a subject, or poetry writing as a practice, but *poetics*. In a 2001 interview with David Meltzer, di Prima notes that the unique contribution of New College was its dedication to exploring "what a curriculum in poetics—as opposed to one in writing poetry—would be and what it would constitute."[37] One can see this process at work within di Prima's poetry, particularly in her works with epic orientations.

The presence of an epic poem, written by a poet over decades in a gradually accreting style, is surprisingly common in postwar American poetry; examples include Charles Olson's *Maximus Poems*, Gerrit Lansing's *The Heavenly Tree Grows Downward*, and Robin Blaser's *The Holy Forest*. Likewise, the majority of Diane di Prima's major poetic works—namely *Revolutionary Letters* and *Loba*—have each unfolded over decades, adhering to a strategy of not revising or reworking but rather accretion as each work gains new poems over the years and is reprinted accordingly. This vision of a body expanding ever-outward is particularly salient given di Prima's interest in cosmology, the branch of science that studies the origins and development of the universe, which she explores in *Revolutionary Letters* and her work more broadly. For di Prima, forms of knowledge and understanding are not in the provenance of academic or theoretical research (as with Claude Shannon's mathematical concept of information) but inherent in an attentive life.

During her time teaching at the New College of California in San Francisco, where di Prima was core faculty in the Poetics Program from 1980 to 1987, she recounts a class visit from Robert Duncan: "Toward the end of the class there was a general discussion, and I don't know what came up, but he said 'I don't want to see the whole picture, I just want to see my little piece that I have to work on, and just work on that little piece, I don't want to see the whole thing.' And I said, 'I want to know, I want to know it all, even if I never pick up a pen again.'"[38] The desire "to know it all," and the risk di Prima is willing to take for this principle, is embodied in her explorations of cosmology and cosmogony in *Revolutionary Letters,* as well as her investigation of goddess cultures in *Loba.*[39] Her occult library, however, might be considered a material corollary to her poetics of *sourcery.*

Di Prima traces the conceptual genesis of her occult library to 1976, when she lived in Ranchos de Taos, and spent hot summer afternoons meditating on the Tarot, dreaming, and working with visualization. Before then, in 1971, she taught herself cabala, and by the 1980s, when she was teaching at New College in San Francisco, this intuitive approach grew into an "understanding of how it wove itself into European consciousness, and which parts came at which point."[40] While books accumulated through the decades, likely one of the first significant additions to this particular collection is di Prima's full set of *The Golden Bough,* including all thirteen volumes, dated "Christmas 1960."[41] Thus, the collection is, on a material level, at least half a century in the making, and likely longer: di Prima recounts that when she left Swarthmore, she used their bookstore to purchase numerous books on credit, including Pound's *Cantos.*[42] In this dimension, we might read this library like di Prima's other poetic projects—morphing over decades, with material traces to attest.

The books represent the wide variety of forms that informed di Prima's own bookmaking and book collecting as she came of age in the mimeograph revolution as a printer, with a mix of small press and trade publishers, as well as items that are handwritten, photocopied, scrapbooked, and otherwise bespoke. This quality makes the library even more unique in its classification as a library, since it is neither books nor archive alone, and is at once comprised of duplicated and original material. And while the physical forms of the items defy mainstream archival or cataloging practices, their contents provide equal subversion, bringing Paracelsus, crystals, Crowley, early mythology, Buddhist traditions, Julian of Norwich, and other esoteric practice into a singular array.

The development of di Prima's occult library speaks to the intuitive mind of its maker. The collection spans hundreds of volumes and shelves upon shelves of books, but it was not built for a singular purpose. The books in the library result not out of need but desire: to know, to explore, to deepen the possibilities of di Prima's poetry and classroom. In particular, "Hidden Religions" was di Prima's signature class at New College in the Poetics Program,

FIGURE 5. Packets and books created by Diane di Prima in her occult library, housed in her garage, San Francisco, 2018.
—Photograph by M. C. Kinniburgh. Permission of Sheppard Powell.

covering Paracelsus, Hieronymus Bosch, Greek philosophy, Gnosticism, and Indo-European goddess mythology.[43] On a copy of a syllabus for this course, at the very end, she writes an initialed "Note About 'Clumps,'" articulating that "one might say that each clump is the center of a node from which excursions radiate in various asymmetrical directions."[44] Thus, the topics and themes of "Hidden Religions" remained open to excursions, explorations, and diversions based on what they sparked in both student and teacher: a hallmark of the occult library, as well, and similar to the way that Ed Dorn frames a good bibliography (as a kind of map) in his Charles Olson Memorial Lectures, or how Lorde designed her CUNY syllabi.

Given this commitment to pleasure and intuition, di Prima's library evolved through accumulating elements over decades, with openness to new acquisitions rather than a strict collecting style. She notes that she bought some volumes for her course on "Hidden Religions," out of general curiosity, and out of relationships with people like bookseller Louis Collins who would help locate books.[45] The collection formed organically: books that friends sent (accounting for the high volume of signed first editions in her overall library), books purchased for others, or books purchased to enjoy. Given di Prima's history as a printer, it is unsurprising that community would serve as a fundamental source for her collection.

In *Recollections,* di Prima recounts the intuitive way in which she has encountered certain occult texts, and thus, how they may have made their way into her collection. She describes encountering a silver locket that contained a small carved skull, likely made in Tibet, and feeling a mysterious attraction to the object. She recounts,

> One day, as I . . . star[ed] into the carved eye-sockets of the tiny skull, I heard/ saw the word MILAREPA in my head. Had no idea what it meant, but noted it down. It took me a week to get around to it, but I went to visit my old friend, the magus of stage lights, Nicola Cernovich, at Orientalia Bookstore where he worked—it was then the only place in town to find out about things Eastern— and asked him, 'What's a Milarepa?" . . . [He] pulled a beautiful boxed two-volume hardcover set off the shelf and handed it to me. *The Hundred Thousand Songs of Milarepa.*[46]

In this sense, we might consider the way di Prima collects books as directly related to her poetic practice, listening closely to the strong voice of her intuition and using this as a means of discovery. Her occult library makes good on the promise of her poetry: "The work is part of the life . . . what you don't control is the spirit, the voices, coming through you."[47] For di Prima, the voice might bring poems, or it might bring the next thing to read. Intuition is a force for connecting di Prima's instinctive knowledge (MILAREPA) with its material counterpoints in the world (the book itself).

Like other poets' libraries, the question of the library's completeness remains uncertain. On an immediate level, Diane di Prima's recent passing means that the ultimate location of the library is yet to be determined. In this process, books from the occult library that found their way elsewhere in the house will have to be reshelved, and full cataloging of the library will reveal additional information about the nature of the collection. As a library that has been decades in the making, though, this question of completeness or final form has had many twists and turns. For instance, di Prima notes that after Soren Agenoux housesat one of her New York City apartments, the majority of her floor-to-ceiling bookshelves were emptied, with not a "single art book left on the shelves . . . every art book I had ever managed to get my hands on had been sold."[48] Who knows if these books might have joined the

occult library or another "wing" of di Prima's collection? Likewise, her recollection of Alan Marlowe's fundamental betrayal—throwing out two boxes
"full of letters from my friends from the early days . . . and the other held my
journals, starting from when I was fourteen and wrote the 'No day without
a line' notebooks"—highlights the archival resources that no institution will
ever recover.[49] Di Prima remembers the importance of books as currency,
especially during lean times, such as selling first editions of *Howl* and *Gaso-
line* to pay the electric bill for the Poets Theatre for a show that evening.[50]. Di
Prima's libraries thus are shaped by the requirements of her life, even as they
reflect aspects of her poetic and readerly practices.

Yet on a conceptual level, di Prima's library recovers and preserves occulted
knowledge, especially related to wholeness as a type of healing, rather than an
archival or bibliographic concept. Many of the books in this library, especially
the prolific section on crystals, are preoccupied with questions of completeness from a perspective not of comprehensiveness but rather wholeness as
a spiritual and mystical state. For di Prima, with xerographed books, handwritten manuscripts, workbooks, and evidence of active reading, this process
is part of the practice, a spiritual devotion to "doing the work" that enables
the poetry to come. Like her poetry, it resists conclusions—focusing on "the
process, the bloody process."[51] This structuring echoes di Prima's ars poetica,
from *Recollections:* "THE REQUIREMENTS OF OUR LIFE IS THE FORM OF OUR
ART"—in which "art" can be substituted for "library." If the library is the temple, her poetry is the liturgy—the crystallization of how poetic transmission—
through dictation, through "being open to the stuff," as di Prima would say,
synthesizes and preserves knowledge traditions that would otherwise be
erased. Or even how it preserves the self-knowledge of our own experiences
(or others before us) that our conscious minds can scarcely acknowledge. In
the spirit of "women's alchemy, quick arms / to pull down walls," our arms
might also pull down, one at a time, di Prima's careful collection of books.
And the knowledge they contain, but also stir within us, will crack the mortar.

The Poetics of Diane di Prima's Occult Library

The library itself contains a dizzying variety of materials, worth describing in terms of the larger material categories they embody, but also in
terms of themes and genres represented. Some books are printed very
recently, with spines still firmly intact to suggest they have yet to be read or
ingested. Some books certainly qualify as rare, in the provenance of special

collections—especially those from the late nineteenth century, or small press chapbooks such as Jack Hirschman's translation of Eliphas Levi's *Dove Rose*, inscribed to di Prima in May 1979. Still others are copies or facsimiles of medieval or early modern texts, spiral-bound and labeled by di Prima. Given her reflections on Pound's Vivaldi, the relatively frequent occurrence of materials she has duplicated and bound herself indicates the need to preserve the knowledge of the book in some material form (without fetishizing the authority of a publisher's printing or binding). To this end, the library contains numerous books that have been copied, placed in binders or binding, and then thoroughly annotated—such as *The Nature of Substance*, by Rudolf Hauschka, which di Prima heavily annotates for correspondences between metals, definitions of scientific terminology, and observations on matter.[52] The form that these nonbook media might take can also appear highly ephemeral, such as a printout on the Irish soma ritual that sits in a folder with eight pages of notes taken on a yellow legal pad, titled "Peter Lamborn Wilson 7/26/94 Celts + Soma." Even more ephemerally, there are items such as an extensive typed book outline with notes, titled *Women's Work: The Lives of the Great Women Alchemists*, although no information exists on author or publisher, and it is difficult to determine whether the book exists or was perhaps a plan for one by di Prima or another scholar.

Still other items challenge the idea of a reference library as a static place for print materials; di Prima's teaching notes intermingle with writings on ritual and magical practice. The collection holds a booklet, dated 1985, of a three-night ritual for the "Gold Circle"—a group of practitioners, including di Prima and Sheppard Powell, who have met regularly since 1978 to "investigate through group visualization the five elements and twenty-five subelements and the Major Arcana of the Tarot."[53] In the booklet, di Prima's hand (dated 1985) notes that the worksheets are constructed from her notebooks and journals for Gold Circle members only, cautioning new students against using them. Items like this demonstrate the ongoing and iterative nature of these materials; the booklet contains a revised 1986 section. And materials like this, which enumerate performance and ritual, often leave other archival traces: di Prima's collage notebooks from the 1970s and 1980s, now held at the University of North Carolina at Chapel Hill, contain photographs of the ritual described in the booklet.

To consider the more theoretical dimensions of the library: if we take the Maud/Olson Library as both an embodiment of Charles "Olson's brain," to use Gregor Gibson's term, as well as a conceptual unit for unique materials that lead in a variety of vectors away from their original subject (such as the rare Yeats editions, never read, in Maud's collection of Olson's reading), di Prima's occult library has a similar dimension. For instance, di Prima's hand is not the only one in the collection. Certain used books, with bright yellow highlighting, contain annotations not in di Prima's own hand—sometimes even inscribed to others. Other inscriptions reveal that the books are gifts to di Prima: Mary Greer, influential author of Tarot manuals, inscribes a copy of *Tarot for Yourself* (1984) to Diane, thanking her for poetry, conversation, and teachings. That a well-respected and popular Tarot writer would learn from di Prima's own work with Tarot is not a surprise to those who know di Prima, or took one of her numerous Tarot-focused workshops in San Francisco. Thus, in this instance, while the nature of the collection suggests the variety of acquisition as vectors into material conditions beyond the physicality of the library itself—used books, gifts from friends, printouts, handwritten notebooks—it is nevertheless di Prima's at its core, replete with her writing, her ephemera, and her knowledge-building project. Many of di Prima's books contain multiple items used for bookmarks—paper towels, bookstore-branded bookmarks, a flyer for her son's piano instruction service, pressed flowers, a folded page here and there—marking the process of reading. The ephemera further speak to di Prima's lesson from Pound's Vivaldi—capturing fragments that give a sense of her lived experience, that if not for their repurposed use as bookmarks, would otherwise not persist.

Annotation

While annotation only provides a partial story of the structure and use of di Prima's occult library, certain instances of annotation are nevertheless very revealing. Containing inscription by others, or note-taking by di Prima, these books often show deep engagement with the text. Of special note is her copy of *Comfortable Words for Christ's Lovers* by Lady Julian of Norwich, inscribed on the flyleaf with the initials "C. R. A.," "d. d. G. A. A., " and "Norwich Jan–July 1918." In a different hand, Bob Wilson begins his inscription: "For Diane di Prima from W. H. Auden via Bob Wilson," and notes "G. A. A. is our Auden's father. He gave it to Charles Auden, Wystan's older brother, who then gave it to Wystan. I got it from Auden when I bought his library, and now I give it to you. Who next in the chain? Love, Bob," followed by the date "March 1975."

Bob Wilson, owner of the Phoenix Book Shop, was a friend of di Prima's and a book dealer—and was also largely responsible for a variety of her materials that are located at the Henry W. and Albert A. Berg Collection of English and American Literature in The New York Public Library. *Comfortable*

Words for Christ's Lovers is from the two-thirds of Auden's library that he "abandoned," and sold to Wilson in 1972, when he left America to return to Oxford.[54] While the inscription is remarkable in that it places di Prima in direct poetic lineage with Auden and his family, under the auspices of reading medieval mysticism, my conversations with di Prima reveals further nuance. She remembers reading this copy, and how in the process of reading it she envisioned a poem that became part of *Loba*: an image of a white unicorn erupting between two lines of text.[55] In this sense, Auden's former book not only places di Prima in poetic lineage but becomes a substrate on which to perform her work. *Loba* in particular, a poem that incorporates extensive source-based knowledge of pre-Christian Western traditions, hermeticism, and Greco-Roman mythology alongside di Prima's own intuitive approaches, is a prime work to receive dictation from in the context of an occult library.

In fact, we might compare certain elements of the very composition of *Loba* and the library as an act informed by a similar poetics. One of the features of both the publication and editorial history of the poem is that it was composed chronologically, with no "map," as it were, to sketch out the dimensions of the poems or their narrative or thematic arcs. Di Prima described this process at length in a June 2, 1976, reading at the Bay Area Writers series at Novato, California:

> I never really made any plan for what shape it was going to take and the first four parts kind of evolved themselves in an order and they got to be notions on my part of what I wanted to do. As soon as they became notions, the poem veered in opposite directions to the notions, constantly, so that I have parts that exactly fit my notion of what I wanted to do next and then other parts that are just the next insistent part of the poem, and how part five and part six are going to eventually shape up [this is 1976]. I don't know. But I'm just going to read odd pieces from it, from the first parts, not in any particular . . . I mean, I'll go in order through the manuscript, but I won't read, like, page one, two, three, and four, I'll, like, you know, flip through, until I find something I want to read. . . . And I'll probably start to read low and read things that take more energy later because I'm still driving the freeway, if that's ok with you guys.[56]

By the 1978 Wingbow edition, this sentiment of "still driving the freeway" in the compositional process of the poem remains: an author's note states,

> The Work is, like they say, in "progress."
> The author reserves the right to juggle, re-arrange,
> cut, osterize, re-cycle parts of the poem in future editions.
> As the Loba wishes, as the Goddess dictates.

Roseanne Giannini Quinn takes this note as a "secret handshake . . . where di Prima sets forth a way of writing that destabilizes conventional ways of reading," cautioning that "we should not get too comfortable with any ideas of 'master' narrative here."[57] Indeed, this opening note changes the nature of the poem to a living creature with a pulse, rather than an artifact to be examined. This shift is particularly important in light of the question of sources or bibliography, and the tracings of various allusions or references throughout the work. It advises: best not to get bogged down in the details but instead watch for movement, breath, the living line.

This aliveness also appears on the pages of di Prima's occult library, especially since certain poems are directly inscribed in the books themselves. Considering di Prima's entire library, many poems are likely contained in the books. She recounts teaching Charles Olson's poetry in 1976, and receiving a dictated poem for her ongoing work *Loba*, which she rediscovered in her notes in 1978 as she prepared the Wingbow Press edition: it was jotted down in her copy of Olson's *Selected Writings*.[58] In her occult library, in *Inanna: Queen of Heaven and Earth, Her Stories and Hymns from Sumer*, di Prima writes a poem on the verso of a page of the index:[59]

> Before the first days, when no one numbered
>   the moons
> Before the first nights, when no one numbered
>   the hills
> When no one mapped the rivers, or
>   set sail on the seas
> From the steppes she came
> From the place of tall grass she came
> From the inland desert she came
> She rode a lion
> Arrows she brought w/ her, arrows
> She rode a lion
> A sword she carried, a flail
> She carried the measuring rod
> The ray of the sun @ her back
> ~~She came forward~~
> She came to the sea

The poem evokes ancient, dreamlike landscapes and the women who stride over them, with the presence of an alchemical lion as means of conveyance and ceremony, and juxtaposition between earthly elements in sea, desert, sky, and grass. The presence of the "measuring rod" is significant; this item, while its purpose varies across cultures, is often considered a device for measuring the dimensions of sacred sites or as a protective talisman that is found in premodern to early modern burials. Between "sword," "flail" (or threshing device), and "measuring rod," the woman in the poem holds powerful symbols of strength, fertility, and sacredness as she walks her mythic landscape. The poem was delivered to di Prima with clear transmission from its source—only one line ("she came forward") has been crossed out. This poem appears in *Loba*, part 14, with the title "Inanna: The Epiphany," with a few changes—mostly typographical.

This poem, alongside the story of dictation between the lines of Auden's Julian of Norwich, gives a distinctly mystical edge to the singularity of the occult library. Just as with the Maud/Olson Library, we might think that all objects within a literary collection, even those that are meant to attest to a theme, such as Charles Olson's reading, contain their own distinct materiality that leads in different vectors (such as annotations by another hand, or unopened pages in a library meant to symbolize what has been read). For di Prima, the materiality of her library is special, specialized. It allows us to experience the source texts that inform her poetry, without overdetermining a path for negotiating how the bibliographic and the poetic inform each other. Its annotations offer us correspondences and invite us to produce our own, and its bespoke indexes honor ways of producing knowledge that are specific to di Prima and hold possibilities for future readers. And, at times, we are welcomed into specific vectors that lead us to *Loba*, as well as di Prima's other poetic projects.

Yet with the Maud/Olson Library, annotation can be a difficult metric to analyze textual engagement. While annotation almost certainly indicates a book has been read, the annotation may evidence another type of practice; di Prima casts the *I Ching* on a letter repurposed for scrap paper and a bookmark in Henry Corbin's *Spiritual Body and Celestial Earth: From Mazdean Iran to Shi'ite Iran*.[60] Likewise, an absence of annotation does not necessarily mean a book has not been read. For instance, di Prima has clearly read Jacob Boehme extensively—marginal notes about him appear throughout her collection—but her copies of Boehme are not annotated.

With this in mind, almost every book contains some sign of having been opened and explored, and dust jackets are often used as bookmarks to mark this process. And in the collection, there are items with significant annotation. This generally takes the form of underlined passages, stars next to key points, argumentation in the margin, and even entire flyleaves or inside covers annotated with summaries, questions, and other divergences. In particular, margins will often feature the annotation "HR"—as in the case of *The Chalice and the Blade,* by Riane Eisler—which demarcates topics relevant to "Hidden Religions," di Prima's extensive course at New College.

A general characteristic of these markings is di Prima's detailed engagement with the intellectual premises and historical details of the works she annotates. She is an incisive reader who corrects, questions, and elaborates in the margins to the edification of both herself and any given book's author. Of the influential *History of Magic* by Eliphas Levi, di Prima writes in a lower margin on page ninety-one: "The errors this man makes are incredible." Later in the book, in a chapter that purports to address "the magic of public worship," di Prima writes, "He places the shackles on his own wrist" and notes on page 131, "Too bad this chapter has had so little to do with public worship." Di Prima is not hesitant to call out lack of rigor, flaws, or even structural racism in the materials she reads. Of Dion Fortune's *The Esoteric Orders and Their Works,* she writes "racist" in the margin next to a statement that describes white men as masters in the "First Emigration Tradition" of the "Three Great Traditions" on page forty-seven.[61] Occultism and esotericism historically tend to engage with elements of cultural appropriation, racism, and sexism, and di Prima's annotations show awareness of this, and how she challenges these observations in her own research.

Robert K. G. Temple's *The Sirius Mystery* is largely unmarked except on the back flyleaf, which is fully annotated with di Prima's criticisms of the work: "Lack of imagination . . . no knowledge of alchemy / or the importance of transformation/transmutation . . . does not understand the 'bow & arrow' as symbols of <u>astral</u> travel . . . nor that the stars themselves & the gods derive from the <u>numbers:</u> hence the triple goddess the 50 yr orbit of Sirius B, the <u>necessity</u> to never be too accurate as this wd lead to all material creation being subsumed into Number. He's also suffering from classicism—insists on bringing it all back home to Egypt, Sumer, Greece when obviously the traditional is purer + more meaty among the Dogon."[62] In di Prima's estimation, Temple's failures boil down to short-sightedness and narrow-mindedness—he is too stuck in a disciplinary tradition to examine more relevant and less Western sources, not to mention occult traditions such as alchemy, and di Prima notes that the combined lack of research and "imagination" mean that he is unable to see the patterns (such as Sirius B's orbit) and their cultural consequences. This type of critique reveals di Prima's strengths as a historian and critic—her ability to read across traditions, patterns, and rituals to consider relationships between humans and divinity, as well as the diligence required to read occulted knowledge sources that thicken the possibilities of historical research. She enumerates her criticism on the back flyleaf of the book, as a type of reference or indexing device. Yet, as an annotation style, this pattern-sensing insight shines through in the poetics of *Loba*, which considers what type of poetic experience or knowledge might be produced by intermingling traditions across time, instead of consolidating them to their narrow geographic and historical windows.

At the same time, di Prima's annotations are not limited to the book or topic at hand. At times, her annotations function on a meditative level that captures experience beyond the book's covers. A blank page in Aleister Crowley's *Book of Thoth,* one of the most heavily annotated books in the collection, lists the following:

The Things to Be Done
Ajapa breathing
Meditation
Walking
Study (language / poetics—> alchemy—healing / tarot / kabala)
Writing
Makko-Ho
Piano
Drawing
Correspondence

These "things to be done" echo the "no single thing, no singular purpose" of di Prima's library in the daily rhythms of her own life; the task of staying open to the poetry as it comes requires a variety of efforts, some physical (Ajapa breathing, Makko-Ho, walking), some social (correspondence), some spiritual (meditation), some intellectual or creative (writing, drawing, piano, etc.)—but none of these activities falls neatly into a single category of benefit. Rather, the "things to be done" always exist in complex interrelation with each other, achieving wholeness in di Prima herself, and even more so, in the reception of the poem. The occult library can have no singular purpose or benefit, because like everything else that di Prima did within her lifetime, the maxim remains: do the work, and the rest will follow.

Symbol, Correspondence, Index

An entire shelf of di Prima's library is devoted to the works of Aleister Crowley, whose *Book of Thoth* and *Tarot Divination* are both highly annotated. Di Prima taught workshops on using the Crowley Tarot Deck—in a copy of Mary Greer's *Tarot for Your Self,* a flyer is inserted as a bookmark that advertises a course on the Tree of Life Tarot Spread, noting that this one-day workshop, offered on February 6 (no year noted) and taught by di Prima, "is a prerequisite for the Thoth Deck Study Group" set to begin a new series on February 20. In the Crowley section are three notebooks of di Prima's, with handwritten notes that meditate on the correspondences of symbols, images, plants, Hebrew alphabet, planets, and days of the week. These notebooks appear to function as a writing meditation or as workbooks, whose purpose is their processual nature, intermingling knowledge traditions and forms into a unique understanding forged by di Prima herself.

A significant portion of the books in the library address visual history, including sacred geometry, inscriptions, symbols, hieroglyphics, the Hebrew alphabet, and Islamic patterns. Patterns, proportion, and correspondences between inner and outer worlds of knowledge predominate the visual terrain of di Prima's library—rather than maps, geographies, or the history of art movements (although the library does not exclude any of these subjects). When considering the compositional process of di Prima's work, in which poems are received, chronologically and thematically unfurling over the course of decades as the poem dictates, one considers the question of organization and proportion: how to remain perceptive to these incoming forces while at the same time rendering them legible?

Indeed, many of di Prima's annotations are designed to draw parallels across traditions, matching symbols with words, and archetypes with their many iterations, to build a density of knowledge across traditions. In Dion Fortune's *The Mystical Qabalah,* di Prima annotates the margins with planetary symbols, turning the prose that describes the four elements and their planetary correspondences into equations.[63] These equations, while they function as mnemonic devices, are accompanied by extensive annotation in Crowley's *Tarot Divination,* which has, at times, entire pages of symbols that illustrate the correspondences between elements, planets, and principles of the Tarot. With these annotations, di Prima is not only engaging the cosmological principles of the Crowley deck but also mystical traditions on the whole. For instance, di Prima annotates aspects of the ten Sefirot, from the Kabbalah's Tree of Life, another object of her intensive study. Blending the Kabbalah and the Tarot is generally considered part of the twentieth-century Tarot tradition (practiced by di Prima's friend, Mary Greer), yet the body of di Prima's annotations shows extensive interest in not just reading but also in *generating* these symbols, writing out these correspondences, and making them vivid across traditions.

In particular, di Prima has created a Kabbalistic workbook, adorned with the cover of Paul Riccius's *Portae Lucis* (1516), known as one of the first texts that elucidated the Tree of Life in the Kabbalistic tradition. Di Prima's workbook contains no fewer than forty-eight drawings of the Tree of Life, in a variety of colors and styles, and with annotations that draw together traditions of Tarot and its associated elements. Di Prima's devotion to this type of practice attests to a broader theme in her approach to the syncretic, synergistic way that occult traditions inform each other, and the possibilities of harnessing this as a holistic form of understanding.

One of the most powerful outcomes of this type of correspondence-based work that appears so readily in di Prima's occult library is her teaching, particularly during the 1980s at the San Francisco Institute of Magical and Healing Arts (SIMHA), an institute she cofounded with her partner, Sheppard Powell, that ran from 1983 until 1992.[64] In addition to her teaching at New College, SIMHA was a key vector for di Prima to share the syncretic wisdom of the traditions she studied, as an "educational organization presenting a grounded approach to the hermetic tradition," staffed by her and members of the Gold Circle. In the spring of 1985, di Prima taught "Structures of Magic," a course that covers the polarities, the four elements, and the numbers one through ten in order to "evolve the Tree of Life and the 78 cards of the Tarot. Relationships of the cards to the Tree, correspondences between the Major Arcana and the Hebrew alphabet, etc., will also be explored. Whenever possible we will use both reason (discussion) and imagination (visualization) to approach the material."[65] Di Prima's annotations speak to this same theme—exploring reason and imagination as they work across traditions, seeking not just to understand the Tree of Life or the Tarot but to "evolve" it by building from polarities (light and dark) and the four elements. "Evolving" the Tarot and its correspondences was also a preoccupation of di Prima's friend, Timothy Leary, whose *Game of Life*, coauthored with Robert Anton Wilson, was a multidecade project that explored the correspondences between the Tarot and the periodic table of the elements. This symbolic and connected approach exists in an even greater context; that same semester, in the spring of 1985, di Prima taught "Principles of Homeopathy" on "the great "polycrests" or type-remedies," as well as "Psychic Self-Defense" for "tak[ing] power back into our own hands." Her annotations show the interconnectedness of esoteric traditions, highlight the depth of her teaching expertise, and suggest that the greatest application of this knowledge is for it to be used to visualize possibilities for personal transformation and lived experience.

While a strong impulse to annotate symbols and correspondences pervades many of the manual-like books in di Prima's collection, her books often have indexes that she writes herself. In *The Murdered Magicians: The Templars and their Myth* by Peter Partner, the back cover states "some real stuff" and then lists a series of page numbers that point to relevant topics. Likewise, Uma Silbey's *The Complete Crystal Guidebook* is practically indexed by di Prima on the back flyleaf, including notes to purchase white silk, salt, a box, as well as what appear to be notes in preparation for teaching various aspects of crystal use—programming for protection, healing, focus, and protection—even writing.[66] In fact, books about crystals and precious stones form a surprising bulk of the collection—with no fewer than twenty volumes on the first shelf alone, including books on geology, crystal healing, gemstones, precious stones, crystal guidebooks, and workbooks, from pocket-size books to coffee-table offerings. Of these, Silbey's is the most annotated, likely a well-used teaching tool for both di Prima and her students.

In Lewis Spence's *The History of Atlantis,* di Prima uses the pastedown and flyleaf to index the book, writing key themes and page numbers across the pages.[67] For this particular text, the index contains "Atlantis in the Far North 34–35," "Egypt 41," "Bullfighting 48 (cf 22)," "Neolithic Culture as coming from Atlantis 78–79," and more, over the span of two pages. In this dimension, di Prima's indexical annotations make good on her conception of these books as a "reference library," meant to be used and explored. Like Lorde's glossary and bibliography in the back matter of *The Black Unicorn*, di Prima's handwritten indexes utilize a well-known technique of reading infrastructure to present understudied and underrepresented information. The index, while it may traditionally have a reputation as a sterile device for navigating reference material, becomes energetic in di Prima's hand. Her indexes are rigorous and focused on the topic but also subjective because they are hers. These indexes make explicit the way that di Prima navigates research through particular themes, symbols, and motifs, rather than extant infrastructure in books such as titles or page numbers.

For di Prima, reference is not a genre but a way of approaching books as fundamentally useful objects. She remembers Bob Wilson's chagrin at her regular habit of reading first editions with breakfast and coffee, but has always persisted in her belief that books are meant to be used. This impulse to parse texts, note their themes, and draw connections from this information is a part of di Prima's poetics. She once mentioned to me how she wished books like *Revolutionary Letters* and *Recollections of My Life as a Woman* had an index for easier navigation, especially when she used copies of these books for her poetry readings. This idea, that an index would assist her in navigating her own work in new ways, also suggests to us as readers a type of comprehensiveness: a new way to explore or arrange our experience of the poems. And, in many ways, this intuitive approach to indexing is related to di Prima's poetics of dictation, particularly as she describes in *Loba*.

Staying Open: Dictation

When di Prima and I spoke about her library, I found that we often were also simultaneously speaking about *Loba*. Many of my questions for her focused on the relationship between sources and poetry itself, as I considered her occult library as a possible resource for *Loba,* with its extensive allusion and occult orientation of dictation. The genesis of *Loba* occurred around the start of di Prima's occult library in the 1960s, when di Prima describes a shift in her writing toward a different style of poems, "with their longer lines and almost deadly certainty," beginning after her "first peyote trip" and the "vast permission" of her composition classes with Jimmy Waring. She recounts how "a powerful voice found its way through me and into the world," which was "the first of many voices that would speak through me, now that I no longer sought to control the poem."[68] This type of poetics requires an availability and a vulnerability to the poem that sometimes necessitates dramatic action, as di Prima recounts of her reception of *Loba*. She was "teaching in a high school in Watsonville," and remembers, "I just had to let the other guy take over the class and write it down. And I (had) no notion of what she was talking about and no notion of what the next part and (part) two was about and slowly began to realize they all had this wolf."[69] In Jerome and Diane Rothenberg's anthology *Symposium of the Whole: A Range of Discourse Toward an Ethnopoetics,* di Prima frames this moment teaching in Watsonville with a two-week stint teaching in Wyoming that left her ill for a month—partially, since, as she describes it, "there was nothing to eat but steak and liquor," and perhaps mostly because of the heaviness of experiencing a "situation of people living in total pain" without anyone to blame yet also without recourse.[70] Di Prima describes how integrating this information resulted in her dreams shifting from replaying experiences she had had in Wyoming to becoming more deeply symbolic—including a significant dream that involved her and two children attempting to escape from being eaten by a wolf, gladiator-style, for the entertainment of the wealthy—only to have to wolf begin to walk alongside her. She recounts "And at some point, I turned around and looked this creature in the eye, and I recognized, in my dream, I recognized or remembered this huge white wolf, beautiful white head, recognized this as a goddess that I'd known in Europe a long long time ago. Never having read about any European wolf-goddesses, I just recognized this as deity. We stood and looked at each other for a long moment."[71] Later, di Prima describes how this dream is the only one that she has directly transcribed into a poem—in part 4, titled "Dream: The Loba Reveals Herself." And while it would take another year for what di Prima identifies as the first *Loba* poems—while teaching in another emotionally heavy space, "with barbed wire around the playing field, guards all over the place," the dream-genesis of the poem is essential from a perspective not just of technique but also of the question of intuition.[72] Referencing a past life, "a goddess I'd known in Europe a long long time ago," and experiencing a sense of recognition—not cognition, not analysis, just the experiencing of "look[ing] at each other for a long moment"—di Prima foregrounds the principle that source work ("never having read about any European wolf-goddesses") and witnessing are often not chronological or hierarchical experiences but are interwoven.

In the third section of *Loba*, by the time of its publication in Wingbow Press in 1978, two poems are litanies: "Some of the People This Poem Is For" consists of two pages of names, including Lenore Kandel, di Prima's daughters, Muriel Rukeyser, Mary Korte, H. D., Mother Mary, and a host of other women writers in the twentieth century. A few poems later, another untitled poem consists of a block of text that enumerates multiple names of mother goddess figures across historical era and cultures: Duna, Ishtar, the White Lady, Cerridwen, Diana, Kali, Maat, and Freya. The effect of this poetic practice is incantatory; the reader repeats the names of the goddesses and poets in the act of reading that, by virtue of its repetition, becomes devotion. Likewise, poetic effect occurs not only within sound, rhythm, and association but also in the consolidation of often-occulted knowledge—the names of the goddess. This twofold (at the very least) effect requires the reader to calibrate their interpretive style: should we lean on research, intuition, or both? Thus, in a work like (but not limited to) *Loba*, the poem invites meaning through multiple layers: firstly, through the intuitive work of reading words and bodies of knowledge not yet familiar to the reader, and secondly, through the investigative work that the poem makes so seductive. Resisting a solely bibliographic or source-based approach even as it calls for rigor, di Prima's work reminds us that a variety of reading practices can create comprehensive meaning in the act of the poem.

Rather than a process of planning, mapping, and execution, di Prima receives poems and does not heavily edit by either rearranging or rewriting. This act of reception appears vividly in the first section of *Loba*, whose poems veer heavily toward images of wolves and Kali, evoking the surrender needed from poet and reader: "If he did not come apart in her hands, he fell / like flint on her ribs" and "If you do not come apart like bread / in her hands, she falls / like steel on your heart."[73] To "come apart" is a mystical concept at its core: from the medieval era onward, the practice of dissolving the self (to "come apart") in order to reform in perfect union with God ("come a part" of) is fundamental to the experience of conversion. Likewise, the verb "falling" connotes surrender and penetration at once—"flint on her ribs" and "steel on your heart" suggest sacrifice, in the sharpness and strength of the materials di Prima references. The repetition, and also paradox, of both "falling" and "coming apart" constitute the mystical initiation of both di Prima and reader: an invitation, and perhaps requirement, to surrender to the terms of the poem.

This notion of surrender embeds itself fully by the end of the poem, when the poet asks, "does she look / w/ her wolf's eyes out of your head?" Di Prima advises we read *Loba* without sources, like the *Cantos*—reading with an intuition and imagination before reaching for the dictionary (or now, search engine). This type of reading creates space for an immersive and, indeed, inhabited experience. The looking with wolf eyes out of a human head might be read as a type of ars poetica for the possession aspects of di Prima's visitation by *Loba* as a poetic figure but also for the necessity of the reader adopting an immersive stance—or willingness to be seduced into one.

However, seduction may be hard to come by, depending on the reader. Di Prima recounts, "When *Loba* was being written, if I read it in New York, people had a million intellectual questions and they didn't understand," while if she "read it in Sonoma, all the young, single moms with their babes would come out of the woods, and they'd hear it and dig it."[74] The poem "The Critic Reviews Loba" speaks to the New York–style reception, written in a slew of italicized questions that attempt to gain intellectual control over the nature of the work. The poem begins, with urgent italics:

> *Where is the history in this, & how*
> *does geometry of the sacred mountain give strength*
> *to the metaphor*

Here, the figure of the critic is at first concerned with a viable concept of "history"—chronological, perhaps even geographic, but certainly preoccupied with establishing a concept of poetic authority. The question "where is the history in this" almost suggests an absence, a missing core, or a failure on the part of the poet. The speaker goes on to ask formal and mathematical questions—how is metaphor affected by the "geometry of the sacred mountain," or how could questions of the body or emotions trump the mathematical perfection of "proportion?" So too, the speaker longs for concrete details to anchor the poem in lived experience:

> *where are the dates, street names*
> *precise equations?*

Of course, *Loba* will offer no such reassurance. The poem continues with a plea:

> *Must we accept*
> *that star clouds burst with feeling*
> *Hermes dances*
> *in blood & bone*

The disdainful—or groveling, for the poor, overwhelmed critic—"must we accept" shows, in part, a realization of the terms of the poem, a rhetorical question that answers itself with the language that follows. For a skeptical critic, the speaker of the poem begins to descend into *Loba*-like language—"breathless beauty," "dodecahedron / form the mind's light," then

> *cutting lines of Force*
> *thru this quivering*
> *flesh seedpod/*
> *Cosmos*

While the poem initially evokes the beside-the-point type of poetic criticism that seeks to not understand the poem on its own terms but rather to force it into context with the critic's own consciousness, by the end of the poem the language suggests that the figure of the critic may have experienced a bit of *Loba* possession in the manner of the poet herself. So, if even the critic must too yield to a sense of possession in the experience of the poem, and even if the variety of sources within the text appear to reach ever-outward into new sites of meaning, no reading experience can escape the premise of the poem's composition. We must inhabit the world of the poem on its terms if we are to understand it, and there is no substitute for intuition and imagination in this process.

In conversations with di Prima, she reminded me of the power of reading intuitively, focusing on what could be understood in the first moment of reading—reading like a child for the experience itself. She shared that she'd been rereading mostly nineteenth-century classics, and that if she didn't follow her own advice she'd be reading more dictionary than book. Writing on the *Maximus Poems*, Ammiel Alcalay flags a related concept and its stakes for understanding twentieth-century poetry: "The false assumption . . . that one needs all kinds of erudition in order to approach something . . . it's as if there were two strains of American poetry: those deriving from Pound—one needs all kinds of esoteric knowledge in order to even open their books—and those deriving from Williams—their work is vernacular and emotional. These origins and splits are posited so that everyone else becomes derivative or an imitator and can then be erased."[75] Looking at Alcalay's and di Prima's wisdom side by side, one must examine poetry for the immediate experience it produces, within its historical and material context. Skipping anywhere else first—lineage, the dictionary, erudition—distorts what is happening in the moment itself. This requires a certain unmediated interaction with poetic materials. Time to flip through pages, time to browse titles and books, the physical space to perform these actions. Taking this time, like Lorde's formulation of self-care, is a political act of rearranging attention to prevent the erasure of difference, to first understand what is *there* before rushing to interpret or seek new information. As Olson tells Dorn in the *Bibliography on America*, one doesn't have to know everything there is to know, just the tight particulars and context of a few prime things.

Primary sources offer significant recourse in allowing us to experience what feel like unmediated materials, which absorb us with their immediate qualities. However, contemporary discourse in academic spaces often frames institutional archives as the ultimate in primary sources. Of course, archives are often highly mediated even before they arrive at an institution, and then undergo archival processing, or the procedure by which materials are described and physically arranged for research use. Even when few physical adjustments are made to the order of documents—which is rare, since items often must be refoldered and house according to archival standards—the act of description alone is a layer of interpretation that is a first step to "gain intellectual control" over the materials.[76] This practice is acknowledged even in the more theoretical works in the field of archives, such as Derrida's *Archive Fever,* which underscores the necessity of titles, hierarchies, and classification for the "archontic principle of legitimization" that occurs in the process of assimilating materials to the archive.[77] As I spent a week documenting di Prima's occult library, sensing viscerally the importance of the books and also the fact that *all of this material was contained in the consciousness of Diane di Prima the poet,* the archival processing instinct to try and "gain control" kicked in. Looking at di Prima's library, I was asking for *"the dates, street names . . . precise equations."* I was New York, not Sonoma. Archival processing is a necessary step in custodianship, but especially as the archives profession contemplates postcustodial practices for supporting resources and maintaining collections, we are due to revisit the importance of initial encounters and unmediated approaches. This can happen only if we invite more people into the archival process, not just reading rooms after collections are acquired, processed, and made available on institutional terms.

———

When Virginia Woolf suggests that "to admit authorities, however heavily furred and gowned, into our libraries and let them tell us how to read, what to read, what value to place upon what we read, is to destroy the spirit of freedom which is the breath of those sanctuaries," and notes that "everywhere else we may be bound by laws and conventions—there we have none," she underscores the juxtaposition of "the spirit" of forms reading and collecting and the question of oversight and control.[78] To return to Alcalay's and di Prima's instructions—*come as you are, see what's there, hold off on categories*—this is the necessary dance with poets' libraries, given how heavily they sit in their materiality. On the one hand, to find them homes, it is difficult to avoid subjecting them to "the dates, street names, precise equations" of "gaining intellectual control" over their contents—asking the poet, "What is this library for?," "How does this library relate to your poetry?," and any number of questions that can tell an archival story but might be wholly artificial in the context of a living, breathing, working library. At times, if we can answer these types of questions, it puts us in a position of strength to advocate for these collections to those who hold institutional sway and funding, and who need those precise street names and dates (so to speak) to advocate for purchase or preservation. It is historically imperative to make plans for the poets' libraries of our recent generation, and this inevitably entails working within current systems to ensure that their importance is legible. This may mean placing these libraries within formal institutions, generating new institutions to house them, or reimagining the resources of these libraries' current and future communities. At the other end of the spectrum, this may also mean returning to Jack Clarke's "biblio. & library," and creating extensive documentation of these libraries and others as a means for advocating for their preservation, or preserving them in bibliographic form if other avenues are not possible.

But first, we must seek out libraries like di Prima's, and encounter these collections on their own terms. Di Prima's vast shelves of books contain a profusion of themes, annotations, and evidence of a poet in the act of investigation and absorption. At the same time, these sources are not always linear to poems, information does not accumulate chronologically, and, for most of the library's existence, anything could be rearranged at any time. By yielding to these overtures toward intuition, we might more fully inhabit the possibilities of di Prima's vision for her occult library as an act of preservation, poetics, and, indeed, *sourcery*.

FIGURE 6. Gerrit Lansing in his "magic room," Gloucester, 2015.
—Photograph courtesy of Joshua Kotin.

CHAPTER 4

"ON EARTH, PARTICULAR"
Gerrit Lansing's House and Library

IF, TO PARAPHRASE Maurice Merleau-Ponty, meaning occurs in between things, then one must look for the hidden elements that form the connective tissues. In the networks that comprised postwar American poetry, particularly on the East Coast, the poet Gerrit Lansing is not necessarily a canonical name but likely one of the most frequently occurring people among the constellations of friends that characterize the New York School, Black Mountain, the Boston Occult School, and New American poetry more broadly. Lansing was friends with Frank O'Hara, John La Touche, Charles Olson, Diane di Prima, John Wieners, Stephen Jonas (for whom he was literary executor), and countless others across spans of decades and geographies. With his wide range of companions, Lansing was responsible for introducing numerous poets to each other—Jonathan Williams and Thomas Meyer, for instance, as well as other fateful encounters, such as arranging Charles Olson's first reading in Gloucester.

Like many others from the era, Lansing created poetic *polis* through print, editing the little magazine *SET*. This relatively short but rich project was published in two issues in 1961 and 1963, with the editorial mission to share "the poetic exploration of the swarming possibilities occult and/or unused in American life," in a style equal parts "historical & magical, the emphasized characters of Time."[1] Lansing made his ideas about the purpose of *SET* known in short expositions for both issues titled "The Burden of *SET*" in which burden refers not to obligation but rather a "droning undersong."[2] The idea of a *burden,* as opposed to a manifesto or even a melody, can be used as a method of appreciating Lansing's broader poetic contributions: a constant presence in Gloucester and Boston poetry scenes, a steady and understated tone that propels the music.

Lansing's own work took the form of a constantly unfolding serial poem, first titled *The Heavenly Tree Grows Downward* and mimeographed at Bard College in 1966 by Robert Kelly with a letterpress cover, then reissued in an expanded edition by North Atlantic Books in 1977.[3] Poet John Wieners contributed a preface to the first edition, noting that Lansing's poetry was invested not just in the question of poetics but also in the rhythms and contours of life itself: "This is not a book of poems to read by; it is to live with."[4] Lansing continued to rework the poem over decades—*Heavenly Tree/ Soluble Forest* (Talisman, 1995), and *Heavenly Tree, Northern Earth* (North Atlantic Books, 2009). Beyond poems in little magazines, other publications by Lansing include *A February Sheaf* (2003), with his collected essays and short works; *Turning Leaves of Mind* (Granary Books, 2002), an artist book collaboration with Lignorano/Reese containing Lansing's text intermingled with close-up photographs of thirteenth- through eighteenth-century Spanish luxury book bindings; and numerous one-sheet poetry broadsides and publications in periodicals such as *Conjunctions*.

Robert Kelly notes that Lansing's poetry is "the most important unrecognized body of work" from the latter half of the twentieth century, alongside contemporaries more well-studied, including poets and friends such as Frank O'Hara, John Ashbery, Robert Creeley, Jack Spicer, Charles Olson, and Philip Lamantia.[5] Patrick James Dunagan in "The Poet's Aura" notes that Robert Duncan wrote to James Hart, the then-head of the Bancroft Library at University of California, Berkeley, contextualizing Lansing's poetics alongside those of Robert Kelly, Charles Stein, and Harvey Bialy, and wrote of Lansing in particular: "The deeper currents of writing are understandable finally, not in literary terms, but in terms of a particular culture, involving daily rituals and spiritual allegiances, rather than taste or judgement." Duncan goes on to state how these poets refuse the "challenge" of the expectation that "the poet will seek to find his/her place in the literary 'establishment.'"[6] And indeed, Lansing was a poet for whom poetry was a vast historical stream to tap into, not a livelihood or initiation to prestige. This has affected his visibility in the history of American poetry accordingly; the bulk of critical writing about Gerrit Lansing and his poetic legacy exists in memoriam on *Dispatches from the Poetry Wars*, a now-archived website that focuses on poetics and poetry in direct contrast (the editors might say antagonism) to mainstream, university-based poetics today.

Lansing's interests across forms—poetry, music, philosophy, history, art—meant that he was a voracious reader and observer, often writing reviews and short essays in addition to his poetry. To describe Thorpe Feidt's project of 333 paintings, titled *The Ambiguities*, Lansing quotes Robin Blaser's definition of serial poems: "This is a narrative which refuses to adopt an imposed story line, and completes itself only in the sequence of poems."[7] By suggesting that the technique of the serial poem—a form that was critical to Lansing in his own work—is applicable beyond poetry, Lansing suggests a possible lens for understanding his own library. Like his poetry, it contains daily details (tubby custard, Blue Moon beer) and heavy occult sources (suns, moons, eggs, goddesses, the color red). It is conversational and introspective, highbrow and lowbrow. And like his poetry, it resists classification—one must just join in for the ride and the pleasures and lessons therein.

Lansing lived in a four-story Victorian house in Gloucester that was well-known to all his friends, whose rooms on the two main levels were completely filled with books.[8] His obsession for books has a professional background, given that Lansing was the proprietor of two bookshops during his lifetime. The first was Circle West Books, an antiquarian bookshop with specialization in occult subjects, established in Annapolis, Maryland, where Lansing and his partner, Deryk Burton (a yacht captain), moved in 1972. In 1982, they returned to Gloucester, where Lansing ran Abraxas Books for ten years, upstairs above a local downtown dive bar. In addition to these ventures, Derek Fenner remembers that Lansing's history with Weiser Books, a Boston-based bookseller, dated back to their beginnings in New York City's famed Book Row.[9] Yet Lansing was an equal fan of antiquarian shops and church sales. By Eileen Myles's account, he would often run into her mother at yard sales and rummage sales, scouring for books.[10]

In his introduction to John Clarke's *From Feathers to Iron*, Lansing invokes a maxim: "*Lege et relege*, the alchemists say, and 'One book opens another.'"[11] True to this lesson, the repetition of books, their necessity, and their interconnectedness constituted not only Lansing's intellectual life but his social life as well, especially within the Gloucester community. Robert Podgurski remembers Abraxas as Lansing's "own personal platform for meeting people first and foremost," with a secondary purpose of "selling some books as well as the means for culling the overflow of his own personal library."[12] Books were part of Lansing's work as a host; he had a habit of giving "gateway books," or books that later became essential to poets he encountered—such as introducing Eileen Myles to Robert Walser, and Charles Olson to Wilhelm Reich. Lansing remembers, "When I lent Charles a great essay on *Orgonomic Functionalism* . . . he returned it only half read, saying it was too close to the heart of his work for him to deal with it at that time."[13] Derek Fenner notes that "Gerrit has a book for all of us, not just any book, but the book we were missing all along."[14]

When Lansing "retired" in 1992, he placed the Abraxas dead stock throughout his house by subject, with a large deposit in an upstairs closet-turned-bookshelf, and kept an Abraxas poster above the desk in his upstairs office. For an average person, ingesting the dead stock of a bookstore into their house would constitute a monumental feat of rearranging, but the Abraxas books were just a drop in the proverbial bucket. Lansing's house had few walls—if any, besides bathrooms—that were not completely occupied by bookshelves.[15] Accordingly for his generous demeanor and numerous friends, the house itself was a fixture of Gloucester's poetry scene, and also a pilgrimage site for a younger generation of poets. Lansing stayed in this house in Gloucester for the rest of his life, building his collection of books and hosting an ever-expanding circle of poets that spanned generations. He continued to contribute regularly to the local Gloucester Writers Center, the Maud/Olson Library, and poetry communities in Gloucester and nearby Salem. Lansing passed away on February 11, 2018. I attended the memorial ceremony at Hammond Castle, where numerous friends read tributes, most of which are now documented on *Dispatches from the Poetry Wars,* and almost all of which mention a book that Lansing had shared with them. At a later memorial for Lansing at Poets House in New York City, Ruth Lepson noted that the day before Lansing passed away, he was still ordering books.[16]

"It Is as if Dr. Dee's Library Were Available for Our Perusal"

In the first installment of the Gerrit Lansing papers at the Beinecke Library, in an archival folder labeled "notes and fragments," an undated slip of paper torn from a notebook contains poems, reading notes, and a list of authors to be read: "Benlowes, Jacob Boehme, Huidobro, Strattion-Porter, Cabell, De Man, Geoffrey Hartman," and others, along with call numbers. This is one page among many that chronicles reading lists by Lansing. David Rich, Lansing's longtime friend and the cataloger of the second installment of his archive, has also transcribed a blue notebook found in Lansing's house with further reading lists, including check marks for what had been read, with topics ranging from Japanese folk religion to the relationship between computers and the brain. Lansing led a life physically arranged by books, and his house at the time of his death was the best evidence for understanding this infrastructure that undergirded his writing and relationships.

Charles Stein, in November of 2018, noted "that Gerrit's library is at the moment in tact: it is as if Dr. Dee's library were available for our perusal."[17] However, despite a collection that was, by accounts of friends, in excess of thirty thousand volumes, though likely topped out around twenty thousand at the time of his death, his library can now only ever exist as "notes and fragments." In his will, Lansing ordered the dispersal of his house of books, with sales to benefit his estate, and as of 2019 the library was sold to book dealers. Moments like this occur often in the making of literary history—the dispersal of a collection to the winds—and at this point we know from other examples (such as Charles Olson's collecting of Herman Melville's library) that even if they might be obscure at the time of their death, if a poet ever becomes an object of study, the whereabouts of their library will inevitably become a question.

Through Ammiel Alcalay and my participation in *Lost & Found: The CUNY Poetics Document Initiative*, part of whose editorial work is coordinating actively with literary estates, I heard in January 2019, nearly a year after Lansing's death, that the estate was rapidly putting plans in motion to sell the library, and the work was imminent. Given how important books were to many of our friendships with Lansing, I knew that the dispersal of the library would be a turning point in our ability to understand our relationships with Lansing in the future, in the world without his physical presence and without his library as we all knew it. Likewise, future readers of Lansing's poetry would be missing important context—to the tune of well over twenty thousand books of background reading. So, with permission from the estate, I returned to Lansing's house over the course of a few days in January 2019 to produce documentation of the library. I took photographs of the books' spines on and each and every shelf, and diagrammed the location of bookcases in every room of the house, noting the major themes and authors contained within them.

In this process, I calculated the linear feet of books in the house—1,237 feet, which translates roughly to twenty thousand books, not accounting for a purported ten thousand that Lansing had been thought to have donated earlier.[18] And now the volumes that Lansing kept with delight in his home are making their way onto new shelves and into the ether in ways we might imagine but that will be challenging to trace. Though the booksellers who purchased Lansing's books, which I will discuss later, have been careful custodians of the portion of books they have cataloged, most books have no identifying information, such as inscription or bookplate, even as their traces of Gerrit's reading in them (bookmarks, bent pages, pencil marks) still remain. And the books are mostly unannotated, with few exceptions— leaving even less trace of their association with Lansing.

If one cannot detangle the poet from the library, as has been said by Ralph Maud of Lansing's friend Olson, then one cannot view the library without his worldview, either. Lansing was a lifelong occultist, with early encounters in this field of study and practice in New York City in the 1950s. Materials he collected on this subject were housed upstairs in a room devoted specif- ically to magic, with shelves for Crowley, astrology, magickal practice, and other branches of occultism. As Podgurski notes, Lansing's interest in magic adhered to secrecy as a fundamental component: "As Ovid stated in his *Tris- tia*, of which Gerrit was quite fond, *qui bene vixit, qui bene latuit*, he who lives well hides well."[19] This aspect of secrecy seems relevant in Lansing's stated wish to have his library dispersed, though from what I understand, this was not necessarily a straightforward choice. While I have heard that toward the end of Lansing's life he was reconsidering his options for the library, the man- date to disperse the collection nevertheless remained in his legal documents. It may be that Lansing did not feel that his library was a particular reflection of his legacy, unlike his poetry or friendships, and this is why it was dispersed. It may also be that given the nonexistent marketplace for collections of Lan- sing's size and the utter unfeasibility of a special collection acquiring it on the whole, the poet would have known full well that the collection would need to be disassembled. It may also be that because this overwhelming collection was a magical collation in its own right, as David Rich has wondered, Lan- sing ordered it to be sold; by removing the books from their specific locations on the shelves, their resonances with nearby texts, and their context in the house, more than a few secrets would be preserved.

George Quasha notes that the hermetic aspect of Lansing's knowledge structures are part of his very identity: "For me the 'real Gerrit' was the keeper of a domain that has no name outside his actual being and yet stands for a vast realm of the possible. . . . On so many matters of great importance he never quite gave a straight answer, as if preventing the hypnosis of answers and resolution of complexities from taking hold."[20] This practice is part of a deeper poetic commitment, akin to Diane di Prima's, of resisting neat categorizations of knowing. Lansing notes in an interview with Podgurski that having Neptune opposed to the Sun in the tenth house in his astrological chart lends "a great nebulosity about the persona or the way one is conceived by other people. . . . I don't care, as Diane di Prima said long ago, one has no control over the way one is pigeonholed or categorized or thought about or dealt with. It's something you learn to accept, I mean, instead of pigeonholing yourself or putting yourself in these categories. That's without one's control[,] and your poetry changes over time too. That's already happened in my lifetime, changes in my own perception of my work."[21] Or, as Lansing notes in "The Soluble Forest I," "naming is gaming" and to count, name, or otherwise consolidate something is often to change its very nature.[22] And indeed, Lansing's poetry is a complex blend of alchemical and esoteric knowledge, observations of real places, and emotional experience that necessarily resists categorization as part of its power. The similarities in perspective between di Prima and Lansing are significant; both worked on decades-long poems and studied premodern and occult history intensively. So, if Diane di Prima's occult library was a specific archival act to consolidate fields of study that were difficult to find in the pre-Internet era during the effects of Cold War censorship, and in an era that valued intellectual homogeneity, Lansing's library disperses these same possibilities—under the hermetic principle that encoded, dissipated, or secreted knowledge will come to those that seek its full complexity.

My intention, during that trip in January 2019, was to document Gerrit's library and produce a resource that could be housed alongside his archive. I did not document the library in an attempt to expose Lansing's magic but rather to honor it. I often wondered if I was amusing him, wherever he was, as I photographed shelves day after day, overwhelmed by the absurdity, immensity, and indeed, mild futility of my task. By way of a metaphor, dimensionally, it was as if I were photographing each foot of water on the way to the bottom of the Dead Sea—the aforementioned 1,237 feet, a true archival fonds in the depth-oriented connotation of the word—to see if those photographs would allow me to reconstruct some sense of sea life on the way down. But I documented his library because our literary history is preserved through active intervention, managed alongside the complex wishes of authors that sometimes go against our ability to make sense of their contributions later in time. I knew that someday, someone would stumble on "notes and fragments" in an archive, or a reference in a poem, and wonder what Lansing had read or was reading. Of course, it might get passed down in the apocrypha and the lore that his house was full of books, that they were an essential part of the rhythms and the arc of his life. But future researchers won't be able to walk into his house, receiving a warm welcome from him and usually departing with a book of their own. At least now they can see the shelves and understand the scope.

––––––

Born in Albany and raised in northern Ohio, Lansing was from a prominent and powerful Albany family. He attended Harvard for his undergraduate degree, where his circle of friends included Kenward Elmslie (a childhood friend), Frank O'Hara, Edward Gorey, and John Ashbery, with whom Lansing was said to play tennis on a weekly basis.[23] Harvard introduced Lansing to the study of philosophy, as well as a seminar on Blake and Yeats by Richard Ellmann; he also attended readings by T. S. Eliot and Wallace Stevens.[24] After his graduation in 1949, he moved to New York City and worked for Columbia University Press and George W. Stewart Publishers, receiving a master's degree from Columbia on early modern metaphysics (*Dogma and Natural Symbol in a Seventeenth-Century Vision: A Study of Henry Vaughan's "Regeneration"*) in 1955. While he had first encountered the teachings of Carl Jung at Harvard, while working at Columbia, he met the secretary of the Bollingen Foundation (who had published Jung) and later attended the Eranos meeting in southern Switzerland.

Lansing remembers his time in New York City as a time of sexual exploration as a gay man, but also of deeply formed friendships. Lansing formed a close friendship with John La Touche, considered one of the foremost lyricists and librettists for American musical theater, who opened the doors to writers such as Paul and Jane Bowles, Jack Kerouac, Philip Lamantia, and many others. In the city, he met Diane di Prima (Lansing once said to me, "She was wild. We all were!"), Amiri Baraka, Jonathan Williams, Robert Duncan, Allen Ginsberg, and many others. He also met Harry Smith, a poet, occultist, and collector (notably, the compiler of the *Anthology of American Folk Music*), and together they studied magic with Count Stefan Colonna Walewski, who owned the Esoterica shop and had authored *A System of Caucasian Yoga.* Through friendship with La Touche and his then-lover Harry Martin, Lansing came to know John Hays Hammond, Jr., an inventor who pioneered electronic remote control engineering (which informed modern missile guidance systems, among many other uses). For a time in the 1960s, he lived in John Hammond, Jr.'s castle in Gloucester—a replica of a medieval castle, complete with trick doors, a trompe l'oeil pond, and period-accurate antique furnishings, funded by Hammond's former career. At this same castle, Lansing and Harry Martin organized Charles Olson's first reading in Gloucester, where Olson had moved after the dissolution of Black Mountain College in North Carolina.[25] These entwined geographic and social details at length not only underscore the pure poetics of Lansing beginning his time in Gloucester in a literal castle but also show how Lansing's integrality in growing scenes of poetry, Jungian analysis, early modern and medieval thought traditions (not to mention castle replicas), occult forms of magic, and philosophy.

To return to the library with these details in mind: there is an important difference between information and infrastructure—the content and the structures that house it. This is particularly operational in the documentation of Lansing's library, in which the information—the actual bibliography or catalog of all the books, their annotations, and contents—is preserved in a fragmentary way, whereas the library's infrastructure—the rooms in which they resided and the ways in which they were organized—is in fact quite legible. This visibility stems not from any formal library infrastructural plan but rather a system of organization rooted in psychological realms. Both William James and Sigmund Freud identified houses as metaphors for memory itself, and earlier practices of classical memory often use dwellings as mnemonic devices for storing information in individual rooms. On the shelves of Lansing's "magic room," one of the most important rooms in his house, are two copies of Gaston Bachelard's *The Poetics of Space,* a seminal work that explores this imaginative significance of the image of the house as "topoanalysis," or how memory maps itself into the imaginative presence of physical spaces, like rooms in a house.[26] The function of these memories is comfort, of remembering a space that wants only to be inhabited, possessed. In contrast to Jung's emphasis on shared unconsciousness as a site for archetypal meaning, Bachelard notes the embeddedness of "the virtues of shelter" in human consciousness are inherently comingled with the intimate experience of house-related memories, whose personalization takes the form of secrecy: "All we communicate to others is an *orientation* toward what is secret without ever being able to tell the secret objectively."[27] Thus, the power of the image of the house is that it provides a vector for memory, and the very poetic qualities of these memories are such that at times, their secrets cannot even be named or revealed.

Lansing's occultist background makes clear beyond the two copies of Bachelard on his shelves that he was well aware of the power of the mind in creating reality. That, of course, is the purpose of magic.[28] The imaginative and generative capacities of the mind are crucial to the power of the image of the house. While we might be tempted to understand a house architecturally, this impulse quickly gives way to the psychological power of the image of the house to facilitate daydreaming.[29] There are deep historical roots to this practice, especially as it relates to the history of print, which makes it a fitting approach for remembering a library. The arts of memory were particularly important through the medieval era, before the widespread adoption of the printing press and the increase in textual production during the early modern period; a key text for both Lansing and di Prima was *The Art of Memory* by Frances Yates, an influential Renaissance scholar whose research addressed hermetic traditions in their historical context.[30] There is thus good reason to consider the potent intersection of textual culture, memory, and houses as a perfect confluence in the documentation and meaning of a poet's library. Furthermore, as poet-librarian Shannon Tharp has explored, poems and rooms can function similarly, as sites to inhabit, especially when books are involved.[31] Combined with high-level enumerative bibliography, listing major themes, authors, and titles in Lansing's library, we have the basic infrastructure to proceed with Bachelard's recommended technique: daydreaming. While scholars of book history tend to advocate for more clearly defined or objective methods, the precarious nature of our cultural record requires us to explore methods that allow for subjectivity and ambiguity. Lansing himself was resistant to preserving his library, to categorizing his poetry or his practices, or otherwise reducing the complexity of his life of reading. Thus, instructive here is Diane di Prima's "Revolutionary Letter #58," which reads, "What we need to know is laws of time and space they never dream of." To seek to write about Lansing's library now is to actively attempt to plumb the alternative realities in these unknown laws, to dream as a means of reanimating an archive that is now only imaginary. I turn now to the image of the house: Gerrit's house, high on the hill overlooking the water.

Structure of the House

In early conversations with me, David Rich suggested that the structure of Lansing's house was "exothermic" based on the themes of its major book spaces—including the kitchen, a lower hallway, a living room, a library room, the upper front hallway, a guest room, an office, an upstairs closet and upper back hallway area, the so-called "magic" room, and the bedroom. The basement and the attic floor did not formally house any books that belonged to Lansing at the time of my visit. However, of the populated rooms, one could navigate all them in a spiral pattern that proceeds according to the house floor plan, facilitated by connecting hallways and adjoining spaces, in a movement that ascends inward and upward from the moment one steps into the kitchen to the time one arrives in Lansing's bedroom—the room with the greatest "heat" of the house and where the most important books were placed.

The idea of directionality and its patterns appeared often in Lansing's poetry, embodied in the shifting title of *The Heavenly Tree Grows Downward*, his major poetic work that evolved over decades. George Kalamaras has noted the yogic root of this title, which describes the theory that the human body develops like an inverted tree, growing downward along the spine, with the hair symbolizing the roots.[32] Lansing's poem "The Heavenly Tree Grows Downward" uses anaphora to emphasize those "who bury the dead," referencing the ritual placement of bodies in the fetal position for their eventual resurrection, beneath the soil to "rise again."[33] The poem "The Great Form Is without Shape" features a Tarot card–like dictation to instruct the reader, requiring them to look at the center, a "middle level," and "vertical axis" of an alchemical image, and then careens toward its final lines with a moment of vertical axis relief, bringing together the heavens and the earth: "all life long / the dew falls from heaven / all life long / trees climb up from underground."[34] In Lansing's poems, planting trees is a persistent motif, and forests themselves operate on the experiences and connotations of canopy and the underbrush. This sense of direction, oriented for spiritual and religious ritual, is evocative in conceptualizing Lansing's collection of books.

Likewise, one of the primary principles of Bachelard's work echoes this sense of directionality, drawing on the work of Carl Jung to specify how the phenomenology of imagination occurs at the polar opposites of the cellar and the attic, which alternately symbolize higher and lower forms of consciousness and even a primal sense of good and evil.[35] If the image of the house operates on these directional forces—across vertical poles, held by centripetal force—Lansing's careful placement of books in particular rooms adds to the specific tension that gives shape to the library on the whole. In "The Soluble Forest IV," Lansing echoes this Bachelardian idea: "The house stands on its cellar and grows up. Also grows down from its garret invisible, as the crown of a tree flourishes the idea of its root."[36] Like the thousand-petaled lotus that emerges from the top of the head as consciousness, so too Lansing's own house mirrors this psychological and even alchemical act of enlightenment.

By the time that I arrived at his house, many books had already been moved, rearranged, boxed, or otherwise modified from their original placements. This was not uncommon during Lansing's lifetime as well, though after his death the rearrangement was primarily facilitated by booksellers and the estate. These modifications included shifting books on shelves, moving bookcases within rooms, extracting three banker boxes of annotated volumes, extracting nine banker boxes of unsaleable items (due to condition, which may be because they were highly read and annotated; these items were inventoried and reassessed after January 2019), and ten boxes of chapbooks and rare books that were extracted and inventoried. In addition to this, three volumes of rare materials from earlier centuries had been removed from house, taken to a safe deposit box, and then returned. These chapbooks and books largely represent friends and contemporaries of Lansing as well as small press publishing, and David Rich (who produced these inventories) noted that among those included were large volumes of Diane di Prima and Robert Duncan, Pressed Wafer projects, and the poets Kenward Elmslie, Pierre Joris, Lewis Warsh, Charles Olson, John Wieners, Eileen Myles, Anselm Hollo, Robert Kelly, Kevin Killian, Robin Blaser, Clark Coolidge, Joanne Kyger, and Kenneth Irby, as well as numerous others. David Abel and Lansing's estate oversaw this process at the onset, leaving the structure of rooms and themes within them largely intact but nevertheless modified. Yet if we consider the library not as individual books in arbitrary individual spaces on a linear shelf but rather as an assemblage held in place by axial tensions in the three-dimensional space, these shifts after Lansing's death might not hold the same consequence as they would for a more tightly curated collection.

What follows is an exploration of this universe-as-library, containing a discussion of each room and the type of books it contains, and proceeding in the spiral pattern that guides readers from the threshold of Lansing's house to its center. For each room, I will list a general overview of themes and authors held within each room based on the notes that I took while documenting. My intention is not to analyze Lansing's reading and collecting but rather to present it as it appeared on the shelves—combined with anecdotes or references to his poetry where appropriate. In this sense, my primary methodology here is to describe attentively, a methodology that Sophie Seita likewise engages in her work on avant-garde little magazines. Citing Sharon Marcus, Heather Love, and Stephen Best's formulation in their article "Building a Better Description," Seita asserts that attending to description without privileging interpretation or hastening toward broad claims is a critical mode of hospitality.[37]

Marcus, Love, and Best note the derogatory attitude toward "mere description" that is unique to humanities research, noting the idea that description on its own terms is valuable, and not just "as a stepping-stone on the way to interpretation and critique" but also as a mode of generosity that "attends not only to its objects but also to the collective, uncertain, and ongoing activity of trying to get a handle on the world."[38] My perspective on description is also formed by the poets I study, especially Diane di Prima. Discussing negative capability and Keats in a talk at Naropa Institute in 1975, di Prima stated the importance of "leaving behind opinion and judgement—the first requirement for tuning the instrument in poetry, and meditation."[39] Thus, description is part of my bibliographic methodology and also practiced out of fidelity to the poetics of the poets I study as a broader ethic for my engagement with poets' libraries on their own terms.

For the most thorough record of Lansing's books, I invite researchers to use my original notes and the photographs of all of the books' spines, which are now located with Lansing's archive in the Beinecke Rare Book and Manuscript Library. Together, my hope is that both notes and images of the books can allow future readers to go much deeper into the possibilities of Lansing's library, and what it meant to him as well as to us. Lansing's poetry and his library are both formidable bodies of knowledge, which deserve monographs in response. My intention here is to lay a type of groundwork, to establish a few key principles based on his house, in a moment that finds us vulnerable to this information being disseminating before it is captured. As Jacques Derrida states, "The archive takes place at the place of originary and structural breakdown of the said memory."[40] My method sits at the crossroads of Derrida's idea of the archive and Bachelard's daydreaming: an attempt to integrate my personal memory of Lansing's house with the archives—both preserved and dispersed—that it generated.

The Kitchen

Lansing's house was visible from the road, looming over a downward slope that looked out toward the ocean. If you were driving over the Cut, from the Gloucester Writers Center, Charles Olson's apartment, or other Gloucester landmarks, you'd make a sharp right turn up his steep driveway and pull into an asphalt driveway in his backyard. Rhododendrons and other woodsy plants began soon after a small area of grass, on which there was a shed where guests might stay, but on prior visits where Lansing had kept a large record collection he was distributing to friends (on one visit he gave us some records of Erik Satie and sitar music). Instead of using the front door, the way to enter Lansing's house was through the back porch, which opened into a sunroom and kitchen space.

The kitchen had a modest thirty linear feet of books on eleven shelves, along with copious plants that enjoyed the sunshine constantly streaming through glass walls. This space of entryway and hearth, with its plants and open walls, maintained an identity on the cusp of indoor and outdoor. At times, the space was even more literally permeable; Lansing was known for feeding a crew of feral cats, and kept the windows open in the winter so the cats could seek shelter inside.[41] The subject of the books in the kitchen also reflects their liminal space, focusing heavily on topics related to the outdoors and the domestic, including plants, herbs, gardening, cooking, and cleaning. Subjects on the shelves included edible wild plants, foraging, herb gardens, wellness encyclopedias, foraging guides specific to New England, backyard birds, insects of North America, medicinal books, field guides to natural history, witches' almanacs, Chinese tonics, recognizing plant species, flowers, potluck suppers, pasta cookbooks, holistic herbs, practical Ayurveda, Chinese casserole cooking, *The Five Elements of Self Healing*, light French Provençal cooking, the classic bestseller *The Joy of Cooking*, Martha Stewart books, books on the German Romantics (perhaps migrated from another room in the house, perhaps not), and cookbooks on fish and seafood, tempeh, and chiles. Almost all of these books were produced for the mass market, with perhaps a few rarer volumes interspersed; their purpose hews toward use in the room in which they are located.

Lansing's interest in food can be traced back to "The Burden of Set #2

(Editorial)," in which he describes the alchemical belief "There is no division between electricity, poison, medicine, food, drug, elixir. We cannot avoid absorbing microdilutions. All foods are drugs."[42] Accordingly, even this mundane room was imbued with Lansing's understanding of the occult history of daily life. In another room, a section on natural history expanded Lansing's collection of books on herbalism and mushroom foraging; he was known to collect mushrooms in Dogtown (a crucial, quasimythological location in Olson's *Maximus Poems*). These activities were part of his larger connection with the natural world, understood alongside writers like Emerson and Thoreau, the latter whose *Walden* Lansing calls one of "the last great religious books of the West."[43] In "On the Right Use of Simples," Lansing writes, "If your mouth is dry, the berries of the meadow will sweeten it, / safely enough if you only remember / that 'creatures unfit for human consumption / are not the normal order of nature,'" alluding to his own foraging practices and the research that informed them.[44] This trustingness of the natural world, that it will provide and is safe, given the right respect, runs deep. In "Weed Udana," Lansing calls weeds "so many friends to play with:" "what we smoke, / we eat, we work with, what we are, how we joyously do and are done."[45] While books in the kitchen tended toward how-to guides, quick reference, or introductory texts (such as *The Idiot's Guide to Gardening*), they mark the important threshold between inside and outside for Lansing, his respect for the bounty of sustenance and learning that plants provide. As if to bring these two sacred elements together, bookshelves were often topped with wildly growing plants, with the occasional spider setting up shop among the volumes.

The Lower Hallway

After Lansing offered his guests something to drink—though he practiced sobriety for most of his later life, he often had a jug of wine for others—visitors would make their way through the kitchen and through a long hallway that faced the front entrance. Looking at the front door, a room known as the library (despite the status of the entire house) was at the end of the hall on the left, and the living room was on the right. Lansing made good use of hallways and transition areas in his home for more books, and this slim hall contained thirty-eight shelves of books across eight large cases, with 113.5 linear feet of books. Beyond the reference reading located in the kitchen, this hallway contained significantly more in-depth reading material that began to align with Lansing's influences and what he enjoyed reading. Here, visitors would encounter Spanish, South American, French, German, and other non-Anglophone authors, as well as art books and books on music. A case near the front entrance was also dedicated to Olson books, since, as David Rich notes, Lansing expected people to ask. Many of the books in this front hallway and entryway section connected to other parts of the house, including books on symbolism, Novalis, Goethe, Borges, and music and art, making it not only a physical but a conceptual entryway to the house.

On these bookcases, a large concentration of Surrealist and Native American art books comingled with works by German philosopher Johann Wolfgang von Goethe, composer Ludwig von Beethoven, and author Octavio Paz. Overall representing a wide range of Western European and South American literature and art, the hallway also includes authors such as Bertolt Brecht, Julio Cortázar, more Octavio Paz, Italo Calvino, Amos Tutuola, Jorge Luis Borges, Fernando Pessoa, Franz Kafka, Mikhail Bakhtin, Novalis, Jean Paul Hoffman, Rainer Maria Rilke, Jean-François Lyotard, Maurice Blanchot, Walter Benjamin, Robert Walser, Friedrich Hölderlin, Thomas Mann, Aimé Cesaire, and Herman Hesse, accompanied by anthologies of Cuban and Chilean poetry and Bohn's *Standard Library* volumes. The combination of volumes such as *Bohn's Libraries*, published by Henry George Bohn beginning in 1846 as mass-market standard editions with translations in classics, history, archaeology, science, and theology, and author-specific books hints at the distribution of books throughout the house; at once generalist, acquired for Lansing's love of a bargain or bookseller reflexes, and highly specific, Lansing's library contains a variety of types of books.

This hallway had the highest concentration of art-related materials, particularly in the form of art and coffee table books. Artists and movements represented included Symbolism, Chinese art, Egyptian art, prehistorical art, Surrealism, and Outsider Art from Poland, as well as books related to Jane Freilicher (who did the artwork for *A February Sheaf*, and a portrait of in the 1966 mimeograph edition of *The Heavenly Tree Grows Downward*), Edward Hopper, Paul Klee, Max Ernst, Leonora Carrington, Caspar David Friedrich, Wassily Kandinsky, Marcel Duchamp, Rembrandt, Pablo Picasso, Edgard Varèse, and Giorgio Vasari, who helped establish the field of art history with his foundational biographies of Italian Renaissance artists.

Music texts also lined the hallway shelves, as if preparing a guest for the nearby living room, where Lansing, an accomplished pianist, kept his piano. A few such books include various songbooks and lesson books, music by

Johannes Brahms and Ludwig von Beethoven, and an opera guidebook. In the hallway too, perhaps having migrated from another room, were two critical objects: Carl Jung's *The Red Book,* a seminal work that speaks to Lansing's own experiences with Jungian analysis, and a book of Mother Goose—which he mentioned reading shortly before his death.

Beyond the long series of bookcases in the hallway, the front door was flanked by two bookcases, one with books belonging to Lansing's housemate, John, and another special dedicated bookcase to Charles Olson, with books by and about the poet. With Olson as a symbolic guardian of the front threshold of Lansing's house, Lansing knew that Olson was a primary frame of reference for many poets who visited Gloucester. Nevertheless, the relationship and its legacy were also important to him, and Lansing's participation in local Gloucester projects with the Gloucester Writers Center and the Maud/Olson Library kept Olson's legacy alive in the local poetry community.

On either side of the lower front hallway were two rooms: a living room and a library. The living room was a large and prominent space, with Lansing's grand piano, a couch, and all sorts of paintings and artworks by friends. While this was not the case during his life, by the time of this survey, a selection of books deemed the most valuable in terms of their resale price had been removed and stored here by bookseller David Abel, and a list of these titles was created by David Rich. This room was mostly for entertaining guests, and part of the public sphere of the house; there was a large table in the room, where Lansing piled his new acquisitions and library books checked out from Harvard (as an alumnus, he had borrowing privileges) so they were handy for discussion, and the omnipresent question between poets—"What are you reading these days?" Perhaps because of the dearth of books arranged by Lansing within it at the time of my documentation, it was the room with the widest array of differing experiences that we might remember. Sitting on Lansing's couch, perhaps with his cat Hektor, this was a room of conversation and a space where many of us were likely to have encountered Lansing's understanding of his books, if not the books themselves.

The Library

While the whole house represents Lansing's library, a specific room was also designated as such, located across the hall from the living room. If "library" implies a variety of liberal arts subjects, the wide-ranging contents of this room, combined with a specific strength in contemporary American poetry, makes its name apt. On ninety shelves that stretch across nineteen book-cases and 222 linear feet of books, this room also contained boxes of heavily annotated material. These materials were pulled aside after being deemed unsellable by Abel due to their condition, though at the time of my documentation, David Rich was conducting an additional inventory to determine whether certain annotations were valuable and should be kept with Lansing's archive. There was significant flux between the living room and the library, since these two rooms were established as the ongoing headquarters of the effort on behalf of the estate to sell Lansing's library to prepare the house for its post-Lansing life.

Still, the library room retained a strong element of its character: as an ongoing repository for contemporary poetry books given to Lansing by friends, with the room itself heavily focused on the history of poetry and literature in the Western tradition. Accompanied by clusters of books on natural history, geology, ecology, and the natural sciences, as well as sections on Western and American History, the room was a broad gloss of a liberal arts education. It is important to note that Lansing was not uncritical of Western history and liberal education, particularly given the prominence of these books in his house. Like di Prima, he shared a healthy distrust of Western-centric ideas of post-Renaissance and Enlightenment "science and progress." Rather, Lansing was interested in the interactions across knowledge systems, the possibilities that arise from studying systems that had been pushed underground by the traditional conception of the Western canon—and in particular during the time of *SET*, how this information could fuel the exciting energies that propelled new ways of writing and sharing poetry in the 1960s. Writing on Jean Baudrillard, Lansing notes, "It is possible that the seeds of a new conception of human being in nature can be found even in certain Western sources, occulted under the 'Renaissance' by the 'collective consciousness' of the West, arcane in its canon."[46] Thus, the intention here was to collect the histories, even the known Western ones and to read between the lines for new ways forward that conceptualized history not as a rehearsal of facts but as an opportunity for a generative poetics. The dual historical and poetic mission of this room, combined with its location on the lower level nearest the living room where Lansing hosted guests, made it an especially resonant room for most people who visited. With inscribed chapbooks and the foundations of a liberal arts education, the room itself was an excellent conversation piece. Anyone could find anything to talk about with Lansing in this room. And as master of his own domain, he knew it all.

Authors featured most prominently in this room included Hart Crane, Ezra Pound, and Henry James, yet the room was so wide-ranging that few subjects or authors had significant space to reappear with much notable frequency. The first three bookcases in the room included music-related texts, with books on Johannes Sebastian Bach, Pyotr Ilyich Tchaikovsky (edited by James Huneker), Frédéric Chopin, Franz Schubert, Franz List, Wolfgang Amadeus Mozart, and works on jazz and music theory. These music texts were intermingled with the works of Henry Wadsworth Longfellow, Thomas Pynchon, Willa Cather, Edith Wharton, Henry James, Fanny Howe, Walt Whitman, a good deal of Herman Melville, Ralph Waldo Emerson, Edgar Allen Poe, Margaret Fuller, Cotton Mather, John Metcalf, Louisa May Alcott, Fanny Fern, Mark Twain, and others. Generally engaging the nineteenth-century strains of thinking and writing that informed British and American culture, these authors were readily known, and easy opportunities for conversation. At the same time, they represent deeper affinities for Lansing, as with Emerson, who was so dear to Lansing as a writer and a thinker that the bulk of Lansing's Emerson collection was stored in his bedroom, among the most intimate books and subjects.

In the library, in built-in bookcases on either side of a hearth, the collection of American authors continued with Washington Irving, then Percival, and turned toward New England and North American history, including books on the Lansing family, the Gansevoort family (like the Lansings, another prominent Albany family), the Civil War, and the Federalists. On the opposing built-in bookcase, the musical theme continued with books on rags, opera, and music of the 1920s and 1930s, before looping back to poetry with Dylan Thomas, W. H. Auden, William Shakespeare, and Ovid.

Two large bookcases flanking a large window that looked out to the side of the house contained Lansing's contemporary poetry collection, including many copies of works inscribed to him from his peer generation of poets. These shelves likely had chapbooks and inscribed materials removed for sale, given the value of inscribed items, small press books, and little magazines in the literary market. However, at the time of documentation, these shelves still included the little magazines *Open Space, Compost, Sulfur, Fulcrum,* and *Talisman,* as well as books from *Dispatches* editions. Authors included a wide array of what might broadly be considered New American poetry and the various strains that both precede it and inform it, including books by Richard Grossinger, Emily Dickinson, John Wieners, Bill Berkson, David Meltzer, Charles Bernstein, George Quasha, Alice Notley, Clayton Eshleman,

Audre Lorde, Joanne Kyger, Annie Finch, Anne Waldman, James Schuyler, Hart Crane, Frank O'Hara, Ed Sanders, Helen Adam, Seamus Heaney, Larry Eigner, Allen Ginsberg, Kenneth Patchen, Robert Lowell, Ted Hughes, Sylvia Plath, J. H. Prynne, Robert Kelly, Ezra Pound, Kenneth Irby, Duncan McNaughton, Gertrude Stein, Kenneth Koch, Clark Coolidge, C. D. Wright, Diane di Prima, Ed Barrett, and Benjamin Hollander. Toward the front of the house, the shelves continued with e. e. cummings, Vincent Ferrini, John Bayliss, Homer, Ed Dorn, Eileen Myles, Jack Spicer, Robin Blaser, Wallace Stevens, James Merrill, William Carlos Williams, Wallace Stevens, and Edmund Wilson.

Below the window two smaller bookcases included more works on music, John Cage, science and music, Grove Books editions, more Beethoven and Schubert, along with music history, African rhythm, modern art, *The Social History of Art* in four volumes, John Savage's history of punk titled *England's Dreaming*, the yoga of sound, Georges Bataille, Georges Perec, iconology, and Greek anthologies. The classical turn here continued with books on Seneca, Boethius, Cicero, Virgil, Sappho, classical history and literary studies, Tacitus, Pliny, Ovid, Euripides, and others. In an impressive forty-eight volumes, the *Ballantine British Poets* series sat with Julius Caesar, Robert Creeley, New American anthologies, Robert Duncan, *Ironwood* and *Sagetrieb* magazines, lyrics from the Middle Ages, and Pindar. The bookshelf at the corner closest to the front door contained books on food and herbals, mushrooms, rocks and fossils, natural history, the history of Boston and Cape Ann, herbalism, plant teachings, healing mushrooms, leechcraft, Darwin, geology, Beatrix Potter, and ecology. While one might interpret this cluster of books as an extension of the themes in the kitchen—or perhaps an allusion to another nearby threshold, the front door—they might also be considered as the practical extension of Lansing's interest in Emerson and magic, as tools to learn about and appreciate man's relationship to the natural world, and for Lansing to cultivate his love of mushroom collecting and foraging.

Three bookshelves sat in the middle of the room, containing books on cuisine and class, American history, *Caterpillar* magazine, Marianne Moore, and more Gertrude Stein, as well as books with fine bindings from the nineteenth and twentieth centuries. Multiple *Library of America* volumes were present, including works on Henry Adams, Thomas Paine, the Dutch Republic, more Shakespeare, the French Netherlands, and the history of the United States; there were also nearby books on Thomas Jefferson, Alexander Hamilton,

Goethe, John Burroughs, and optical illusions. Eclecticism pervaded this room, with chunks of arranged subjects in history and literature peppered with more unlikely titles, and no small amount of repetition of authors or subjects across shelves. The space delighted with its array of little magazines, small press books by contemporary authors, multivolume publishers' anthologies, and foundations of Western and American literature, philosophy, and history. One got the sense that anything was possible to discuss, which might evoke any number of responses that would then lead to subjects represented in other rooms of the house or undocumented rooms within Lansing's mind. And, since many people did not go upstairs unless they were overnight guests, as the last downstairs room in the house this room represents a sort of holding and liminal space, pointing to possible areas of greater intimacy and knowledge in parts of the house yet to be seen.

Upstairs and Upper Front Hallway

While Lansing was generous with tours of his impressive book collection, fewer people went upstairs. The increased intimacy of these rooms corresponds with the increased intimacy of the books within, closer to Lansing's inner workings and study and less for public display. Likewise, we might also remember Lansing's vertical orientation in the title of his work, *The Heavenly Tree Grows Downward*, as well as Bachelard's theory that the image of the house operates on a vertical axis to create meaning and mood. Thus, the upstairs rooms represent a critical part of the tension of themes within the house, skewing toward the more personal and occult.

The upstairs rooms in the house included a guest room, an office, a large closet, a second study known as "the magic room," and a bedroom. These areas were accessed by a staircase, whose upper landing provided additional wall space and nooks for bookcases. Directionally speaking, the curved staircase began in the lower front hallway a few feet behind the front door, with stairs pointing back toward the kitchen then curving up toward the left. At the top of the staircase, one would arrive at the magic room. However, to follow the spiral pattern of increased intimacy throughout the house, one would begin on the landing itself. After passing a bookshelf with *The Spectator* in eight volumes, books on Egyptian mysteries, consciousness, the quantum mind, Afrocentrism, the universe, molecules, and the Gospels, the upper front hallway opened into a small room, flanked by seven facing bookshelves with a faded pink couch nestled on the far wall in between them. Facing the window of the room (which overlooked the harbor), and the sofa beneath it, four bookcases on the right contained books on Eastern philosophy and religion, and three contained books on these topics in the Western tradition. Most of the books were paperbacks, and represented a sort of introductory syllabus to different strains and practices of philosophy. In their meditative opposition, with an inviting sofa to match, the area felt like a breath of contemplation. And in its position directly over the front entrance area downstairs, the room held any visitor aloft within the heights of Lansing's books and the inquiries they represented.

On fifty-five shelves, with 129 linear feet of books, the Eastern section was larger by practically three bookcases. It also contained a greater mix of texts that inform philosophical traditions in the East—including religious or spiritual practices, classical literature, and other themes. In contrast, the Western section mostly contained the texts of specific authors in the history of Western philosophy, illustrating the more confined way in which the Western version of this tradition is both conceived and received. Philosophers on these shelves included Thomas Hobbes, Merleau-Ponty, Friedrich Wilhelm Joseph von Schelling, Martin Heidegger, Marshall McLuhan, Immanuel Kant, William James, Alfred North Whitehead, Bertrand Russell, David Hume, John Locke, Arthur Schopenhauer, Friedrich Nietzsche, Georg Wilhelm Friedrich Hegel, Jacques Derrida, Friedrich Kittler, and Gilles Deleuze, along with books on the Enlightenment and the history of Western philosophy.

Topics on the Eastern side included Chinese medicine, Chinese mythology, Taoism, *The Tale of Genji*, Sanskrit poetry and criticism, the *Lotus Sutra*, Japanese literature, yoga, Kundalini, classical Indian literature, texts by Alan Watts, Saivism and philosophy, the *Upanishads*, Kali, sexual magic, the *Bhagavad Gita*, Hinduism, Indian philosophy, Tantra, neo-Vedanta, the history of yoga, Sri Aurobindo and Alfred Whitehead, the *Mahabharata*, large art books on philosophy and yoga, the role of evil in Hindu mythology, the Ramacha Raka Yogi Publication Society, and *Yoga for Dummies*. In particular, publications such as the latter suggest that in the same spirit as the library room, the breadth of the collection appears as though it was meant to provoke others in conversation or serve as an introductory bibliography-made-flesh to its subjects; Lansing's own research was much farther progressed.

With the thematic yogic roots of *The Heavenly Tree Grows Downward*, it makes sense that these types of texts were particularly important to Lansing's own reading as well as the reading he shared with others. George Kalamaras remembers Lansing's knowledge of Paramahansa Yogananda and Swami Sri Yukteswar, noting that Lansing's recommendations proved essential for Kalamaras's dissertation topic, forming part of his chapter titles and chapter arguments.[47] This advisory quality, of knowing such a vast amount of information and doling it out to students according to their interests and level of engagement, speaks to the type of role this particular room embodies—books to remind Lansing of topics close to him, to educate others, and to provide further avenues for research, conversation, and, indeed, generative writing.

A final shelf, located closest to the guest room, contained a more eclectic mix of books still speaking to Eastern and Western traditions, including works by Baruch Spinoza and Plato, and books on ancient China, prehistoric religion, mysticism, vision, Zen and the brain, bodymind, and the first five volumes of the magazine *Tenemos*. From there, a visitor would proceed to the guest room.

The Guest Room

Many people stayed in Lansing's guest room over the years, given his centrality to the poetry scene in the Northeast and his generous spirit. At the time of my arrival, the room was flanked with nineteen bookcases, and wall space was only otherwise occupied by a bed. In addition to the 113 shelves, Mitch Highfell remembers how a pile of books was there to greet him on the guest bed whenever he visited Gloucester; when I arrived, there were numerous stacks of books on the floor as well.[48] Given its eclectic range, the guest room was a likely spot for Lansing's known habit of visiting church and secondhand book sales; to add to this symmetry, the room was directly above the library room downstairs, which had a similar eclecticism that was likewise anchored by poetry and literature. Upstairs in the guest room, J. K. Rowling sat next to Charles Dickens on the shelves, along with Dan Brown, three copies of *Infinite Jest* by David Foster Wallace, and books on radical sex, alien encounters, and Barnes and Noble mass-market books. Clusters of books featured crucial writers of the Western literary canon, including Victorian (Emily Brontë, George Eliot, more Dickens), modernist (Virginia Woolf, John Dos Passos, Djuna Barnes, Jean Toomer), and an assortment of writers who appeared often across the shelves, including H. P. Lovecraft, Kenneth Burke, Machiavelli, and Robert Anton Wilson. With sly touches, like the location of books by Anaïs Nin right next to the bed, the room read like a pick-your-fancy of literature and poetry, with brows high, low, and everywhere in between.

During the period of my documentation, a bookcase that had been located in the upper front hallway had been moved into the guest room, containing books related to the *I Ching, The Idiot's Guide to the I Ching,* wonders of the natural world, oracles and demons of Tibet, the *Book of the Dead,* and other topics related to Eastern spiritual practice that were resonant with other books in the hallway. Books on the floor were largely positioned there for ease of dealer's access, mostly including mass-market publications of contemporary or classic fiction, anthologies, and pulp paperbacks. In this room also, a shelf was relocated from the bedroom that contained books that were exceedingly important to Lansing. This shelf included the complete works of Emerson published by Houghton Mifflin in 1914; the complete works of Thoreau published by Houghton Mifflin Riverside Press in 1982; the essays of Michael Lord of Montaigne edited by David Nutt in three volumes published in Edinburgh in 1893; *North's Plutarch* from the Limited Editions Club; the *Upanishads;* books on the Vedic experience; works by Michael Drayton, George Chapman, and François Rabelais; *The Revelation in the Wilderness* by Dr. G. H. Mees; *Plutarch's Lives* (in ten volumes); *Pliny's Natural History* (in six volumes); and even more Thoreau and Emerson.

Otherwise, the shelves contained a large amount of poetry—likely appealing for Lansing's guests, who were by a majority poets—as well as Western literature and some historical topics. To give a sense of the gradual unfolding of themes in this room, I enumerate themes and authors in counterclockwise order as one would have encountered them: self-help books (*There Are No Accidents*), *Alphabetic Labyrinth,* George Bernard Shaw, Algernon Charles Swinburne, Godfrey Higgins's *Anacalypsis,* Jed Rasula, Edward Bulwer-Lytton (whose novels are located elsewhere around the room), *Talismans,* the *Nag Hammadi,* Ben Johnson, H. P. Lovecraft paperbacks (also located on multiple shelves), Sir Thomas Browne's works in three volumes, *The Decline and Fall of the Roman Empire* in three volumes, William Blake, Algernon Blackwood, radical sex, John Dos Passos (on multiple shelves), Sherlock Holmes in a nine-volume issue by Doubleday, Harold Bloom, Umberto Eco, Guy Davenport, cults, cult rapture, *The Omnibus of Crime,* Robert Anton Wilson, literary biographies and commentary, Harry Mathews, Jack Kerouac, S. P. Elledge, Jonathan Strong, Raymond Queneau, French language poetry, James Branch Cabell, Brion Gysin, Henry Miller, Iain Sinclair, gay literature and detective anthologies, William Faulkner, Jean Toomer, *The Paris Review,* *Poems for the Millennium* anthology, Eudora Welty, Thornton Wilder, Richard

Brautigan, Mina Loy, African American literature, ancient mysteries, Henry George, Karl Marx and German ideology, social thought and economics, revolution, the cult of information, *Das Kapital,* an anthology on Vladimir Lenin, Adolf Hilter's *Mein Kampf,* Neil Gaiman, Truman Capote, Rudy Rucker, Philip K. Dick, A. Merritt, Salman Rushdie, Lord Dunsany, *The Illuminatus,* Oscar Wilde, J. G. Ballard, *The Inklings,* Aldous Huxley, ghost stories, Ayn Rand, Paulo Coelho de Souza, Ivan Turgenev, Bram Stoker, Dan Brown, science fiction paperbacks, Edward Lear, *The Mind Map Book,* Jewish fantasy and the occult, Guy Debord, future science, anarchists in Russian revolution, Niccolò Machiavelli (significant amounts), *Kropotkin's Revolutionary Pamphlets,* Max Stirner, Kenneth Burke (significant amounts), Samuel Butler, William Godwin, Anthony Powell, alien encounters, *What Is Marriage For?,* homosexual desire, poetic meter and form, Charles Dickens, J. K. Rowling, Virginia Woolf, Thomas Hardy, Mary Web, A. E. Housman, Ford Maddox Ford, Donna Tartt, David Foster Wallace, Angela Carter, Dawn Powell, George MacDonald, Katherine Mansfield, Jane Austen, Neal Stephenson, Evelyn Waugh, Ivy Compton-Burnett, Djuna Barnes, Chris Isherwood, John Crowley, Miguel de Cervantes, Don DeLillo, Tennessee Williams, Cowper Powys, Paul Auster, Henry Fielding, math and the universe, the Brontë sisters, William Makepeace Thackeray, D. H. Lawrence, George Eliot, Elizabeth Gaskell, Angela Carter, and Samuel Beckett.

The Office

Next in the clockwise circle, and within the realm of the top three intimate rooms in the house—also including the magic room and the bedroom—lay the office, which at the time of my visit still had an Abraxas poster from Lansing's bookshop displayed above the desk. Lansing would write and research in this room on a desktop computer, surrounded by thirteen bookcases, most of which were built using a system of cinderblocks and wooden planks. While the contents of the computer have been lost (the system crashed shortly before Lansing's passing), the books remained to tell the story of thought in the room. On these seventy-six shelves, including a closet stacked high with books, the books become more expert-oriented and decidedly more mystical and esoteric, even as they remained literary and historical in nature. This room housed significant collections of George Ivanovich Gurdjieff, Mircea Eliade, William Butler Yeats and materials related to the Golden Dawn, and the history of language, along with histories of religion and magic. The books began next to the

doorway with Celtic subjects, including Druidry and folklore before veering
into medieval North Atlantic sagas, with a closet stuffed with Christianity and
linguistic subjects. The largest bookshelf, made of cinderblocks and wooden
planks, contained canonical literary texts by mostly British and Irish authors,
including Yeats and Joyce, as well as Shakespeare and other early modern and
Renaissance authors up through the Victorian era.

In the same manner that I presented the books, authors, and themes of the
guest room—in counterclockwise order from the entryway, I will proceed
here. I understand that this method produces a wash of information, rather
than a synthesis better suited to digestion. However, this aspect of enumera-
tion is important to maintaining the fidelity of this project. Lansing's books
resist neat summary, and by their sheer volume, important works can either
be needles in a haystack—that is, what someone is looking for, a beacon of
clarity for further study—or significant for their inclusion and blending into
this tapestry of authors and subjects. In the spirit of Bachelard's method of
daydreaming the image of the house to understand its full power, I present
these lists in order, given that these are the most intimate rooms in Lansing's
house, to offer readers the same opportunity to meditate with the books
before drawing conclusions.

Subjects and authors in this room included mythologies, the Golden
Dawn, an encyclopedia of the Kabbalah, mythology and folklore, Druidry,
Celtic shamanism, *Wylundt's Book of Incense*, Lynn Thorndike's eight-volume
History of Magic and Experimental Science, strange planet binders, dreams,
spirits, magician handbooks, birthday guides, the *Oxford English Dictionary*
in fourteen volumes, pagan Europe, the *Kalevala*, Druids, Norse mythology,
the medieval Icelandic sagas, volume four of *TYR: Myth Culture Tradition*,
Teutonic mythology, Paracelsus, alchemy, more Celtic Golden Dawn, science
fiction, supernatural themes, astrology and outer space, Gurdjieff, encyclopedia of witchcraft and demonology, German linguistics, Spanish, language
studies, English, phonetics, a family bible, Mircea Eliade, signs, religion, dictionaries, Rumi, Sufi mysticism, Ismaili gnosis, the Islamic *Book of the Dead*,
the Koran, logic, hexalogy, Alan Turing, geometry, mathematics, Old Testament, New Testament, Christianity, Bibles, Henry Hart Milman, Robert G.
Ingersoll, apocalypses, Church history, Irish writing, Fiona MacLeon, W. B. Yeats,
A. E., Seamus Heaney's *Beowulf*, James Joyce, *Ulysses*, Old English translations,
Celtic saints, John Skelton, Thomas Campion, Shakespeare paperbacks, John
Milton, numerology, William Morris, *Pilgrim's Progress*, Thomas Malory,

Knights Templar, Vikings, Thomas Nash, Sir Philip Sidney, Grail legend, Celtic magic, medical dictionary, the medieval Icelandic *Poetic Edda*, dictionary of quotes, the Merlin quest, Geoffrey Chaucer, surveys of literature, Matthew Arnold, John Dryden, Ben Jonson, British poets, Gerard Manley Hopkins, originality and imagination, more Shakespeare, the history of England, Walter Savage Landor, Henry Vaughan, Lewis Mumford, Samuel Pepys's diary, more Milton, James Boswell's *London Journal*, Paul Bunyan, Richard Corbett, Samuel Taylor Coleridge, John Clare, Robert A. Wilson's *Modern Book Collecting* (Wilson of the Phoenix Book Shop), and Thomas Gray.

Having listed the thematic arc of the room, there are certain authors and themes that are particularly significant to Lansing. In particular, Henry Vaughan was the subject of Lansing's master's thesis at Columbia University, and likewise, the foundational work of Yeats (especially in *A Vision*), who describes his composing technique as receiving dictation from a spirit speaking through his wife Georgie, was highly influential on poets of Lansing's generation, including Charles Olson and Jack Spicer, who also read and studied Yeats extensively. Through these two small examples among many, one can see the cosmicity of the books within the house—some books are the night sky, and some are the stars. By this metaphor, suggested in part by Bachelard's idea that "an immense cosmic house is a potential of every dream of houses," all books are necessary phenomena in the gravitational pull and shape of themes in Lansing's library.[49]

The Closet and Upper Hallway

The closet in the hallway immediately next to Lansing's office contained solely books: fifty linear feet on shelves that stretched from floor to ceiling. Nearby, thirty two linear feet of books sat on three cases in the hallway area. The closet specifically was known to house a portion of the dead stock from Lansing's bookshop, Abraxas, and because of this they contained a higher percentage of *Astrology for Dummies*-esque books than the rest of his collection. The closet contained multiple multivolume sets, such as the *Waverly* novels, *Life of Scott*, Thomas de Quincy in twenty-six volumes, and Jeremy Taylor's works, and also books on astrology, Nostradamus, transcendental astrology, divination, prophecies, hermetic sciences, how-to astrology manuals, dictionaries and lexicons (Greek, Italian, French), crystal magic, occultism, Buddhism, Jacob Boehme, esoterica, Joseph Campbell, and *Auld Lang Syne* by Friedrich Max Muller.

The hallway included material on energy, medicine, chakras, energy bodies, ten volumes on Robert Southey, a significant volume of Walter Pater, Celtic miscellany, rhetoric, Giacomo Girolamo Casanova, the epic *1001 Nights*, and a number of multivolume sets, as well as Chinese health and healing, qigong, somatics, Tai Chi, qi energy, acu-yoga, esoterica, anatomy, reflexology, Jung, *Spring* magazine, Freud, Marie-Louise von Franz, archetypes, dreams, symbolism, Jungian analysis, *The Red Book* (another copy was located downstairs in the lower hallway, thus stitching these hallways together), and criticism on Jung and psychoanalysis. Together, the themes drew from the office and the upper front hallway, including Eastern spirituality and medicine, combined with literary histories veering toward esotericism and shared unconsciousness of cultural experience, and embodied by epic texts that draw on premodern history such as the *Sagas* and the *Kalevala*. This momentum drew one toward the magic room, where the hints of magical and occult study offered in the closet reached their fullest form in the house.

The Magic Room

Perhaps the most significant room in the house, the magic room contained seventeen cases, 107 shelves, and 256 linear feet of books at the time of my arrival. Certain shelves had been moved and rearranged for booksellers, but the principle themes of the room remained, as did a large desk with various occult materials still held within its drawers—including a black mirror, a scrying ball, and a few sets of Tarot cards. The room was a master class in magical, esoteric, and occult practices, embodying decades of study, beginning with Lansing's time in New York City studying with Count Stefan Colonna Walewski alongside friend Harry Smith. Walewski owned the store Esoterica and had authored *A System of Caucasian Yoga* in 1955, the year of Lansing's thesis deposit, and his mentorship proved highly influential on Lansing's pursuit of magical and occult studies.[50]

Bookseller Adam Davis summed up this room in particular by noting that "reading through Gerrit's library could make one an exceedingly well-informed heretic," and the magic room would be the first stop for this type of education.[51] Notably, the room contained not just occult and magical works, but also a good measure of French Surrealism, Symbolism, Oulipo, and Dada. Lansing's work in French literature is particularly notable, especially as he was the first translator of Mircea Eliade, whose *The Forge and the Crucible* provided critical research in thinking through the history of alchemy in the twentieth century. In this French milieu, key authors present in the magic room included Arthur Rimbaud, Guillaume Apollinaire, Charles Baudelaire, André Breton, René Daumal, Paul Verlaine, Antonin Artaud, Salvador Dalí, Philippe Soupault, Robert Desnos, Jacques Roubaud, Théophile Gautier, Paul Valéry, Joris-Karl Huysmans, Michel Leiris, Gaston Bachelard (from whose framework my exploration of Lansing's library is drawn), René Crevel, Stéphane Mallarmé, and Michel Deguy. And indeed, there is something magical and occult about the practices of Symbolism and Surrealism at the level of language in that they often deal with chance protocols, the summoning of presence through image alone, and subversive political themes. Hovering near the doorway, they provided an excellent introduction to the core of the room, as the bookshelves snaked into various nooks and corners.

Additional authors represented in this room included Heinrich Cornelius Agrippa, whose masterpiece *De occulta philosophia libri tres* is one of the most valuable books in Lansing's library (Lansing owned Walewski's 1533 first edition). Aleister Crowley is the most thoroughly represented author in this room, with *The Equinox* and many other texts, given his centrality to the Thelemites, an occult order that Lansing at times visited in at their Salem, Massachusetts, outpost. Other authors and texts in the magic room included A. E. Waite, Helena Blavatsky, Dion Fortune, Henry S. Olcott (in old diary leaves), Baird T. Spalding's *Life and Teachings of the Masters of the Far East*, Frances Yates on John Dee, Ebenezer Sibly's *A Key to Physic, and the Occult Sciences*, Edward Sanders's *The Family* (notably not with books by other friends downstairs in the library), Agrippa, Hudson Tuttle's *Arcana of Nature*, Robert Anton Wilson's *Cosmic Trigger*, Marsilio Ficino, *The Fenris Wolf* (an esoteric journal), Proust, C. F. Russell, Meister Eckhart, Jacob Boehme, Pseudo-Dionysius, Plato, Homer, Jung, Charles Stein, Plotinus, Pythagoras's *Golden Verses*, Aristotle, George Robert Stow Mead's *Echoes from the Gnosis*, Paul Foster Case's *The Book of Tokens* for Tarot meditations, Rudolf II, Proclus's *The Elements of Theology*, *The Book of Numbers* and *The Book of Moses* (from the Bible), Robert Temple's *Oracles of the Dead: Ancient Techniques for Predicting the Future*, the *Necronomicon*, *The Magus*, Nicholas Goodrick-Clarke's *Black Sun*, and many volumes of *Red Flame: A Thelemic Research Journal*, edited by J. Edward and Marlene Cornelius in Berkeley, California. There were also significant volumes of works published by Scarlet Imprint and Golden Hoard Press on these shelves.

Subjects in this room spanned the occult gamut, including astrological geomancy, popular magic, mythology, occidental mythology, Surrealist women, Dutch interiors, ritual wolf magic, the Sphinx, spiritualism, Enochian physics, Freemasonry, the Gnostic Circle, Atlantis, consciousness, the history of magic, Moses, dream culture and Neanderthals, wind power, Jesus, sexual alchemy, occult philosophy, the Golden Dawn, theosophy, Enochian dictionaries, Platonic theology, Rosicrucianism, the Zohar, the Kabbalah, cycles of time, astral projection workbooks, healing magnetism, crystal gazing, numerology, new age instructions for Tarot via mail order, Wiccan magick, Satanism, body time, reality, occult and the supernatural, art, magic, Santería, orphic songs, Jung and American moon cycles, anatomy and destiny after Freud, old goddesses, DMT, the Marian (a Catholic religious community), and techgnosis.

The large desk in the center of the room was piled high with papers, including reference copies of additional works related to magic and the occult, broadsides, flyers, magazines, and other ephemera. While this is one of the most essential rooms in terms of its alignment with Lansing's poetic practice, it is also one of the most inscrutable and does not easily give up its secrets. In contrast to Diane di Prima's occult library, which provided small clusters and clumps of specific themes meant to represent different approaches to occult topics, from Atlantis to the Kabbalah, to Dogon religious practice to Crowley's *Cocaine*, Lansing's library has the feel of a working space in progress—a series of visible volumes built on having read other volumes in other libraries, other homes, and other spaces. Thus, to know the volumes in Lansing's library does not reveal his magic; even if one were to trace each book and read it, the connections might not prove clear. The room simultaneously claims magic as its subject while concealing the payoffs of such study.

The Bedroom

The bedroom, the most intimate place in Lansing's house, was also perhaps the most significantly altered by the time of my documentation. John, Lansing's longtime housemate, had placed a large yellow sectional beneath a curved wall with windows, and the books had also been rearranged. Many items were moved from this space and placed in the guest room as enumerated, sometimes as entire shelves. These items primarily included a mix of multivolume sets with fine bindings, as well as some light reading, magic, Egyptology, Romantic poetry, and an intensive section on runes from the closet.

With five cases, twenty-nine shelves, and sixty linear feet of books, Lansing's bedroom was one of the rooms in the house least populated by books. What the room lacked in volume, it made up for in density of books and authors that were important to Lansing. A single bookcase remained in the main room, containing works by Gerald Masse, Giordano Bruno, Marsilio Ficino, Thomas Vaughan, and John Patrick Deveney, as well as *The Testament of Cyprian the Mage, Living Witch, Geosophia: The Argo of Magic, Grimorium Verum*, books by the publisher Scarlet Imprint, and books on the Kabbalah, Tarot, talismans, angels, psychomagic, hermeticism, and soul flight. In the closets, more books were stowed. Subjects and themes include Frater Ud's *High Magic*, a gnostic workbook, a guide to the Crowley Tarot, witchcraft, occult, Crowley magic, Sir Philip Sidney, John Donne, Egypt, Shaftesbury, Muriel Rukeyser's *Life of Poetry*, Lord Byron, George Herbert, John Campbell Colquhoun's *Isis Revelata: An Inquiry into the Origin, Progress, and Present State of Animal Magnetism*, Caroline and Elizabethan poets, Symbolism, Fyodor Dostoevsky, Leo Tolstoy, Malcolm Gladwell, Egyptian magic (very well represented), the *Book of the Dead*, Andrei Bely, Nordic runes, dreams, chakra energies, the healing power of trees, Celtic themes, runic astrology, Icelandic witchcraft, William Blake, Percy Bysshe Shelley, John Keats, William Wordsworth's *Prelude*, Edward FitzGerald's *Rubaiyat of Omar Khayyam*, Dante Alighieri, Robert Browning, scholarly criticism on Romantic literature, information theory and aesthetic precepts, Lewis Spence's *Myths and Legends*, Edward Carpenter, Laurence Sterne, and Helena Blavatsky.

Thoreau is especially instructive in his influence on Lansing; Lansing writes of his admiration for Thoreau that he "made of his daily and local experiences a rich mythological fabric, a cosmos as complex and as individual as any system of totemic classification."[52] This was part of Olson's work on Gloucester with the *Maximus* poems, and part of Lansing's own poetry as well. Thoreau's careful attention to Walden Pond is likewise an attribute shared by Lansing's observations of Cape Ann in his poetry: a white moon on a beach, cedar berries in winter, fields and forests and gardens. Lansing's poems are full of rocks and boulders, like Gloucester's glacial erratics in Dogtown and nearby rocky coasts, that seem dually characterized as Philosopher's Stones and as the geological and ecological truths they represent in the landscape.[53] Crucial here is the clarity of the mission: the devotion to what just *is*, not yet subsumed into systems of classification. This, too, is the poetics of Lansing's library.

Dispersal

As with any library, Lansing's book collections took a lifetime to assemble. It was approximately a year and a half before his library disbanded as part of probate. As this chapter proves, there is no neat summary possible for Lansing's library, nor for its meaning to him. Likewise, considering the close relationships of houses to memory, it is impossible to fully capture the meaning of Lansing's library to each of us who encountered it, or the possibilities we might have for understanding his work in the future. I mention this not as a lament but as a core feature of certain poets' libraries; because of their eclecticism in the face of twentieth-century American knowledge categories—as inherently precarious collections, designed to collect what was not being collated—they are in most cases destined to be dispersed.

However, there is an additional resource we have for working with the memory of Lansing's library, courtesy of the booksellers who eventually purchased a few thousand volumes from the collection. Grey Matter and Division Leap produced a thirty-six-page catalog that provides further context for 120 specific books, with detailed descriptions and photographs of items, accompanied by essays by Sam Burton and Adam Davis. To have detailed descriptions of these important works, many inscribed or otherwise annotated by Lansing, offers even further possibilities to the type of documentation I created. In his foreword to the catalog, titled "The Immanent Library," Adam Davis cites the importance of presentation copies within the library as critical evidence of Lansing's involvement in the postwar American poetry community, and mentions David Rich's work on the influence of Lansing's library on Stephen Jonas's Tarot poems. Davis also cites the importance of the house in his initial experience of the library, walking through with David Abel: "It felt like that indefinite space that begins after recognizing a passage of music, but before being able to name it."[54] And likewise, Davis notes, the physical qualities of each of Lansing's books become "the impression of a subtle geometry of the library's place in the world," giving the image of the library a shelter-like quality not unlike Bachelard's image of the house.[55]

Sam Burton's afterword to the catalog, "Brief Chronicle of the Acquisition," addresses the complicated nature of the actual dispersal of the library. He notes by first initial the multiple booksellers involved, the concern that Lansing's friends felt over the dispersal of the library, my own documentary work (though as a small correction: thankfully I did not attempt to catalog every book). And, importantly, it establishes that Grey Matter and Division Leap were the ultimate purchasers of a significant portion of Lansing's library; their website indicated that six thousand volumes of Lansing's library were in their possession as of mid-2019. The process of selling the library was not straightforward. Other booksellers that had entered the space as of January 2019 included Passages, Weiser, Brattle Bookshop, Commonwealth Books, and Manchester by the Book. In some cases during this process, entire shelves were designated for booksellers like Weiser, whose sale did not proceed. At this point, David Rich and David Abel, followed by Adam and Kate Davis and Sam Burton, likely know the most about the particulars of books that were in Lansing's library, as well as Lansing's housemate for many years, John (to whom Lansing left his house). Those who visit Lansing's archive, preserved in two installments at the Beinecke Library under the curatorship of Nancy Kuhl, will be able to learn further by examining a few dozen volumes determined to be significantly annotated or otherwise archivally valuable.

In his foreword to the catalog, Davis notes that he pursued bookselling because it "seemed to offer an intellectual freedom that was eclectic, sensual, and offered the prospect of serendipity in a world that each day becomes further narrowed by algorithms." He continues, "Gerrit's library was the furthermost example of this freedom that I've yet encountered, and cataloging it has been one of my greatest joys as a bookseller."[56] When I think of Lansing's library on the whole, small details stick out: his love of beautiful multivolume sets that pepper the house; the constant presence of Emerson, Yeats, Campion, or Shakespeare in a variety of rooms as a testament to the reassuring historical reminder of poets past; books on magic that remain difficult to find and hard to tell how he might have even read them. The mysteries, especially when it comes to magic, remain preserved even in exploring Lansing's library on the whole. Lansing's library is not a concentrated thesis in a few hundred volumes, like di Prima's. Rather, it is a whole barrel of fish, complete with red herrings, sand, and sediment—*Astrology for Dummies* in the house of the magus.

The story of Lansing's library is its presence in his house, part of the infrastructure that guided his daily life and work for so many decades. Following a path from public to occult through the tension created by the vertical axis and centripetal force of the house, one can see where the repetition of books across rooms—such as Emerson—suggests centrality in Lansing's canon. While certain key texts may emerge, the books are also like pixels on a screen, aligning to make a complete picture of Lansing's intellectual and social life. One could not isolate the pixels or books deemed important and extract them as the true essence of the library. Only within the structure of the house is the image complete.

Lansing's library is also entwined with some of the more concrete details about Lansing's economic status. While his life trajectory was a clear repudiation of his family lineage, their family wealth did provide him with the stability necessary to weather the profession of bookselling by providing basic living expenses through an inheritance. While this demonstrates an economic privilege not afforded to the other poets in this book, Lansing's class position through his genealogy is not echoed in his style of book collecting. He was not often interested in first editions or expensive books but rather the wild expanses of cheap paperbacks, library books from the Widener, books from friends, and the like. Every time I saw Gerrit, he sported a comfortable, well-worn sweater. Like his contemporaries, he built an intellectual life of poetry from the ground up, focusing his gentle attention on plants, language, magic, and community. Part of Lansing's life, too, was his house. Bachelard notes that the house is "a real cosmos in every sense of the word," and claims "the house is one of the greatest powers of integration for the thoughts, memories and dreams of mankind," in which daydreaming is the method that facilitates this integration.[57] This perspective recalls Audre Lorde's invocation of her Staten Island home that once housed her books and family, also now dispersed. The imaginative properties of *remembering* the house, and its close relationship to practices of memorial arts, give unique possibilities not afforded by physical archives.

Bachelard notes that each of us has an "oneiric house, a house of dream-memory, that is lost in the shadow of a beyond of the real past."[58] The reasons for this are emotionally instinctive at times, especially when confronted with loss; Bachelard argues that the house, or the image of the house, derives its power from its ability to act as an "instrument with which to confront the cosmos," as a shelter for its inhabitants.[59] According to Bachelard, if each of us has access to a "shadow house" with the memory of Lansing's house and all the books within, the very power of the image of the house means that others who never stepped foot in his plant-filled kitchen can also have imaginative access to his library through the existing documentation. Beyond the details of its infrastructure, the content of the actual archive here is not Lansing's books but rather our memory of them. The actual archive in question here is not even Lansing's house but rather our shadowy constructions. The archive itself is imaginary and memorial.[60]

In a sense, suggesting the generative power of imagining archives is almost callous given the context of most precarious archives globally, which are constantly destroyed for political purposes in countries besieged by war, burned or flooded in household accidents, or neglected into rot. For these archives, "a good death" is justice that resists these conditions in the first place. But Lansing's library, while subject to dust, spiders, and the occasional mouse droppings, are not in this category, though many of his friends may have wished the deadline for selling his books could have been interpreted more generously. Because of this, it is important to note that while the physical dispersal of Lansing's books cuts off certain avenues of exploration at this juncture, the way in which Lansing structured his library affords us memorial and imaginative methods to understand it.

We either have to feel that he did not understand his own library, and thus ordered it dispersed, or there may have been a logic to this unfolding that left us with some secret magic after all. In "Gerrit Plays Scriabin," Robert Kelly remembers that Lansing "was able to confirm those who listened to him, a quiet, almost sacramental confirmation of their own nature: they had enough to go on with, they had what it takes."[61] While it may not be what we wanted, we may well have enough to go on. His library still teaches, even in its absence.

CONCLUSION

a poem as fragment
a book as fragment
a library as fragment of the library at large
the library at large as a fragment of the galaxy
the galaxy as fragment of the cosmos

—Alan Loney, *"What Book Does My Library Make?"*

WHILE THE LIBRARIES I discuss in this book are ephemeral, every poet in this book has a large archival deposit in a major research collection. Institutional practices shape our expectations of the use and value of poets' libraries, just as they shape our understanding of the archival materials and research collections that they house. In the relatively short history of literature-focused repositories, the Poetry Collection at the University at Buffalo–SUNY is particularly instructive given the richness of its collections and its influence on collecting practices in the field more broadly. Charles Abbott, the first curator, knew that assembling a prestigious rare book collection in the 1930s would be cost-prohibitive for the Poetry Collection; instead, he personally reached out to poets in order to gather their draft materials by donation.[1] Despite the initial perception—by both poets and other curators—of working papers as merely trash, a literary papers market would soon emerge from Abbott's example, and the practice of cultivating donors by engaging active literary communities directly would eventually become common practice.[2]

Abbott's strategy led to a particularly notable acquisition in 1950: a groundbreaking collection for Joyce scholars, with manuscripts, correspondence, notebooks, and Joyce's Paris library, preserved in large part by Paul Léon.[3] Scholars immediately recognized the value of Joyce's personal library for their research, given his densely allusive writing style. Furthermore, scholar Thomas Connolly's thorough descriptive bibliography, complete with edition information and transcription of annotations, scaffolded clear connections between Joyce's book collection and his writing.[4] This early acquisition at the Poetry Collection paved the way for certain assumptions about what to do, in a scholarly sense, with an author's library, and how a library might be stored and used as an archival resource. Researchers continue to access the Joyce library frequently, and a digital project is underway to explore the connections between Joyce's books and his work more comprehensively.[5] In this sense, Ralph Maud's methodology for examining Olson's books relates to, and may stem from, this foundational modernist example, which entails producing an exhaustive bibliography with reproductions of annotations, negotiating the presence and absence of certain texts, and arguing for a direct connection between the poet's library and their literary works.[6] This model is used by many others, and is highly practical to consult even when the library is not physically present. For instance, by noting editions of books, as Connolly does, readers can obtain similar copies and explore how annotations might function in context.

However, sometimes books within a library refract light back on lived experience, and not just literary themes. The Poetry Collection at Buffalo is also home to the Robert Duncan papers and his library. Like Lansing, many of the rooms in Duncan's house, shared with his partner, the artist Jess, were lined with books. And like Lansing, the positioning of books within the house was also significant, not in the least because of the creative importance that Duncan and Jess dedicated to their household, which Tara McDowell describes as a "politics, an ethics" embedded in a radical transformation of the "domestic" as a creative space for two men's artistic practices. McDowell argues that in making their own household, Duncan and Jess established and inhabited their own physical and conceptual architecture as a sanctuary, when no models were available either through the heteronormative happy couple with two and a half children, nor the itinerant tendencies of the Beats or other poetry-based countercultures.[7] As in Lansing's house, the walls were buttressed with books; McDowell cites a collection exceeding five thousand volumes in the Duncan/Jess household in the Mission District of San Francisco, with several rooms functioning as libraries for "in-depth holdings in fiction, art history, poetry, literary theory, philosophy, classics, world religion, history, architectural history, biography, fairy tales, science fiction, magic and the occult, Theosophy, drama, psychoanalysis, physics, and biology."[8]

When the Poetry Collection acquired Robert Duncan's papers, it also acquired his vast library shared with Jess, comprising approximately nine thousand volumes that were ingested shortly before and after Duncan's death in 1988. This type of acquisition would be challenging for any institution to replicate today, given the size of the collection and the likelihood of duplicate copies. However, the Duncan acquisition is notable not only for its size but also for how it was cataloged by the Poetry Collection. While the books are cataloged individually, the Poetry Collection uses Cutter numbers to assign Duncan a call number (D86.226R), adding a .8 to indicate a book from his personal library. While the technique of using Cutter numbers to provide personal call numbers for poets' libraries is used for the Poetry Collections' other similar collections—including the library of Duncan's friend, Helen Adam—Duncan's books are further categorized by the room in which they appeared in Duncan's house using additional decimals. Thus, the books can be "kept together" conceptually, and their relationships made visible through thoughtful cataloging.

It is important to note that this type of specific information and the Poetry Collection's attentiveness to it, are a result of their relationship with the poet and his circle. The then-curator of the Poetry Collection, Robert Bertholf, was also the acting literary executor for Duncan, and facilitated the boxing-up of the books. Likewise, the current curator of the Poetry Collection, James Maynard, was a graduate assistant to Bertholf at the time of the acquisition, and unpacked and cataloged the books, which shaped and facilitated his own studies on Duncan.[9] Without this aspect of community, the ambient information that surrounds the individual books—including the significance of their place in Duncan and Jess's house—would likely not be preserved.

Memories from friends continue to provide important context for the library, too. In Lisa Jarnot's Bagley Wright Lecture at the University at Buffalo in February 2021, titled "Abandon the Creeping Meatball: An Anarcho-Spiritual Treatise," she remembers Duncan and Jess's "big looming Victorian house" as a "sacred place" with several rooms of libraries, "especially the first floor library to the left of the living room, where the hermetic/Gnostic/theosophical/theological books were shelved." Inviting listeners in—"Let's peer into that room"—Jarnot remembers "the feeling of being totally enveloped in the dark wood and towering shelves, and the books salvaged variously from Duncan's parents' library and from bookstores that Duncan had regularly gone to during his reading tours," and that "that room was for me a portal, it was a room where one might actually be transported, it was a room that, as far as I was concerned, could raise the dead."[10] The house for Jarnot was assemblage, museum, repository of the materials that informed her poetic guide, Duncan's *The H. D. Book,* and an irrepressible object of memory. Her recollection continues to preserve the library within its sense of community: those who experienced it as an embodied presence.

Jarnot's observations, though, remind us of another dilemma in terms of the research life of the collection. Even if the Duncan library is cataloged in such a way that it is legible as a complete library, this lack of *visibility* as a complete library can often be an impediment to research. Without open stacks to browse, and without clear information on finding aids or catalog records, it can be difficult to discover even those poets' libraries that are cataloged and available at institutional research collections. As I discuss in relation to the Maud/Olson Library, the question of open stacks and the type of "performance" of a library that they invite can be a valuable tool for interpretation. The architectural rhetoric of the reading room in special collections— monitored tables, closed stacks—alters the reception of information from a poet's library by requiring analysis at the book level. However, the Poetry Collection's layout offers an intriguing possibility. The personal libraries of Oscar Silverman, Helen Adam, Basil Bunting, John Logan, Charles Abbott, and George Butterick are all in a glass-enclosed room, visible to researchers. While this architecture functions in a more ornamental or allusive sense, it nevertheless suggests the nature of the stacks beyond, as well as the books' close associations to their former owners.

As Alison Fraser, associate curator of the Poetry Collection, observes, Abbott's initial strategy of collecting unpublished manuscript drafts focused on the idea of an unknowable future. Abbott articulated that the Poetry Collection "wanted to be in a position to provide [the scholars] of the future with the kind of evidence that nobody had thought of saving."[11] Now this practice is commonplace, and literary papers, their markets, and special collections have all matured to the point in their identities where a poet's archive is most likely destined for an institution. Thus, it is little surprise that the Poetry Collection at Buffalo contains a significant number of poets' and writers' libraries, given its early experimental forays in collecting. While many institutional repositories may have conducted similar experiments in acquiring poets' libraries, the challenges of scale, duplicate copies, and other physical considerations with poets' libraries makes one wonder whether those who work at institutions will one day be shocked that minor poets' libraries were once considered detritus (Helen Adam's library was literally salvaged from the curb), not unlike literary manuscripts in the early twentieth century.

It is equally important to note that not all poet's libraries *should* necessarily be collected by institutional repositories, for a variety of reasons. Perhaps as in the case of Gerrit Lansing, the poet has expressed that he does not want the library to be maintained as a collection. Perhaps also, as in the case of the Maud/Olson Library, it is important to use the books to engage a local community (in Gloucester) in ways that would be prohibitive were the books be ingested into a special collection. Given the fact that these libraries were often created because poets found institutional collections to be lacking in some way, it is paradoxical that these collections may enter those very same institutions. Instructive here are ongoing conversations and critical frameworks for antiracist practices at institutions that interrogate the ways in which materials created by Black or Indigenous people, as well as people of color, exist at institutions that historically marginalized or excluded these same voices. Furthermore, studies such as Shannon Mattern's "Fugitive Libraries" suggest ways to highlight independent collections created by individuals within marginalized communities alongside mainstream conceptions of libraries, using these spaces to mutually inform similar yet distinct goals. Mattern cites projects like the Free Black Women's Library that "express a debt to the library-proper—to its logics and logistics, and to specific administrative, architectural, and aesthetic practices" yet are "also committed to working outside the constraints of the traditional library, which too often limit or invalidate Black voices and perspectives."[12] While community-based projects have their own significant challenges in terms of raising and maintaining resources, histories of these types of projects have much to teach us—especially in the ways in which they transform what Foucault called "the fantasy of the library" into reality, by taking direct responsibility for knowledge production and distribution within a community.

Flexible and imaginative preservation will soon become an even more profound necessity in the face of increasing volumes of digital materials in poets' libraries. After all, the poet's library of the future will not look like the Maud/Olson Library, Lorde's library in Saint Croix, di Prima's occult library, or Lansing's house. Future libraries will present new storage and retrieval issues in their forms as digital data, which will produce its own challenges and rewards. The fact that a poet's library composed of only printed or holograph items may soon be an obsolete format makes the importance of documenting, and even collecting them, all the more important for institutions and communities, since examples will become increasingly ephemeral and may no longer be produced by a future generation. Raised with the Internet as a primary infrastructure of information, future poets will create in ways that react to this new architecture—perhaps reminding us of the mimeograph revolution, using a new technology to fuel innovations in format and to share texts more readily. This remediation, in Jay David Bolter and Richard Grusin's sense of the word, is already apparent in certain digital spaces, such as Jed Birmingham's *Reality Studio*, a blog with images of mimeograph magazines, or digital bibliographies such as the *From a Secret Location* website by Granary Books. In any event, techniques like di Prima's xeroxing of alchemical texts are fading quickly as means of preservation and transmission, which make the media specificity of libraries like hers all the more compelling.

But what matters, for today and the future, is the hand of the poet in the library. The entwined histories of information theory, scientific infrastructure, and political surveillance in Cold War America, especially during the 1960s and the civil rights movement, teach us that poets were labeled government adversaries, arrested, investigated, and harassed. To be a poet in this manner was to be a radical, a renunciant. The way these poets collected and organized knowledge underscores the political and historical realities of their era, and their shared mission to recover occulted threads of intellectual inquiry. The process of collecting and organizing allowed poets to grapple with ideas of profusion, overload, and messiness—but also the precarious and delicate nature of ballooning information in its material forms.

George Herms's assemblage piece from 1960 titled *The Librarian* captures this energy, in its appearance as an anthropomorphic structure with outstretched arms made of jumbled books found at a local dump. *The Librarian* shows the disorder of information, and how books pull together disparate ideas and contents that align about as neatly as leaves on a forest floor.[13] Books are a messy body indeed. And while the libraries—occult, dispersed, imaginative, preserved—that document our recent history might slip through the cracks of community and institutional preservation, given their shaggy and unwieldy forms, their ethos nevertheless remains. As Sanders notes in *Investigative Poetry*, "poetry / should again assume responsibility / for the description of history."[14] And when the bards speak—through poems and through the books they collected—we must listen.

AFTERWORD

THE ORDER OF the chapters in this book does not reflect the order of my encounters with each of these libraries. Revealing that chronology, however, shows that the longer one researches this topic, the greater the entropy of the books themselves. The Maud/Olson Library was the first collection with which I worked, and was the most stable I encountered—thanks to its close association with the Gloucester Writers Center and its initial funding agreement through André Spears. It was housed in a dedicated space, cataloged, and made available in a standardized though intimate way. Diane di Prima's house was the next library I worked with, and taught me much about the in-processness of poets' libraries, as well as negotiating the work of making them legible to an institution versus maintaining their fidelity to the poets' own perception of their book management practices. By the time I arrived at Lansing's library, whose dispersal was imminent, I sought to gather as much as possible of the textures of the library and to commune with the house of a friend I had cherished. In the early phases of my research, I truly thought I was studying "books." On a walk in Gloucester, I realized that I was more accurately studying the memories and structures of imagination that surrounded those books—books at a distance, books dispersed, books unseen, books whose significant was felt by their collectors but not materially encoded in any visible way. By the time I delved into Lorde's librarianship, this entropic transformation of books into memory felt painful. Seeking her library only to find out that the books she took to Saint Croix for the last years of her life were destroyed in a hurricane moved me to tears.

Yet even when the books were in my hands, their context was within peoples' memory: books calcified as references in poems (like Diane di Prima's hallucination of a *Loba* poem in her Julian of Norwich book, owned by Auden) or in the amber of enumerative bibliography (the Maud/Olson Library, or Gerrit Lansing's jotted notes of books). Obtaining this necessary evidence from memory required speaking at length with poets and their friends, sleuthing through published works, finding interviews and other traces. These conversations, especially with Diane di Prima and Gerrit Lansing, showed that a life lived with books, far from the solitary bookworm stereotype that persists in our culture, was a life full of people who gave books, read them, forgot to return them, put coffee cups on them, shelved them, sold them, and bought them as a lifelong practice. Poet and printer Alan Loney encourages us to keep a "picture of books swarming in and out of the bookcases over a lifetime firmly in mind as a fluxual context for all else that might be said."[1] In Loney's formulation, we might observe how "the movement, constant, continuous, of books off the shelves and back again" reminds us that "as long as there are people who have to do with books, books will have this traveling life of small or large journeyings in which humans can seem little more than participatory factors."[2]

I have been witness to this movement of books in a prismatic fashion, from most of the professional or interpersonal vantage points that one might see a poet's library. As a graduate student, I experienced poets' libraries as part of house tours, topics of conversation, and places to share excitement about a particular volume that we both loved. As a specialist in the Berg Collection, one of my initial tasks was to prepare the collection space for additional storage, which essentially involved moving or touching almost every item in its holdings. There, author libraries and association copies were hidden gems of the collection, often uncatalogued and marked only by a note. As I spoke with my librarian colleagues in special collections across the country, I noticed a tacit (though not uniform) assumption that for a prestigious poet exceptions could be made, but a certain kind of poet's library was too big, full of useless things like *Astrology for Dummies* (see Lansing's library), too messy, or too full of duplicate copies of what a library already holds. Now, as a rare books and archives dealer with Granary Books, I see libraries at the tipping point. Steve Clay, the proprietor of Granary for nearly forty years, has done important work in placing libraries like Robert Creeley's at Notre Dame, and has observed that this type of effort is often most successful when an institution wants to augment their base collection of poetry materials and there is not a significant amount of duplication between the poet's library and the institutional library. Sometimes, libraries can be neatly carved as opposed to scattered to the winds; Anselm Hollo's library went partly to an institute at Finland (the country of his birth), and partly to the Beinecke Rare Book and Manuscript Library at Yale University with his archival papers, with additional items for sale separately. His complete library exists in the memories of his widow, Jane Dalrymple-Hollo, and his friends. I saw his beautiful study in his backyard, where numerous books still remained.

But it is not always so happy, how the books end up, and sometimes imagination is our only recourse. As I read the *Collected Poems of Bob Kaufman,* I think of the man who lived on the streets of San Francisco for years after shock treatments and wonder what his library was like.[3] A few books on a windowsill, near a sink, on the floor? Libraries require homes: seemingly, the ultimate privilege in our era of natural disasters and widening economic gaps. Many poets traveled frequently, lived transiently, or, like Kaufman, found their lives torn apart by overlapping forces of racism and poverty. Likewise, I read *Yours Presently: The Selected Letters of John Wieners,* and think of how Wieners often lived in poverty, and was in and out of mental institutions even as he was writing poetry and working at Eighth Street Bookshop before finally settling in Boston.[4] By the time of his death, his most important books consisted mostly of a shelf. Dedicating a life to poetry, especially in di Prima's words, as a "renunciant," was never easy, and the necessities of stability and resources to build a library could be scarce. In light of this, poets overcame great odds to acquire the books that were meaningful to them; Vincent Ferrini maintained an enormous and meticulous library (which now resides with the Cape Ann Museum) even though he was broke. Of course, not every poet collects a library—sometimes they just have books. But when the library exists, the labor and politics of its creation are sometimes invisible to us, and this invisibility leads to actual physical precarity or disappearance. I know that sometimes when I imagine libraries, the possibilities may end there: with imagination as the only way in.

When it comes to history, we are in a very large ocean on a very small ship. It is important to remember how our understanding of this history has been so intensively shaped by the allotment of resources for practicing the humanities in the twentieth century, and the mindset and material considerations this produces. As I discuss in the introduction, the Cold War restructured intellectual and academic environments dramatically—from the rise of MFA programs in which the CIA had a direct hand to an unprecedented increase in large-scale government funding for scientific research.[5] While various arts grants became increasingly available in the 1970s through organizations such as the National Endowment for the Arts or private foundations, on the whole, humanities research was not endowed with a fraction of the private and government funding that scientific research received during the twentieth century. And we have inherited a landscape shaped by the policies of this era. Institutional repositories of humanities-oriented materials, as well as academic departments and nonprofits, consistently operate on the razor's edge with funding and staff. This is a reality with a long historical arc, and, importantly, an intentional one. Limiting one's resources to survival also limits the possibilities of imagination, and I acknowledge this not only for the production of poets' libraries but also for their prospects of custodianship in sustainable ways.

When the poets of this recent era of poetry were collecting, the constant threat of atomic warfare meant that life on this planet could cease to exist at any time. This force was fully present in daily life, totalizing, and scarring to most who grew up in it; there was widespread social agreement on the perceived reality of the threat of destruction in the Cold War. Today, we live with the knowledge that the earth as we know it will become uninhabitable due to climate change, displacing massive amounts of the population through heat (and resulting weather), famine, war, and unbreathable air—the first element of which already destroyed Lorde's library at Saint Croix. However, climate change is not an agreed-upon reality, or even descriptive term, for what is happening to our planet. We debate the reality of this phenomenon at the highest echelons of our governing bodies, and both global and local leaders fruitlessly attempt to impose regulations that would meaningfully slow the thermometer's climb. Many of our decisions for sustainable stewardship of cultural materials are now based on the idea that we have a limited capacity to store and maintain collections, and this is true on a material level for the historical reasons I state. But how might this be different if we considered instead how little time we might have? How might we collect and organize knowledge as an act of survival in the way that the poets before us did?

If poets' libraries throughout history are the night sky, this book is a very small constellation. The immensity of that vault leaves much to be explored. A side effect of my research is that now, whenever I read about a poet, I imagine their library. I invite you to join me in this practice, to imagine as an act of possibility, recuperation. Perhaps together, we can envision a more spacious idea of what a library could be: imaginary, ghostly, stored in one's head like a house of memory, summoned by a bibliography whose recitation works as a magic spell. Shared spaces to dream, to bond, to enumerate in a stable way, for us to revisit. I think of Thomas A. Clark's simple poetry, and his thought: "If you like something, you might want to say its name over and over, as if to draw it near."[6] Like words uttered cyclically as a mantra, books are a repetitive device as they accumulate on shelves. Yet each book is a different object, an opportunity for an ever-receding horizon of closeness to its subject. Together, books form a poet's library: a textual home that reifies its reader, an information architecture in which we might dwell and encounter the distinctively wild intelligence of its creator.

ACKNOWLEDGMENTS

THIS BOOK OWES a deep debt to the poets who paved the way—Charles Olson, Audre Lorde, Diane di Prima, and Gerrit Lansing. I had the privilege of meeting di Prima and Lansing, and will be forever grateful for the ways in which they welcomed me into their homes in San Francisco and Gloucester, and into their cosmoses of books and poems.

I thank Sheppard Powell, longtime partner of Diane di Prima and formidable healer, for his permission to share Diane's library and for his thoughtful insights at each turn. My thanks to David Rich for his perspective on Gerrit Lansing's work and library. I also thank the Gloucester Writers Center and the Maud/Olson Library, including Judith Nast, who helped launch my research, and the Steering Committee, with John Faulise, Henry Ferrini, Paul Cultrera, Gregor Gibson, Barbara Guest, and especially André Spears.

This book would not have been possible without the mentorship and friendship of Ammiel Alcalay, who is a poet and *'istorian* in the truest Olsonian sense. His recruitment of me, while I was still a medievalist, to the graduate English program at the Graduate Center, CUNY, no less than altered the course of my life. I thank him for supporting this book at each turn, and for suggesting *Wild Intelligence*, its title. Ammiel was also essential in connecting me to archives and poets through his general editorship of a remarkable program, *Lost & Found: The CUNY Poetics Document Initiative*, whose methodologies are cited throughout this book. I thank *Lost & Found* and the Center for the Humanities, including Kendra Sullivan, Sampson Starkweather, Shea'la Finch, and Stephon Lawrence, for their support of my work, including research fellowships on multiple occasions.

Steve Clay is another mentor who shaped this book in significant ways. His work at Granary Books involves publishing that centers books as physical objects and reanimates some of the rarer works of twentieth-century avant-garde poetry. Likewise, his quiet and consistent efforts are responsible for placing many poets' libraries, in whole or in part, with collectors and institutions. Steve's inexhaustible *A Secret Location on the Lower East Side* was one of the first bibliographic records that showed me the liberatory possibilities of a life structured by poetry, and I am grateful to him for the objects and ideas he has put into the world and the work that we do together at Granary. In this book, my main methodology is to follow his advice: to tell the truth.

My thanks to Greg Barnhisel, who encouraged this project through his editorial auspices at *Book History,* and as a series editor for University of Massachusetts Press's Studies in Print Culture and the History of the Book. I thank *Book History* for publishing an earlier version of the Olson chapter of this book, and Molly Hardy, who was an initial reviewer. I thank James Maynard for his thoughtful comments and Robert Duncan expertise, as well as all the anonymous reviewers who have shaped this work with their useful insights. Thank you to Amy Hildreth Chen, who read my proposal and provided valuable feedback. I am grateful to Alison Fraser for her friendship, exquisite scholarship, and important leads on poets' libraries at the Poetry Collection of the University at Buffalo; her insights were a significant contribution to the conclusion of this work. And my sincere appreciation to the series editors, the peer reviewers, the staff of the University of Massachusetts Press, and particularly Brian Halley for his support of this project and transforming it from a manuscript to what you hold in your hands.

My thanks to Matthew K. Gold and Wayne Koestenbaum, two critical interlocutors in this work and mentors during its early years. I appreciate also my former colleagues and mentors at The New York Public Library, including Isaac Gewirtz, Declan Kiely, William P. Kelly, and Joshua McKeon, wonderful colleagues in the Manuscripts and Rare Books Division, as well as those within the broader library. My warmest thanks to fellow di Prima student Iris Cushing, who was a trailblazing companion on California research trips with me and continues to inspire with her own work.

I am particularly grateful to the librarians with whom I collaborated along the way. My thanks to those at the University of North Carolina at Chapel Hill, including Emily Kader, Nicholas Graham, Elizabeth Ott, Aaron Smithers, and the staff of the reading room who facilitated my access to the Diane di Prima papers. At the Beinecke Rare Book and Manuscript Library, my thanks especially to Nancy Kuhl, for her advocacy in poetry archives and work with Gerrit Lansing, including a collaboration with me on the Room #15 Discrete Notions Series she curates. My thanks to the Lesbian Herstory Archive, including Deb Edel, Joan Nestle, and Saskia Scheffer, for connecting me with resources related to Lorde's library. I thank also Holly Smith at Spelman College for answering my questions about the Audre Lorde papers, as well as the other important archives in her care. I offer thanks to the staff of the reading room of the Bancroft Library at the University of California, Berkeley, for access to the Jack Spicer papers.

I am grateful to the resources that made it possible to conduct research, gather skills, and create community around this topic, including the Community Grants Program of the Bibliographical Society of America, and scholarships to Rare Book School and the Digital Humanities Summer Institute. I am also grateful to programs at CUNY, including the Pine Tree Fellowship at the Advanced Research Collaborative, the Knickerbocker Award for Archival Research in American Studies, the Diane di Prima Fellowship from *Lost & Found,* and the Digital Fellows Program, as well as my students at Brooklyn College who sailed on Olson's "boat book" with me for a few semesters.

With a profoundly appreciative heart, I also thank the poets, publishers, and colleagues whose conversations with me at various points in my research journey showed the importance of poetics as a foundation to life: Mary Korte, David Henderson, Anne Waldman, Maureen Owen, Kalima Vogt, Elaine Katzenberger, Steve Dickison, Kevin Killian, Whit Griffin, Ann Charters, Ed Sanders, Jolie Braun, Shannon Supple, Bric and Brac of *Dispatches from the Poetry Wars,* Marjorie Welish, Joshua Kotin, and many others.

I feel particularly fortunate that my sister, Virginia Kinniburgh, is an expert on indexing and was able to apply her skill here—instead of her usual habitude of the State Department's Foreign Relations of the United States digital series. She and I have been wild horses running through the humanities—from Old English elegiac verse to the Cold War, we've somehow managed to keep stride together, and I am grateful to her as a writing collaborator and friend always.

Of all the libraries I have gone to and will go to: the high school library was where I met you, Conley. You are deep inspiration and steadfast home.

NOTES

Introduction

1. Muriel Rukeyser, manuscript box Einstein, Albert. 1 TL (carbon) to 1942 Sept., accompanied by: Einstein, Albert. 1 TLS to Muriel Rukeyser, Sept. 12, 1942, Muriel Rukeyser collection of papers, The Henry W. and Albert A. Berg Collection of English and American Literature, The New York Public Library, Astor, Lenox and Tilden Foundations.

2. Amiri Baraka, *Blues People: Negro Experience in White America* (New York: Harper-Collins, 1999), vii.

3. Jennifer Seaman Cook, "Still Happening: An Interview with Ed Sanders," *LA Review of Books,* July 18, 2018.

4. Diane di Prima, *Recollections of My Life as a Woman: The New York Years: A Memoir* (New York: Penguin Books, 2002), 422–23.

5. Jolie Braun, "A History of Diane di Prima's Poets Press," *Journal of Beat Studies* 8 (2018): 11. Di Prima, *Recollections,* 412.

6. Audre Lorde and Adrienne Rich, "An Interview with Audre Lorde," *Signs* 6, no. 4 (1981): 732.

7. Diane di Prima, *Pieces of a Song: Selected Poems* (San Francisco, CA: City Lights), 156.

8. Robin Blaser, *The Astonishment Tapes: Talks on Poetry and Autobiography with Robin Blaser and Friends,* ed. Miriam Nichols (Tuscaloosa: University of Alabama Press, 2015), 81.

9. Don Byrd, *The Poetics of the Common Knowledge* (Albany: State University of New York Press, 1994), 5–6.

10. Daniel Kane, *All Poets Welcome: The Lower East Side Poetry Scene in the 1960s* (Berkeley: University of California Press, 2003), 3–4.

11. Gerrit Lansing, "Planting the Amplitudes," *Heavenly Tree/Soluble Forest* (Jersey City, NJ: Talisman House, 1995), 74.

12. Gerrit Lansing, *A February Sheaf: Selected Writings, Verse and Prose* (Boston, MA: Pressed Wafer, 2003), 163.

13. Charles Olson, *Collected Prose,* ed. Donald Allen and Benjamin Friedlander, and with an introduction by Robert Creeley (Berkeley and Los Angeles: University of California Press, 1997), 168.

14. "Henry W. and Albert A. Berg Collection in Memory of Henry W. Berg: Addresses Made at the Formal Presentation," New York: The New York Public Library, October 11, 1940, 11.

15. See Frances Stonor Saunders, *The Cultural Cold War: The CIA and the World of Arts and Letters* (New York: The New Press, 2013). Greg Barnhisel and Catherine Turner, introduction to *Pressing the Fight: Print, Propaganda, and the Cold War* (Amherst: University of Massachusetts Press, 2010), 6.

16. Di Prima, *Recollections*, 216.

17. Ammiel Alcalay, *A Bibliography for "After Jews and Arabs"* (Goleta, CA: Punctum Books, 2021), 24.

18. Laura E. Helton, "Making Lists, Keeping Time: Infrastructures of Black Inquiry, 1900–1950," *Against a Sharp White Background: Infrastructures of African American Print*, ed. Brigitte Fielder and Jonathan Senchyne (Madison: University of Wisconsin Press, 2019), 82–108, quote on 84–85.

19. Paul Raabe, "Library History and the History of Books: Two Fields of Research for Librarians," *Journal of Library History (1974–1987)* 19, no. 2 (1984): 282–297, quote on 283.

20. Jean Hatfield Barclay cited in Barnhisel and Turner, "Introduction," 5.

21. Betty Bright, *No Longer Innocent: Book Art in America* (New York: Granary Books, 2005), 53, 67.

22. Ralph J. Coffman, "The Working Library of Samuel Taylor Coleridge," *Journal of Library History (1974–1987)* 21, no. 2 (1986): 277–299, quote on 277.

23. Richard W. Oram, editor, with Joseph Nicholson, *Collecting, Curating, and Researching Writers' Libraries: A Handbook* (Lanham, MD: Rowman & Littlefield, 2014).

24. B. M. Watson, "Please Stop Calling Things Archives: An Archivist's Plea," *Perspectives Daily, Perspectives on History: The Newsmagazine of the American Historical Association*, January 22, 2021.

25. Terry Cook, "The Concept of Archival Fonds in the Post-Custodial Era: Theory, Problems and Solutions," *Archivaria* 35 (Spring 1993): 24–37, https://archivaria.ca/index.php/archivaria/article/view/11.

26. Jacques Derrida, *Archive Fever*, trans. Eric Prenowitz (London: University of Chicago Press, 1996), 17.

27. Amy Hildreth Chen, *Placing Papers: The American Literary Archives Market* (Amherst: University of Massachusetts Press, 2020), 122.

28. Amanda Golden, *Annotating Modernism: Marginalia and Pedagogy from Virginia Woolf to the Confessional Poets* (London: Routledge, 2020), 39.

29. Sheila Liming, *What a Library Means to a Woman: Edith Wharton and the Will to Collect Books* (Minneapolis: University of Minnesota Press, 2020), 109.

30. Amanda Golden, "Sylvia Plath's Library: The Marginal Archive," *Contemporary Poetry Archive* (Edinburgh: Edinburgh University Press, 2019), 111; 119.

31. Liming, *What a Library Means*, 201.

32. Allen S. Weiss, *Unpacking My Library, or The Autobiography of Teddy* (Berlin: K. Verlag, 2020), 15–17.

33. Di Prima, *Recollections*, 214.

34. Elizabeth McHenry, "Rereading Literary Legacy: New Considerations of the 19th-Century African-American Reader and Writer," *Callaloo* 22, no. 2 (1999): 477–82, quote on 478. Ted Joans, *Ted Joans: Poet Painter / Former Villager Now / World*

Travellers, Parts 1 and 2, ed. Wendy Tronrud and Ammiel Alcalay (New York: Lost & Found: The CUNY Poetics Document Initiative, 2016), *Part 2*, 2.

35. Audre Lorde, *Sister Outsider: Essays and Speeches* (Berkeley, CA: Ten Speed Press, 2007), 112.

36. To this, di Prima adds "ART IS MAGIC," after Michael Goldberg, a painter who was friends with Frank O'Hara. Di Prima, *Recollections*, 226.

37. Lorde, "Age, Race, Class, and Sex," in *Sister Outsider*, 116.

38. Charles Olson, *Collected Prose*, ed. Donald Allen and Benjamin Friedlander, and with an introduction by Robert Creeley (Berkeley: University of California Press, 1997), 249, 246.

39. Muriel Rukeyser, manuscript box (Rukeyser). United States, War Information Office, Graphics Department, Memoranda (8) relating to various projects, typescripts and typescript carbons, one signed, dated Dec. 14 1942–April 22, 1943, 2 folders, Statement re: her work, typescript, unsigned, dated Dec. 1, 1942, Muriel Rukeyser collection of papers, The Henry W. and Albert A. Berg Collection of English and American Literature, The New York Public Library, Astor, Lenox and Tilden Foundations.

40. Hiromi Ochi, "Democratic Bookshelf: American Libraries in Occupied Japan," in Barnhisel and Turner, *Pressing the Fight*, 90.

41. Peter Middleton, *Physics Envy: American Poetry and Science in the Cold War and After* (Chicago, IL: University of Chicago Press, 2015), 123.

42. Eric Bennett, *Workshops of Empire: Stegner, Engle, and American Creative Writing during the Cold War* (Iowa City: University of Iowa Press, 2015), 10, 37

43. Ammiel Alcalay, *a little history* (Brooklyn, NY: re:public/UpSet Press, 2013), 43.

44. Lorde and Rich, "Interview with Audre Lorde," 731.

45. Baraka, *Blues People*, 230.

46. Brooks Adams, *The New Empire* (New York: Macmillan, 1902), xviii.

47. Adams, *New Empire*, xviii. Adams was not the only scholar of knowledge who argued (and indeed, hoped) for the idea of a "complete" library that meaningfully housed all that could be known. Frederick Kilgour, an American librarian who pioneered the Online Computer Library Center (OCLC), points to multiple instances in his *The Evolution of the Book* (New York: Oxford University Press, 1998) when library databases, which are notoriously specific to institutions, with a variety of standards for cataloging and description, could have merged to form a single descriptive language and database. His contribution with OCLC, whose database is now called WorldCat, is the largest open public access catalog in the world, which enumerates any registered book in its database that encompasses thousands of worldwide libraries. Digitally, rather than physically, this system starts to make good on Adams's wish. Still, completeness is an ever-receding horizon, and Adams's question of how to meaningfully process an ever-expanding array of information remains.

48. Diane di Prima, "Paracelsus: An Appreciation," *The Alchemical Tradition in the Late Twentieth Century*, ed. Richard Grossinger (Berkeley, CA: North Atlantic Books, 1983), 26.

49. Di Prima, "Paracelsus," 29.

50. Alcalay, *little history*, 69.

51. Alcalay, *little history*, 37.

Chapter 1: "Biblio. & Library"

1. Ammiel Alcalay, *a little history* (Brooklyn, NY: re:public/UpSet Press, 2013), 8.
2. Ann Charters, *Olson/Melville: A Study in Affinity* (Berkeley, CA: Oyez Press, 1968), 6.
3. Charters, *Olson/Melville*, 8–9.
4. Charles Olson, "Lear and Moby Dick," *Twice-a-Year* 1 (1938): 165–89; F. O. Matthiessen, *American Renaissance* (New York: Oxford University Press, 1941), 457n6.
5. Merton M. Sealts, *Melville's Reading: A Check-List of Books Owned and Borrowed* (Cambridge, MA: Harvard University Print Office, 1948). Ralph Maud, *Charles Olson's Reading: A Biography* (Carbondale: Southern Illinois University Press, 1996), 39.
6. C. L. R. James, *Mariners, Renegades, and Castaways: The Story of Herman Melville and the World We Live In* (New York: C. L. R. James, 1953).
7. David Herd, introduction to *Contemporary Olson* (Manchester, UK: Manchester University Press, 2015), 1.
8. Charters, *Olson/Melville*, 4.
9. Richard Grossinger, *An Olson-Melville Sourcebook* (Berkeley, CA: North Atlantic Books, 1976). *A Curriculum of the Soul* was based on Charles Olson's "A Plan for a Curriculum of the Soul" published by the Institute of Further Studies in *The Magazine of Further Studies'* fifth issue in 1968. In collaboration with poets in Olson's orbit, Clarke and Glover made twenty-eight fascicles between 1972 and 2002. In 2016, Spuyten Duyvil published a two-volume edition of all fascicles.
10. Charles Olson, *A Bibliography on America for Ed Dorn* (1964), in *Collected Prose*, ed. Donald Allen and Benjamin Friedlander, and with an introduction by Robert Creeley (Berkeley: University of California Press, 1997), 307.
11. Olson was not only invested in textual knowledge that was centered on the book; the influential nature of his time in the Yucatán exploring Mayan glyphs on an archaeological dig has been contextualized by Dennis Tedlock in *The Olson Codex: Projective Verse and the Problem of Mayan Glyphs* (Albuquerque: University of New Mexico Press, 2017). Likewise, see Edgar Garcia, *Signs of the Americans: A Poetics of Pictography, Hieroglyphs, and Khipu* (Chicago, IL: University of Chicago Press, 2019). Benjamin Friedlander, "Charles Olson Now," in *OlsonNow: A Blog on the Poetry and Poetics of Charles Olson*, ed. Michael Kelleher and Ammiel Alcalay, May 27, 2006, http://olsonnow.blogspot.com/2006/05/benjamin-friedlandercharles-olson-now. html. The source of this citation is identified in Rachel Blau DuPlessis's essay "Olson and His *Maximus Poems*," in Herd, *Contemporary Olson*.
12. For more, see Peter Middleton, *Physics Envy: American Poetry and Science in the Cold War and After* (Chicago, IL: University of Chicago Press, 2015).
13. Tara McDowell, *The Householders: Robert Duncan and Jess* (Cambridge, MA: MIT Press, 2019), 156.
14. See also Paul Stephens, "Charles Olson and the Embodiment of Information," *The Poetics of Information Overload: From Gertrude Stein to Conceptual Writing* (Minneapolis: University of Minnesota Press, 2015); Todd F. Tietchen, *Technomodern Poetics: The American Literary Avant-Garde at the Start of the Information Age* (Iowa City: University of Iowa Press, 2018).
15. Maud, *Charles Olson's Reading*, 31.
16. Reitha Pattison, "'Empty Air:' Charles Olson's Cosmology," in Herd, *Contemporary Olson*, 52–63, quote on 62.
17. Gregor Gibson, "Driving Olson's Brain: A Dive into the Maud/Olson Library,"

Gloucester Writers Center, May 27, 2016, https://gloucesterwriters.org/driving-olsons-brain-dive-maudolson-library/.

18. André Spears, "Maud/Olson and Me," *Gloucester Writers Center,* February 15, 2016, http://maudolsonlibrary.org/index.php/andre-spears-maud-olson-me/.

19. Spears, "Maud/Olson and Me."

20. George Butterick, "Olson's Reading: A Preliminary Report," *OLSON: The Journal of the Charles Olson Archives,* nos. 1–7 (1974–77).

21. Typescript letter from Jack Clarke to Ralph Maud, "RE: Clarke's List," January 19, 1989, in the Ralph Maud Papers, housed at the Maud/Olson Library. Published with permission of the Estate of John Clarke.

22. Maud, *Charles Olson's Reading,* 6–7.

23. Spears, "Maud/Olson and Me."

24. Maud, *Charles Olson's Reading,* 26.

25. Diane di Prima remembers that John Wieners borrowed her copy of *Hymns to the Goddess* by Arthur Avalon to give to Olson, and that "Charles never returned the *Hymns,* nor did I ask him for them when we finally met. I simply bought myself another copy." Diane di Prima, "Old Father, Old Artificer": *Charles Olson Memorial Lecture,* ed. Ana Božičević and Ammiel Alcalay (New York: Lost & Found: The CUNY Poetics Document Initiative, 2012), 7–8.

26. Maud, *Charles Olson's Reading,* 25.

27. Maud, *Charles Olson's Reading,* 40.

28. Olson, *Collected Prose,* 307.

29. Richard Pearce-Moses, *A Glossary of Archival and Records Terminology,* Society of American Archivists, 2005, https://www2.archivists.org/glossary.

30. Charters, *Olson/Melville,* 8, cited by Maud, *Charles Olson's Reading,* 8.

31. Maud, *Charles Olson's Reading,* 87.

32. Norbert Weiner, *Cybernetics* (New York: J. Wiley, 1948); Middleton, *Physics Envy,* 157.

33. Maud, *Charles Olson's Reading,* 13.

34. I. A. Richards, *Principles of Literary Criticism* (London: Kegan Paul, Trench, Trubner, 1924), 33. Middleton, *Physics Envy,* 158.

35. Edward Dorn, *The Olson Memorial Lectures,* ed. Lindsey Freer (New York: Lost & Found: The CUNY Poetics Document Initiative, 2012), 12.

36. Dorn, *Olson Memorial Lectures,* 13.

37. Arthur T. Hamlin, *The University Library in the United States: Its Origins and Development* (Philadelphia: University of Pennsylvania Press, 1981).

38. Terry Belanger, "Rare Books and Special Collections in American Libraries: Seeing the Sites," *Rare Books and Manuscript Librarianship* 1, no. 1 (1986): 11–24, quote on 15, https://doi.org/10.5860/rbml.1.1.3.

39. The data about the items—that is, metadata—is the primary means of scoping a collection, and researchers develop techniques accordingly. Keyword search, extensive reading of secondary sources, trial and error: all these methods factor in to navigating a large collection in a reading room that permits limited access to its materials. Particularly with the advent of digital catalogs, the "metadata is the interface" and the means through which certain items may become visible or invisible; Jennifer Schaffner, "The Metadata Is the Interface: Better Description for Better Discovery of Archives and Special Collections, Synthesized from User Studies," *OCLC Research,* 2009, http://www.oclc.org/programs/publications/reports/2009-06.pdf. Depending on

whether its format is extensible, meaning whether it is readily translated into other formats or software applications, metadata can be useful for visualization. Additionally, certain institutions, such as The New York Public Library, have invested in "discovery layers" that are applied on top of the catalog, that allow readers to model patterns, visualize subjects, or possibly use an API to access metadata in innovative ways. However, despite the generative possibilities for visualizing metadata as a means of scoping special collections, there is no substitute for this present-yet-invisible materiality and the insights it holds, often just feet away from a carefully monitored reading room.

40. See *Archival Science*'s March 2016 special issue (16, no. 1), ed. Marika Cifor and Anne J. Gilliland, which builds on a November 2014 symposium at the University of California, Los Angeles, titled "Affect and the Archive."

41. Miriam Nichols, *Radical Affections: Essays on the Poetics of Outside* (Tuscaloosa: University of Alabama Press, 2010), 8, 18.

42. Nichols, *Radical Affections*, 269. Nichols argues that "Olson holds poiesis at the level of affective response rather than that of epistemology, the better that we might tell ourselves to ourselves in our habitudes and responsibilities as a species being here, among others, on the mother rock." See Miriam Nichols, "Myth and Document in Charles Olson's *Maximus Poems*," in Herd, *Contemporary Olson*, 25–37, quote on 36.

43. Olson, "The Resistance (for Jean Riboud)," in Herd, *Collected Prose*, 174.

44. See Karlien van de Beukel, "Why Olson Did Ballet: The Pedagogical Avant-Gardism of Massine," in Herd, *Contemporary Olson*, 286–96.

45. Teresa Brennan, *The Transmission of Affect* (Ithaca, NY: Cornell University Press, 2004), 3.

46. Brennan, *Transmission of Affect*, 7.

47. Olson, *Collected Prose*, 157.

48. Spears, "Maud/Olson and Me."

49. Anna-Sophie Springer, "Melancholies of the Paginated Mind: The Library as Curatorial Space," in *Fantasies of the Library*, ed. Anna-Sophie Springer and Etienne Turpin (Cambridge, MA: MIT Press, 2016), 7.

50. Anna-Sophie Springer, "Reading Rooms Reading Machines," in Springer and Turpin, *Fantasies of the Library*, 52.

51. Buzz Spector, "On the Fetishism of the Book Object?," in *Threads Talk Series*, ed. Steve Clay and Kyle Schlesinger (New York: Granary Books and Cuneiform Press, 2016), 63.

52. Cited in Allen S. Weiss, *Unpacking my Library, or The Autobiography of Teddy* (Berlin: K. Verlag, 2020), 15–17.

53. Alan Loney, "What Book Does My Library Make?" in Clay and Schlesinger, *Threads Talk Series*, 9.

54. Olson, *Collected Prose*, 168.

55. W. B. Yeats, "Three Poems," *New Republic*, October 2, 1929, 23.

56. Thomas E. Connolly, "The Personal Library of James Joyce: A Descriptive Bibliography," originally published in *The University of Buffalo Studies*, 1955; citation from 2nd ed. (Buffalo, NY: Norwood Editions Reprint, 1974), 5.

57. This annotation, which occurs on page 10, responds to Yeats's observation that the spirits "seemed ignorant of our surrounds and might have done so at some inconvenient time or place; once when they had given their signal in a restaurant they explained that because we had spoken of a garden they had thought we were in it." W. B. Yeats, *A Vision* (New York: Macmillan, 1961).

58. I thank Melissa Watterworth Batt for providing photographs of Olson's original annotation, as well as for her keen observations on the differences in the Maud transcription and the original Olson notes.

59. Analyzing Olson's annotations constitute an enormous task that requires a clear angle in, such as Charles Stein's *The Secret of the Black Chrysanthemum* (Barrytown, NY: Station Hill Press, 1987), that explores Olson's annotations of Jung's volumes in particular.

60. Mark A. Greene and Dennis Meissner, "More Product, Less Process: Revamping Traditional Archival Processing," *American Archivist* 68 no. 2 (2005): 208–63.

61. Andrew Stauffer, *Book Traces* (Charlottesville: University of Virginia, 2018-ongoing), http://www.booktraces.org/press-for-book-traces/.

62. Rebecca Knuth, *Libricide: The Regime-Sponsored Destruction of Books and Libraries in the Twentieth Century* (Westport, CN: Praeger, 2003).

63. Alcalay, *a little history*, 17.

64. Walter Benjamin, "Unpacking My Library: A Talk about Book Collecting," *Illuminations* (New York: Harcourt, Brace & World, 1968), 61.

65. Olson, *A Bibliography on America for Ed Dorn*, 298.

Chapter 2: "Don't Forget I'm a Librarian"

1. Audre Lorde, *The Black Unicorn* (New York: W. W. Norton, 1995), 115.

2. Lorde, *Undersong: Chosen Poems, Old and New* (New York: W. W. Norton, 1992), xiii–xiv.

3. Lorde, *Undersong*, xiv.

4. The John F. Kennedy Institute in Berlin, which holds an Audre Lorde Archive, has publications and publication files related to her works; but not books that were possessed by her.

5. "Audre Lorde Collection 1950–2002, Finding Aid." Spelman College Archives, https://www.spelman.edu/docs/archives-guides/audre-lorde-collection-finding-aid -(2012)be59fb34f9bd6490bbe9ffo000b1c0f4.pdf?sfvrsn=b8e49f50_0

6. Christina Olivares, "Thoughts on the Erotic in Audre Lorde's Archive," *Makhzin* 3, November 2018, http://www.makhzin.org/issues/dictationship/thoughts-on-the-erotic -in-audre-lorde-s-archive.

7. Alexis De Veaux, *Warrior Poet: A Biography of Audre Lorde* (New York: W. W. Norton, 2006), xii.

8. Lorde donated her papers to the Lesbian Herstory Archive in 1983 (the twenty-third collection; the first collection was that of Adrienne Rich in 1979). This archive is a collaborative that was founded to preserve and animate lesbian "herstory" outside of institutional bounds, and it is part of its mission statement that it will never be sold or acquired by another institution. Lorde invited the founders of LHA, Deborah Edel and Joan Nestle, to her home to see her papers and photographs. While Edel and Nestle do not remember encountering a specific library, they, along with Saskia Schaffer, kindly suggested a few friends of Lorde I might contact, and sent a few photographs of Lorde's study (one of which opens this chapter).

9. Audre Lorde and Adrienne Rich, "An Interview with Audre Lorde," *Signs* 6, no. 4 (1981): 723.

10. Shawn(ta) Smith-Cruz, "Referencing Audre Lorde," *Reference Librarianship and Justice: History, Practice, and Praxis*, ed. K. Alder, I. Beilin, and E. Tewell (Sacramento,

CA: Litwin Books, 2018), 282. Smith-Cruz identifies these elements as related to Lorde's thinking on the politics of survival, including "1) Acknowledgement of difference, 2) mutual stretching (to hear past the silences), and, 3) resource sharing to ultimately receive each other on her own terms"; *Reference Librarianship and Justice,* 286.

11. Jacqueline Goldsby and Meredith McGill, "Project Rationale," *Black Bibliography Project,* https://blackbibliog.org/about/.

12. Simon Gikandi, "Editor's Column: The Fantasy of the Library," *PMLA* 128, no. 1 (2013): 9–20, quote on 15.

13. Peter Anastas and David Rich, "Reading Ferrini: A Gallery Talk," lecture finding aid and transcript, Cape Ann Museum, Library and Archives, Gloucester, Massachusetts, September 14, 2013, 4.

14. De Veaux, *Warrior Poet,* 232.

15. De Veaux, *Warrior Poet,* 32.

16. Lorde and Rich, "Interview," 718.

17. W. Boyd Rayward, "Melvil Dewey and Education for Librarianship," *Journal of Library History* (1966–1972) 3, no. 4 (Oct. 1968): 297–312, quote on 309.

18. Ruth H. Rockwood, "Melvil Dewey and Librarianship," *Journal of Library History* (1966–1972) 3, no. 4 (Oct. 1968): 329–41, quote on 330.

19. Rayward, "Melvil Dewey," 307.

20. Rayward, "Melvil Dewey," 309.

21. The Spring 2022 Library History Round Table dedicated the sixth volume of *Libraries: Culture, History, and Society* to Black women librarians. The call for papers announcement is an important document in and of itself, with a list of dozens of librarians as possible topics for contributors, across a variety of regions and specializations within the library field.

22. De Veaux, *Warrior Poet,* 99.

23. Melba Joyce Boyd, *Wrestling with the Muse: Dudley Randall and the Broadside Press* (New York: Columbia University Press, 2003), 119. Dudley Randall moved from Detroit to Lincoln, Missouri, for his first librarian position at historically Black Lincoln University (86). Finding the literary environment lacking, he found a new position at Morgan State College in Baltimore in 1954, and then returned to Detroit in 1956, working within the Wayne County Federated Library System at the Eloise Branch, providing library services to hospital patients by taking books to hospitals and mental wards—activities that inspired his poetry (89). He had a formidable library, at the time that Boyd visited she noted, "books appear and disappear in uneven stacks, crowding end tables or ledges, resisting the confines of bookshelves. They generate in piles next to easy chairs or dominate a glass-top coffee table. Titles resurface as they are shuffled and reshuffled from room to room until they are remanded to one of the many wooden shelves that line the walls and hallways" (96).

24. De Veaux, *Warrior Poet,* 68.

25. Audre Lorde, *Zami: A New Spelling of My Name: A Biomythography* (Berkeley, CA: Ten Speed Press, 1982), 181.

26. Lorde, *Zami,* 226.

27. Rockwood, "Melvil Dewey," 335.

28. Laura Helton discusses the particulars of Dewey's 1927 index at length, which Dorothy Porter consulted and attempted to expand. At the time, the term "Negro"

included the following subcategories: "Vocal music—Negro minstrelsy and planta-
tion songs," "Slavery," "Education of special classes," "Negro troops in the U. S. Civil
War," "the 13th and 14th Amendments," "Household personnel," "Race ethnology,"
"Mental characteristics as influenced by race," and "Suffrage," and "for any text that
did not attend to these subjects, the protocol was to place it at 325.26, a number in
political science, 320, under 'Colonies [and] Migration,' 325, for works on 'Emigrants
of a special country or race,' 325.2." Helton further observes, "Nearly every object
relating to African American life and history—aside from those on slavery, suffrage,
minstrelsy, education, or domestic labor—landed in a section of the library reserved
for works about people foreign to the nation." Laura E. Helton, "On Decimals, Catalogs, and Racial Imaginaries of Reading," *PMLA* 134, no. 1 (2019): 103.

29. Laura E. Helton, "On Decimals," 106.
30. Rayward, "Melvil Dewey," 305.
31. De Veaux, *Warrior Poet*, 70.
32. Gikandi, "Editor's Column," 11.
33. Smith-Cruz, "Referencing Audre Lorde," 281.
34. Lorde and Rich, "Interview," 723.
35. Augusta Baker's legacy lives on at the Schomburg Center of The New York Public
    Library today, where they have digitized many of the books in her bibliographies.
36. Audre Lorde, "Eye to Eye," *Sister Outsider: Essays and Speeches* (Berkeley, CA: Ten
    Speed Press, 2007), 148.
37. Lorde, *Zami*, 22.
38. Lorde, *Zami*, 22–23.
39. Karla Hammond and Audre Lorde, "An Interview with Audre Lorde," *American
    Poetry Review* 9, no. 2 (1980): 18–21, quote on 18.
40. The artist Jess had a career as chemist; after studying chemistry at the California
    Institute of Technology in Pasadena, he was drafted, completed three months of
    basic training in chemical warfare, and was assigned to the Special Engineer Detach-
    ment in Oak Ridge, Tennessee, where he worked in a lab. After the war, Jess moved
    to Hanford Engineering Works to produce plutonium. There, in 1948, he had a "very
    strong and convincing dream that the world was going to completely destruct by the
    year 1975. I'm sure the kind of work I was doing had some effect on my state of mind
    at the time. I had a dream—what Jungians call the Big Dream—in which the world
    is being incinerated." Thereafter, Jess quit his job and moved to California, where he
    enrolled at the University of California, Berkeley, in 1949, then the San Francisco Art
    Institute in 1950, and exchanged marriage vows with Robert Duncan in 1951. Tara
    McDowell, *The Householders: Robert Duncan and Jess* (Cambridge, MA: MIT Press,
    2019), 156, 162.
41. Smith-Cruz, "Referencing Audre Lorde," 279.
42. Lorde, *Black Unicorn*, 54.
43. De Veaux, *Warrior Poet*, 7.
44. Lorde, *Zami*, 12.
45. De Veaux, *Warrior Poet*, 210.
46. Lorde, *Zami*, 14.
47. Ted Joans, *Ted Joans: Poet Painter / Former Villager Now / World Travellers, Parts
    1 and 2*, ed. Wendy Tronrud and Ammiel Alcalay (New York: Lost & Found: The
    CUNY Poetics Document Initiative, 2016), *Part 1*, 47. Joans indeed writes of his

reflections on his visits to Africa, especially Timbuktu, which are published in these chapbooks as well.

48. Lorde did not capitalize the "A" in America, because she was "angry about the pretenses" of the country (De Veaux, *Warrior Poet,* 337).

49. Lorde, *Zami,* 132–33.

50. As Elizabeth McHenry notes, early emphasis on "orality vs. literacy" by communication scholars such as Walter Ong often aligned African and African-Diasporic cultures with oral traditions to the exclusion of many historical textual sources, not to mention the unvarnished racism that accompanied eugenics around the turn of the century in the United States. McHenry reminds us that African Americans left traces (though perhaps not as many as European Americans) of their reading practices and literary habits that we are still establishing in contemporary research on Black bibliography. Elizabeth McHenry, "Rereading Literary Legacy: New Considerations of the 19th-Century African-American Reader and Writer," *Callaloo* 22, no. 2 (1999): 447, 477.

51. Laura E. Helton, "Making Lists, Keeping Time: Infrastructures of Black Inquiry, 1900–1950," in *Against a Sharp White Background: Infrastructures of African American Print,* ed. Brigitte Fielder and Jonathan Senchyne (Madison: University of Wisconsin Press, 2019), 82–108. quote on 83.

52. Lorde and Rich, "Interview," 714.

53. Helton, "On Decimals," 99.

54. Helton, "On Decimals," 111.

55. Helton, "On Decimals," 111.

56. Helton, "On Decimals," 101.

57. Jefferson D. Pooley, "Communication Theory and the Disciplines," *The International Encyclopedia of Communication Theory and Philosophy* (Hoboken, NJ: Wiley, 2016).

58. N. Katherine Hayles, *How We Become Posthuman* (Chicago, IL: University of Chicago Press, 1999), 18.

59. Hayles, *How We Became Posthuman,* 50.

60. Lisa Nakamura, "Indigenous Circuits: Navajo Women and the Racialization of Early Electronic Manufacture," *American Quarterly* 66, no. 4 (Dec. 2014).

61. De Veaux, *Warrior Poet,* 40.

62. Lorde and Rich, "Interview," 715, 716.

63. Lorde states, "It might be a line. It might be an image. The poem was my response." Lorde and Rich, "Interview," 714.

64. Lorde, *Zami,* 74–75.

65. Lorde, *Zami,* 76.

66. Lorde, *Zami,* 79.

67. De Veaux, *Warrior Poet,* 136.

68. Lorde and Rich, "Interview," 732.

69. De Veaux, *Warrior Poet,* 151; 154.

70. De Veaux, *Warrior Poet,,* 151.

71. Sam Lohmann, "Sorting Noises: Poetry, Libraries, and the Resistance of Information," *Poet-Librarians in the Library of Babel: Innovative Meditations on Librarianship,* ed. Shannon Tharp and Sommer Browning (Sacramento, CA: Library Juice Press, 2018), 89. Lohmann cites Russell Ackoff, "From Data to Wisdom," *Journal of Applied Systems Analysis* 16 (1989): 3–9; and Jennifer Rowley, "The Wisdom Hierarchy:

Representations of the DIKW Hierarchy," *Journal of Information Science* 33, no. 2 (2007): 163–180.

72. Lorde and Rich, "Interview," 736.

73. Audre Lorde, Marge Piercy, Fran Moira, and Lorraine Sorrel, "Interview: Audre Lorde: Lit from within," *Off Our Backs* 12, no. 4 (1982): 2–11, quote on 2.

74. Lorde, *Sister Outsider*, 171.

75. Lorde, *Black Unicorn*, 8.

76. Lorde and Rich, "Interview," 733.

77. Lorde and Rich, "Interview," 732.

78. Lorde and Rich, "Interview," 732.

79. Lorde and Rich, "Interview," 727.

80. Marion Kraft, "Bonds of Sisterhood / Breaking of Silences: An Interview with Audre Lorde," in *Audre Lorde's Transnational Legacies*, ed. Bolaki Stella and Broeck Sabine (Amherst: University of Massachusetts Press, 2015), 48.

81. Lorde and Rich, "Interview," 727.

82. De Veaux, *Warrior Poet*, 95.

83. Lorde and Rich, "Interview," 721.

84. De Veaux, *Warrior Poet*, 95.

85. De Veaux, *Warrior Poet*, 99.

86. De Veaux, *Warrior Poet*, 101.

87. De Veaux, *Warrior Poet*, 117.

88. Audre Lorde, *"I Teach Myself in Outline": Notes, Journals, Syllabi, and an Excerpt from Deotha*, ed. Miriam Atkin and Iemanjá Brown (New York: Lost & Found: The CUNY Poetics Document Initiative, 2017), 15.

89. Helton, "Making Lists," 84.

90. In light of the poetic genealogy and influences of the poets in this book, Langston Hughes is a particularly interesting figure given his relationship with Ezra Pound. The two corresponded about Frobenius and the idea of "padieuma" related to African American culture; for further reading, see David Roessel, "'A Racial Act': The Letters of Langston Hughes and Ezra Pound," special issue on Ezra Pound and African American modernism, *Paideuma: Modern and Contemporary Poetry and Poetics* 29, no. 1/2 (Spring / Fall 2000). Helton, "Making Lists," 85.

91. Helton, "Making Lists," 89.

92. Helton, "Making Lists," 97.

93. Lorde, "Poetry Is Not a Luxury," *Sister Outsider*, 38. Kraft, "Bonds of Sisterhood," 46–47.

94. Lorde, Piercy, Moira, and Sorrel, "Interview," 2.

95. Kraft, "Bonds of Sisterhood," 51–52.

96. Lorde, *Black Unicorn*, 28.

97. Lorde, "Poetry Is Not a Luxury," *Sister Outsider*, 37.

98. Lorde, *Sister Outsider*, 68.

99. Ekaterini Georgoudaki, "Audre Lorde: Revising Stereotypes of Afro-American Womanhood," *AAA: Arbeiten Aus Anglistik Und Amerikanistik* 16, no. 1 (1991): 47–66, quote on 64.

100. Ammiel Alcalay, *a little history* (Brooklyn, NY: re:public/UpSet Press, 2013), 126.

101. Charles Olson, *Collected Prose*, ed. Donald Allen and Benjamin Friedlander, and with an introduction by Robert Creeley (Berkeley: University of California Press, 1997), 189.

102. Lorde, *"I Teach Myself in Outline,"* 44.

103. Lorde, *Black Unicorn,* 36.

104. Hammond and Lorde, "Interview," 20.

105. Lorde, *Sister Outsider,* 37.

106. Homi Bhabha, "Unpacking My Library Again," *Journal of the Midwest Modern Language Association* 28, no. 1 (Spring 1995): 5–18, quote on 5.

107. Helton, "On Decimals," 103.

108. Lina Garber, "High over Halfway between Your World and Mine: Audre Lorde," in *Identity Poetics: Race, Class, and the Lesbian-Feminist Roots of Queer Theory* (New York: Columbia University Press, 2001), 98.

109. Audre Lorde, "Conference Keynote Address: Sisterhood and Survival," *Black Scholar* 17, no. 2 (1986): 5–7, quote on 5.

110. Kraft, "Bonds of Sisterhood," 46.

Chapter 3: "The Requirements of Our Life Is the Form of Our Art"

1. Audre Lorde Archive, Spelman College, Folder 1.1.039, Atlanta Georgia. I thank Cassandra Gillig for sharing this document with me.

2. Diane di Prima, *Recollections of My Life as a Woman: The New York Years: A Memoir* (New York: Penguin Books, 2002), 410. Jolie Braun, "A History of Diane di Prima's Poets Press," *Journal of Beat Studies* 8 (2018): 11.

3. Di Prima, *Recollections,* 101.

4. David Hadbawnik, "Diane di Prima in Conversation with David Hadbawnik," *Jacket* 18 (August 2002), https://jacketmagazine.com/18/diprima-iv.htmls.

5. Charles Olson, *Poetry and Truth: The Beloit Lectures and Poems* (San Francisco, CA: Four Seasons Foundation, 1971), 42–43.

6. Di Prima, *Recollections,* 186.

7. Tara McDowell, *The Householders: Robert Duncan and Jess* (Cambridge, MA: MIT Press, 2019), 122.

8. Steve Clay and Rodney Phillips, *A Secret Location on the Lower East Side: Adventures in Writing, 1960–1980: A Sourcebook of Information* (New York: New York Public Library and Granary Books, 1998), 10.

9. Clay and Phillips, *Secret Location,* 11.

10. Brenda Knight, *Women of the Beat Generation: The Writers, Artists, and Muses at the Heart of a Revolution* (Newburyport, MA: Conari Press, 1996), 2.

11. Di Prima, *Recollections,* 198.

12. Di Prima, *Recollections,* 114.

13. Di Prima, *Recollections,* 182–83.

14. Diane di Prima, *The Poetry Deal,* San Francisco Poet Laureate Series no. 5 (San Francisco, CA: City Lights, 2014), 5.

15. Clay and Phillips, *Secret Location,* 89.

16. Braun, "History of Poets Press," 15.

17. Di Prima, *Recollections,* 147.

18. Ammiel Alcalay, *a little history* (Brooklyn, NY: re:public/UpSet Press, 2013), 210.

19. Jed Rasula, *The American Poetry Wax Museum: Reality Effects, 1940–1990* (Chicago, IL: National Council of Teachers of English, 1996), 68.

20. Di Prima, *Poetry Deal,* 5.

21. Di Prima, *Recollections,* 110.

22. Di Prima, *Recollections*, 144.

23. Alcalay, *little history*, 129. For a thorough investigation of this topic, see Christopher Simpson's *Blowback* (New York: Weidenfeld & Nicolson, 1988).

24. This postcard is housed in the Diane di Prima Papers at University of North Carolina at Chapel Hill, as well as transcribed and mentioned in her Charles Olson Memorial Lectures (first lecture) at Buffalo in 1985.

25. Ed Sanders, *Investigative Poetry: A New Edition* (New York: Spuyten Duvyil, 2018), 6.

26. Di Prima, *Recollections*, 345–46.

27. David Stephen Calonne, *Diane di Prima: Visionary Poetics and the Hidden Religions* (New York: Bloomsbury Academic, 2019), 8.

28. Diane di Prima, conversation with M. C. Kinniburgh, April 1, 2018, San Francisco.

29. Robert Creeley, "Some Notes on Maximus," in *The Collected Essays of Robert Creeley* (Berkeley: University of California Press, 1989), 114.

30. Kenneth Warren, Kenneth, Dale Smith, and Ammiel Alcalay, *Captain Poetry's Sucker Punch: A Guide to the Homeric Punkhole, 1980–2012* (Buffalo, NY: BlazeVOX, 2012), 346.

31. Di Prima, *Recollections*, 295; and Calonne, *Diane di Prima*, 21.

32. David Stephen Calonne's monograph likewise seeks to situation di Prima among her influences, to observe "key texts in her intellectual development and trace out connections between her own trajectory and other countercultural figures." As di Prima's accomplishments and influence continue to become more well-known, I anticipate others will also explore this rich vein of inquiry. Calonne, *Diane di Prima*, 8.

33. Diane di Prima, "The Birth of Loba," *Symposium of the Whole: A Range of Discourse toward an Ethnopoetics*, ed. Jerome Rothenberg and Diane Rothenberg (Berkeley: University of California Press, 1983), 444.

34. Alicia Ostriker, "The Thieves of Language: Women Poets and Revisionist Mythmaking," *Signs* 8, no. 1 (1982): 68–90, quote on 87.

35. Ostriker, "Thieves of Language," 87.

36. Diane di Prima, "Light / and Keats," in *Talking Poetics from Naropa Institute*, ed. Anne Waldman and Marilyn Webb, with an introduction by Allen Ginsberg (Boulder, CO: Shambhala, 1978), 27–28.

37. David Meltzer, *San Francisco Beat: Talking with the Poets* (San Francisco, CA: City Lights, 2001), 18.

38. Hadbawnik, "Diane di Prima."

39. Hadbawnik, "Diane di Prima."

40. Hadbawnik, "Diane di Prima."

41. Despite the date of inscription, di Prima describes it as a birthday gift from 1961, in fourteen volumes, that she used to prepare for her first winter solstice ritual in Cooper Square, New York. Di Prima, *Recollections*, 370.

42. According to David Stephen Calonne, she would not settle this debt until the 1980s (Calonne, *Diane di Prima*, 24).

43. "Hidden Religions: Reading List for Fall Semester." Unpublished and undated digital document by Diane di Prima in folder titled "Hidden Religions" (not yet located at an institutional repository).

44. "Syllabus," unpublished and undated digital document by Diane di Prima in folder titled "Hidden Religions."

45. Diane di Prima, conversation with M. C. Kinniburgh, March 28, 2018, San Francisco, CA.

46. Di Prima, *Recollections*, 387.

47. Di Prima, *Recollections*, 224.

48. Di Prima, *Recollections*, 329.

49. Di Prima, *Recollections*, 285.

50. Diane di Prima, "Phoenix Memories," unpublished and undated digital document by Diane di Prima.

51. Anthony Libby, "Diane di Prima: Nothing Is Lost; It Shines in Our Eyes," *Girls Who Wore Black: Women Writing the Beat Generation,* ed. Ronna C. Johnson and Nancy M. Grace (New Brunswick, NJ: Rutgers University Press, 2002), 45–68, quote on 47.

52. Rudolf Hauschka, *The Nature of Substance,* trans. Mary T. Richards and Marjorie Spock (London: Vincent Stuart, 1966).

53. A copy of this can be located at the Henry W. and Albert A. Berg Collection of English and American Literature, with the call number Berg Coll Di Prima ZC6 S26 1985, Spring 1985, SF Inst. of Magical + Healing Arts, Classes, Workshops, and Intensives.

54. Robert A. Wilson, *Auden's Library* (New York: Robert A. Wilson and Phoenix Book Shop, 1975).

55. Di Prima conversation, April 1, 2018.

56. "Diane di Prima," *Allen Ginsberg Project,* transcription of June 2, 1976, reading at the Bay Area Writers series at Novato, CA, https://allenginsberg.org/2017/08/diane -di-prima/.

57. Roseanne Giannini Quinn, "The Laugh of the Revolutionary: Diane di Prima, French Feminist Philosophy and the Contemporary Cult of the Beat Heroine," in *The Philosophy of the Beats,* ed. Sharin N. Elkholy (Lexington: University Press of Kentucky, 2012), 22.

58. Diane di Prima, *"Old Father, Old Artificer": Charles Olson Memorial Lecture,* ed. Ana Božičević and Ammiel Alcalay (New York: Lost & Found: The CUNY Poetics Document Initiative, 2012), 16.

59. Diane Wolkstein and Samuel Noah Kramer, *Inanna: Queen of Heaven and Earth, Her Stories and Hymns from Sumer* (New York: Harper and Row, 1983).

60. Henry Corbin, *Spiritual Body and Celestial Earth: From Mazdean Iran to Shi'ite Iran,* Bolligen Series (Princeton, NJ: University of Princeton Press, 1976).

61. Dion Fortune, *The Esoteric Orders and Their Works,* intro. by Gareth Knight (Portland, OR: Llewellyn Publications, 1971).

62. Robert K. G. Temple, *The Sirius Mystery* (New York: St. Martin's Press, 1976).

63. Dion Fortune, *The Mystical Qabalah* (1935; London: Ernest Benn, 1970).

64. Di Prima, *"Old Father, Old Artificer,"* 51.

65. Berg Coll di Prima ZC6 S26 1985 Spring 1985, SF Inst. of Magical + Healing Arts. Classes, Workshops, and Intensives, The Henry W. and Albert A. Berg Collection of English and American Literature at The New York Public Library, Astor, Lenox and Tilden Foundations.

66. Uma Silbey, *The Complete Crystal Guidebook* (San Francisco, CA: U-Read Publications, 1986).

67. Lewis Spence, *The History of Atlantis* (New Hyde Park, NY: University Books, [1926])."

68. Di Prima, *Recollections*, 222.

69. "Diane di Prima," *Allen Ginsberg Project.*

70. Di Prima, "Birth of Loba," 441–42.

71. Di Prima, "Birth of Loba," 442.

72. Di Prima, "Birth of Loba," 442.

73. Diane di Prima, *Loba, Parts I–VIII* (Berkeley, CA: Wingbow Press, 1978), 1, 26.

74. "Passwords" panel on Gerrit Lansing, March 16, 2019, Poets House, https://poets house.org/event/passwords-gerrit-lansing-with-ruth-lepson-kate-tarlow-morgan -robert-podgurski-charles-stein/.

75. Alcalay, *little history*, 104.

76. Richard Pearce-Moses, *A Glossary of Archival and Records Terminology* (Chicago, IL: Society of American Archivists, 2005), https://www2.archivists.org /glossary.

77. Jacques Derrida, *Archive Fever*, translated by Eric Prenowitz (London: University of Chicago Press, 1996), 40.

78. Virginia Woolf, "How Should One Read a Book?" *The Common Reader*, 2nd series (London: Hogarth Press, 1935).

Chapter 4: "On Earth, Particular"

1. Steve Clay and Rodney Phillips, *A Secret Location on the Lower East Side: Adventures in Writing, 1960–1980: A Sourcebook of Information* (New York: New York Public Library and Granary Books, 1998), 134.

2. Gerrit Lansing, *A February Sheaf: Selected Writings, Verse and Prose* (Boston, MA: Pressed Wafer, 2003), 156.

3. Garrett Caples, "Casting Spells: The Quietly Mythic Life of Gerrit Lansing," *Poetry Foundation*, December 19, 2018, https://www.poetryfoundation.org/articles/148770 /casting-spells.

4. Lansing, *February Sheaf*, preface.

5. Robert Kelly observes that the "level of critical acumen in [Lansing's] work is so rare because it isn't immediately coupled with a 'therefore, do this' way, which we saw so much of in the 60's and the 70's," but rather, "we get a far more nuanced analysis of the situation of the cosmos" (Caples, "Casting Spells").

6. Patrick Dunagan, "The Poet's Aura," *Dispatches from the Poetry Wars (Gerrit Lansing Portfolio)*, September 12, 2018. Dunagan cites ten Robert Kelly letters to Harvey Bialy, located in BANC MSS 83/102 c, Box 1, Folder: Duncan, Robert, letter to James Hart, December 9, 1982 at the Bancroft Library, University of California, Berkeley.

7. Lansing, "On Serial Painting: The Ambiguities of Thorpe Feidt," in *February Sheaf*, 98.

8. Ruth Lepson has remarked that Lansing "has one of the fullest libraries I know of & seems to have read most everything in it, retaining most of that, I hear." Ruth Lepson, "'Nor . . . ever Some Place Else': Wieners in Boston," *Dispatches from the Poetry Wars (Gerrit Lansing Portfolio)*, June 2018, 3.

9. Derek Fenner, "On the Star Man in My Heart," *Dispatches from the Poetry Wars (Gerrit Lansing Portfolio)*, November 8, 2018, 2.

10. Eileen Myles, "Gift," *Dispatches from the Poetry Wars (Gerrit Lansing Portfolio)*, November 5, 2018, 1–2.

11. Lansing, "And the Mind Go Forth to the End of the World," in *February Sheaf*, 109.

12. Robert Podgurski, "Thoughts Pursuing a Mercurial Life Well Done: An Appreciation of Gerrit Lansing," *Dispatches from the Poetry Wars (Gerrit Lansing Portfolio)*, November 6, 2018, 5.

13. Lansing, *February Sheaf*, 119.

14. Derek Fenner, "Gerrit Lansing: A Personal Reliquary, or, Notes toward an Essay," *Jacket 2*, Winter 2010. https://jacket2.org/article/gerrit-lansing-personal -reliquary. Furthermore, George Kalamaras remembers the connection fostered by a shared book: "I made a comment in reference to something he had said, in which I mentioned Lewis Hyde's lovely book, *The Gift: Imagination and the Erotic Life of Property*, a book at that point that had only appeared four or five years earlier. Gerrit gave me this look of extraordinary surprise, saying, 'I was just telling Don about that book over dinner before class!' The gaze Gerrit and I shared seemed endless, love pouring out between us, delight dancing in his eyes. At that moment, I knew I had met someone extraordinary—not because we had read the same book, but because of his open expression of awe and childlike wonder at the seeming 'coincidence' of the timing of our shared connection." George Kalamaras, "*The Heavenly Tree Grows Downward*, but It Also Grows into and through Those to Whom We Open Ourselves and Lovingly Meet: A Remembrance of Gerrit Lansing," *Dispatches from the Poetry Wars*, September 2018, 1–2. In certain traditions, particularly academic ones, a shared connection over a book is an invitation to competition, debate, and jousting for intellectual position. For Lansing, the way his friends describe, it was a moment of connection in a spiritual sense.

15. Ruth Lepson describes it as a "treasure, up the hill and across the divided highway from the ocean. . . . The rooms are large and packed and his intriguing housemate John can sometimes be seen moving books up to the top floor, even more books hiding there, waiting to spill over into the living room." "Thirteen Ways of Looking at Gerrit Lansing," *Dispatches from the Poetry Wars (Gerrit Lansing Portfolio)*, November 7, 2018, 3.

16. Poets House, "Passwords: Gerrit Lansing with Ruth Lepson, Kate Tarlow Morgan, Robert Podgurski, and Charles Stein," New York City, March 16, 2019, https://poetshouse.org/audio/2019-passwords-gerrit-lansing-with-ruth-lepson-kate -tarlow-morgan-robert-podgurski-charles-stein/.

17. Charles Stein, "For Gerrit," *Dispatches from the Poetry Wars (Gerrit Lansing Portfolio)*, November 6, 2018, 1.

18. While this was a commonly held belief among his friends, at the Poets House panel in March 2019, the shelf space available in the house did not seem sufficient to suggest that essentially one-third of his book collection had been weeded. For now, the discrepancy between twenty thousand and thirty thousand will remain apocryphal.

19. Podgurski "Thoughts," 3.

20. George Quasha, "The Gerrit Gap," *Dispatches from the Poetry Wars (Gerrit Lansing Portfolio)*, November 6, 2018.

21. Robert Podgurski, "Mercurial in Nature: An Interview with Gerrit Lansing, by Robert Podgurski," *Dispatches from the Poetry Wars (Gerrit Lansing Portfolio)*, November 6, 2018, 2.

22. Lansing, *Heavenly Tree/Soluble Forest* (Jersey City, NJ: Talisman House, 1995), 193.

23. Lepson, "Thirteen Ways," 7.

24. Caples, "Casting Spells."

25. Lansing, "Foreword to *Maximus of Gloucester*," in *February Sheaf*, 117.

26. Gaston Bachelard, *The Poetics of Space*, translated by Maria Jolas (Boston, MA: Beacon Press, 1994), 8.

27. Bachelard, *Poetics of Space,* 12–13.

28. Lansing is very much a poet of community and the places he has lived. As Jed Birmingham has noted, though short-lived, Lansing's little magazine *SET* was like Vincent Ferrini's *Four Winds* in that it contributed to placing Gloucester on the poetic map, especially before Olson centered his poetic project around the city for *The Maximus Poems;* Jed Birmingham, "A Controversy of Poets," *Reality Studio,* 2007, https://realitystudio.org/bibliographic-bunker/a-controversy-of-poets/. In addition to his important friendship with Charles Olson, which continued throughout Olson's life until his death in 1970, Lansing's location in the Northeast placed him in close proximity to the goings-on of the Boston scene, at times called "the Boston Renaissance," with poets including John Wieners and Stephen Jonas, as well as Joe Dunn, Robin Blaser, and Jack Spicer. In Lansing's preface to Steve Jonas's *Exercises for Ear,* he states, "The School of Boston, in poetry, middle this century, is an occult school, unknown. What literary historian has written of Spicer, Blaser, Wieners, Dunn, Marshall, Jonas together?"; *February Sheaf,* 121. This "occult school," circa 1954 to 1970, and currently being studied by Robert Dewhurst, shows considerable "investments in magical traditions and techniques as sources of poetry" that sets its practitioners apart from other contemporaneous poetic movements. Likewise, Lansing's locus in the Northeast, within close distance to Boston, Cambridge, Western Massachusetts, Salem, and the Hudson Valley, would prove important for the rest of his life in terms of the poetic community he created in these spaces.

29. Bachelard, *Poetics of Space,* 48.

30. Frances Yates, *The Art of Memory* (London: Routledge, 1999, first published in 1966). In particular, Mary Carruthers notes that in the medieval period, "the ability to store and recall quickly, easily, and accurately large quantities of textual information" was a key goal of education, embodied by the word *memoria;* friars of the Dominican order widely shared the "architectural mnemonic" in the fourteenth and fifteenth centuries as part of their teaching outreach; Mary Carruthers, "Italy, *Ars Memorativa,* and Fame's House," *Studies in the Age of Chaucer,* no. 2 (1986): 179–88, quote on 181. Carruthers traces the close association between buildings—not just spaces or routes—to medieval Italy and the rise of humanism, showing how both Chaucer and Dante utilize this motif in their poetics (183). She notes that both Chaucer and Dante use housing structures in their work that are both imaginary and tangible—Chaucer's *House of Fame* relying on Ovid and possibly also the Palais de Justice in Paris (186).

31. Shannon Tharp, "The Granting of Grace in an Ordinary Room," *Poet-Librarians in the Library of Babel: Innovative Meditations on Librarianship,* ed. Shannon Tharp and Sommer Browning (Sacramento, CA: Library Juice Press, 2018), 156.

32. Kalamaras, "Remembrance," 1–2.

33. Lansing, *Heavenly Tree/Soluble Forest,* 4.

34. Lansing, *Heavenly Tree/Soluble Forest,* 14.

35. Bachelard, *Poetics of Space,* 17.

36. Lansing, *Heavenly Tree/Soluble Forest,* 196.

37. Sophie Seita, *Provisional Avant-Gardes: Little Magazine Communities from Dada to Digital* (Stanford, CA: Stanford University Press, 2019) 194.

38. Sharon Marcus, Heather Love, and Stephen Best, "Building a Better Description," *Representations* 135 (Summer 2016): 3; 4.

39. Diane di Prima, "Light / and Keats," in *Talking Poetics from Naropa Institute*, ed. Anne Waldman and Marilyn Webb, with an introduction by Allen Ginsberg (Boulder, CO: Shambhala, 1978), 27.

40. Jacques Derrida, *Archive Fever*, trans. Eric Prenowitz (London: University of Chicago Press, 1996), 11.

41. Podgurski, "Thoughts," 6.

42. Lansing, *February Sheaf*, 169.

43. Lansing, "Henry Thoreau and Cosmic Concord," in *February Sheaf*, 123.

44. Lansing, *Heavenly Tree/Soluble Forest*, 112.

45. Lansing, *Heavenly Tree/Soluble Forest*, 117.

46. Lansing, "Production as Metaphor, and 'Nature' in Baudrillard's Mirror," in *February Sheaf*, 94.

47. Kalamaras, "Remembrance," 4.

48. Mitch Highfell, "Thinking about Gerrit," *Dispatches from the Poetry Wars (Gerrit Lansing Portfolio)*, November 3, 2018, 1.

49. Bachelard, *Poetics of Space*, 51.

50. Caples, "Casting Spells."

51. Adam Davis, "The Immanent Library," in *The Swarming Possibilities (Some Occult, Unused) in American Life: A Catalog of Books From the Collection of Gerrit Lansing* (Hadley, MA: Division Leap and Grey Matter Books, 2020), 4.

52. Lansing, "Henry Thoreau and Cosmic Concord," in *February Sheaf*, 125.

53. Lansing writes of Elias Ashmole's "Prolegomena" in the poem "Of Signifying Stones."

54. Davis, "Immanent Library," 4.

55. Davis, "Immanent Library," 4.

56. Davis, "Immanent Library," 4.

57. Bachelard, *Poetics of Space*, 4; 6.

58. Bachelard, *Poetics of Space*, 15.

59. Bachelard, *Poetics of Space*, 46.

60. Bachelard relates this effect in part to the close association of the childhood home with a sense of loss, noting, "We consider the past, and a sort of remorse at not having lived profoundly enough in the old house fills our hearts, comes up from the past, overwhelms us" (*Poetics of Space*, 56). While the motif of the childhood home is not necessarily operational for Lansing in the context of the home in which his library grew into its fully glory (Lansing moved into this particular house in the 1980s), for us as Lansing's younger friends, there is a mentorly and parental element to fellow poets' accounts of their experience in Lansing's house. Or, in Eileen Myles's words, we thought of Lansing as "wise cozy man" and felt accordingly in his presence and home. Eileen Myles, "Gift," *Dispatches from the Poetry Wars (Gerrit Lansing Portfolio)*, November 5, 2018, 2).

61. Robert Kelly, "Gerrit Plays Scriabin," *Dispatches from the Poetry Wars (Gerrit Lansing Portfolio)*, November 5, 2018, 1.

Conclusion

1. Alison Fraser, "Creating the Twentieth-Century Literary Archives: A Short History of the Poetry Collection at the University at Buffalo," *Information and Culture* 55, no.

3 (2020): 262. At this time, private collectors such as the Berg brothers (who had generally accomplished the bulk of their collecting in years prior) began to donate their materials to public institutions, partly as a result of increasing emphasis on public as opposed to private book collections, as well as the desire to reinvigorate a sense of cultural pride after World War Two. See also Sheila Liming, *What a Library Means to a Woman: Edith Wharton and the Will to Collect Books* (Minneapolis: University of Minnesota Press, 2020), 62.

2. Fraser, "Literary Archives," 252.

3. "James Joyce Collection: Collection Overview," University at Buffalo–SUNY, https://library.buffalo.edu/jamesjoyce/collection-overview/. I also thank Alison Fraser for speaking with me about this topic.

4. Thomas E. Connolly, "The Personal Library of James Joyce: A Descriptive Bibliography," 2nd ed. (Tualatin, OR: Norwood Editions, 1974); originally published in *The University of Buffalo Studies*, 1955.

5. Dirk van Hulle, "A James Joyce Digital Library," *European Joyce Studies* 25 (2016): 226–42.

6. Joyce's Trieste Library was likewise haunted by the same absence/presence conundrum that accompanies all author libraries; Richard Ellmann supplemented his initial inventory of this collection with approximately one hundred titles that Joyce was thought to own but were not physically present among the Trieste books. See Michael Patrick Gillespie, "A Critique of Ellmann's List of Joyce's Trieste Library," *James Joyce Quarterly* 19, no. 1 (1981): 28.

7. Tara McDowell, *The Householders: Robert Duncan and Jess* (Cambridge, MA: MIT Press, 2019), 4, 12, 15.

8. McDowell, *Householders*, 36.

9. More of James Maynard's writing on Duncan will appear in a forthcoming book chapter, titled "Unpacking Duncan's Books: Remarks on the Personal Library of Robert Duncan." I thank him for sharing a draft of this work and for providing additional details to me in conversation.

10. Lisa Jarnot, "Abandon the Creeping Meatball: An Anarcho-Spiritual Treatise," Bagley Wright Lecture at the University at Buffalo, February 2021.

11. Fraser, "Literary Archives," 265.

12. Shannon Mattern, "Fugitive Libraries," *Places Journal* (October 2019), https://doi.org/10.22269/191022.

13. George Herms, *The Librarian*, 1960 (held at the Norton Simon Museum). Assemblage was an attempt to bring together disparate objects to manage the chaos of post–World War Two life, and cross-pollinated poetry, film, and other artistic communities from both coasts by virtue of mimeograph magazines and other ephemeral modes of sharing. In response to the overarching cultural motif of containment as a geopolitical strategy and an outgrowth of atomic consciousness, assemblage included collage, printing, multimedia works, and found sculpture. With artists such as Jay DeFeo, Wallace Berman, and George Herms, and drawing on the perspectives of Robert Creeley and John Cage, writers such as Rebecca Solnit have noted the rise of this form in the 1940s and 1950s—outside of a mainstream context and therefore beholden mainly to its experimental cohort of peers.

14. Ed Sanders, *Investigative Poetry: A New Edition* (New York: Spuyten Duyvil, 2018), 6.

Afterword

1. Loney, "What Book Does My Library Make?" *Threads Talk Series,* ed. Steve Clay and Kyle Schlesinger (New York: Granary Books and Cuneiform Press, 2016), 11.

2. Loney, "My Library," 10.

3. Bob Kaufman, *Collected Poems of Bob Kaufman* (San Francisco, CA: City Lights, 2020).

4. Michael Seth Stewart, ed., *Yours Presently: The Selected Letters of John Wieners* (Albuquerque: University of New Mexico Press, 2020).

5. It is important to note that this restructuring of funding was a historical departure, particularly for the sciences; like literary or artistic work, scientific study was sponsored by philanthropy (such as the wealthy patron model or university donor), local industries, or university funding until 1919, when the Massachusetts Institute of Technology rearranged its departmental structure to allow corporations to sponsor academic research. At the same time, the government established highly funded initiatives such as the National Science Foundation, whose budget increased over 1,000 percent from 1957 to 1968, at which point it was channeling five hundred million dollars toward research to aid the Cold War. The scale and funding streams for humanities research were also transforming through government and private programs; the Rockefeller Foundation was critical in the development of institutionalized creative writing programs, since Congress had rewritten the tax code during the Great Depression and World War Two in a way that led to a boom in philanthropic contributions and therefore influence by private foundations. See David Kaiser, "History: Shut Up and Calculate!," *Nature* 505 (January 2014): 153–55; Art Jahnke, "Who Picks Up the Tab for Science?" part 1, *BU Today: Series: Making Research Work,* April 6, 2015, http://www.bu.edu/today/2015/funding-for-scientific-research/; Noam Chomsky, Richard C. Lewontin, Ira Katznelson, Laura Nader, Richard M. Ohmann, Immanuel M. Wallerstein, Raymond Siever, and Howard Zinn, *The Cold War and the University: Toward an Intellectual History of the Postwar Years* (New York: The New Press, 1997), xii.

6. Thomas A. Clark, "Meet the Author: Thomas A. Clark discusses 'The Threadbare Coat'" (Carcanet Press, December 23, 2020), 19:54, quote at 4:10, https://www.youtube.com/watch?v=KvQNr67u2M4.

INDEX